THE
ADVERTISING
EFFECT

HOW TO CHANGE BEHAVIOUR

DEDICATIONS

Dearest Anna and Asterix. I dedicate this book to the A family—you mean everything to me.

Although I doubt any of you will read this, this book is also dedicated to all the 14-year-old boys in the world. Just trust me when I say life has a way of working out. We shun the different when we are young, but as we get older it's the different ones who give us hope.

Finally, this book is dedicated to a series of brilliant bosses and professional partners I've learned from during my career: Catriona McComish and Steve Feelgood from the Department of Corrective Services; Anita Batho from Added Value; Jim O'Mahony from Saatchi & Saatchi; Sean Cummins from The Cummins Partnership; and, of course, the mercurial, beautiful and scatological Jon Wilkins, with Mat Baxter and Mike Wilson from Naked Communications.

THE ADVERTISING EFFECT

HOW TO CHANGE BEHAVIOUR

ADAM FERRIER

WITH JENNIFER FLEMING

OXFORD
UNIVERSITY PRESS

Oxford University Press is a department of the University of Oxford.
It furthers the University's objective of excellence in research,
scholarship, and education by publishing worldwide. Oxford is a registered
trademark of Oxford University Press in the UK and in certain other
countries.

Published in Australia by
Oxford University Press
253 Normanby Road, South Melbourne, Victoria 3205, Australia

© Adam Ferrier 2014

The moral rights of the author have been asserted.

First published 2014

National Library of Australia Cataloguing-in-Publication entry
    Author: Ferrier, Adam, author.
    Tittle: The advertising effect : how to change behaviour / Adam
        Ferrier ; Jennifer Fleming
        (contributor).
    ISBN: 9780195593921 (paperback)
    Notes: Includes bibliographical references.
    Subjects: Advertising—Psychological aspects.
            Consumer behavior.
            Branding (Marketing)
            Influence (Psychology)
    Other Authors/Contributors: Fleming, Jennifer.
Dewey Number: 659.1019

Reproduction and communication for educational purposes

Edited by Pete Cruttenden
Typeset by diacriTech, India
Printed by Sheck Wah Tong Printing Press Ltd
Cover image: Shutterstock/aopsan

Links to third party websites are provided by Oxford in good faith and for information only.
Oxford disclaims any responsibility for the materials contained in any third party website
referenced in this work.

CONTENTS

ABOUT THE AUTHORS

Adam Ferrier is chief strategy officer and co-owner of independent advertising agency The Cummins Partnership. Prior to this Adam founded (and later sold) Naked Communications, one of Australia's most influential agencies. He's also a registered psychologist and one of Australia's most respected and successful advertisers. Adam has been the driving force behind some of Australia's most successful advertising campaigns, and winner of many of the world's top advertising awards. Adam is married to Anna, and has an amazing son called Asterix.

Jennifer Fleming is best-selling author of several books including *Spotless: Room-by-room Solutions for Domestic Disasters, Spotless 2, Spotless A–Z, Speedcleaning, How to be Comfy, Save: Your Money, Your Time, Your Planet* (all with Shannon Lush) and *The Feel Good Body* (with Anna-Louise Bouvier). She's also a senior producer and presenter at ABC Radio.

HOW TO USE THIS BOOK

To my knowledge, this is the first book on influence and behaviour change that draws so heavily on firsthand experiences of real-world advertising ideas. I am an advertising practitioner, not a researcher or academic. However, I and my co-author Jen have taken the approach of talking through how advertisers use advertising to change behaviour, and then dissecting the psychological principles behind each technique (of which there are 10).

This book is written on the assumption that all advertising is about changing people's behaviour. The more effectively and efficiently brands can change consumer behaviour, the better is the advertising.

There are two key stages of behaviour change.

1. Define the behaviour to change.
2. Set about changing it.

This book first discusses how to define and then understand the dynamics of behaviour change, before looking at how to change behaviour using a variety of 'action spurs'—'motivational action spurs' and 'ease action spurs'. I don't believe there is just one way to change behaviour, and the action spurs act as a toolkit for creating behaviour change. As I'm assured this is the done thing for books such as this, here is a chapter-by-chapter overview.

PART 1 WHICH BEHAVIOUR TO CHANGE?

Chapter 1   'The Dark Arts' is an **overview** of the book.

Chapter 2   'Definition' looks at how to **define a behaviour you want to change**. Changing the behaviours of others is difficult enough (people are generally happy doing what they are doing, thank you very much), and if you don't carefully select the behaviours you want to change then you may not have much success. If you don't read this chapter the rest of the book will be less useful.

Chapter 3   'Thoughts, Feelings and Actions' looks at the overall principles of behaviour change. It examines the interrelationship between **thoughts, feelings and actions** and explains how advertising has moved from passive to interactive mediums and the impact that this has on how to influence and change consumer behaviour.

Chapter 4   'Action Spurs' introduces these devices. Action spurs can **increase motivation** to undertake behaviour, or **make the behaviour easier**. The chapter explains how to choose a spur and how to put behaviour change into action.

PART 2 MOTIVATION ACTION SPURS

Chapter 5   'Reframing' outlines how to **present the behaviour** you want to occur in the most motivating way.

Chapter 6	'Evocation' describes how to use the **power of emotion** and **story-telling** to change consumer behaviour. This is perhaps what advertising is best known for, and is the main method used by advertisers when broadcast (non-interactive media) was all they had (although this is rapidly changing).
Chapter 7	'Collectivism' shows how to influence behaviour by **creating a movement**, or larger activity, that people want to be a part of.
Chapter 8	'Ownership' discusses the truism that if you give people **ownership of the behaviour** you want them to do, they'll be much more likely to do it.
Chapter 9	'Play' is one of my favourite spurs. Make the behaviour you want to happen **playful** or **turn it into a game** and people will enjoy doing the behaviour you want them to do. This is one of the fastest-growing areas of advertising.
Chapter 10	'Utility' looks at how to give the consumer **some form of useful incentive** to encourage the behaviour you want to occur.
Chapter 11	'Modelling' examines how this concept can be used to influence and change behaviour. The key is to **find the right model** to demonstrate the behaviour you want to happen.

PART 3 EASE ACTION SPURS

Chapter 12	'Skill Up' shows how to **give people the skills** to do the behaviour you're asking of them.
Chapter 13	'Eliminate Complexity' assumes that people have the skills to do the behaviour you want them to, but perhaps there is **something in the environment** that is stopping them from doing so.
Chapter 14	'Commitment' looks at chunking the behaviour down. If it's too hard to get people to do what we want them to do, we can **make the behaviour smaller** and get them to commit to it.

PART 4 HOW TO BE GOOD

Chapter 15	'Using Your Powers for Good' is about making a **positive change** to the world. Jen and I contemplated making it Chapter 1 because it sets the scene nicely for advertising and behaviour change—so if you prefer to read it before the rest of the book, then by all means go ahead.

Many of the examples used in this book are from my time at Naked Communications, where I have spent the bulk of my career in advertising. I've also drawn from experiences in other agencies, as well as case studies from round the world. Many of the examples have been recognised through Effie Awards as among the most effective pieces of work in the industry. The Effies are the advertising industry's gold standard awards giving focus to the 'effectiveness' of the advertising. The awards are not measured by creativity (like most other awards in advertising) but rather, how effectively did the advertising create sales, build the brand and change behaviour. The winning papers are published on national Effie websites, although I've referenced them here so you can find them more easily. Full references for cited works are also supplied, along with further readings in case you're interested in specific topics. Also, the book doesn't have to be read in order. Each of the chapters are standalone—especially in Parts 2 and 3. Further, the book is written in a similar way to how I like to think, with chunks of information from a diverse reference base, hopefully all coming together to tell a story.

THE INSIDERS

Throughout this book you will hear from a number of 'Insiders'. These are people in, around or (in a couple of cases) adjacent to advertising. The Insiders are interesting people I've met, or I'd like to meet, all of whom have an interesting perspective on how to influence others and change people's behaviour. I'd like to thank them all for generously responding to my request to be a part of this book. The Insiders are:

- Rohit Bhargava—best-selling author of *Likeonomics* (and very likable guy) and founder of Influential Marketing Group
- Anna Bongiorno—my wonderful wife, and mother of Asterix
- Jon Casimir—co-producer (with Andrew Denton) of *The Gruen Transfer*, *Gruen Planet* and *Gruen Nation*, and best-selling author
- Alain de Botton—philosopher, best-selling author and founder of The School of Life
- Andrew Denton—one of Australia's most talented and successful TV producers/ presenters
- Claudiu Dimofte—associate professor at San Diego State University and an editorial board member on *The Journal of Consumer Psychology*
- Bob Garfield—renowned advertising journalist and media commentator
- Arjan Haring—founder of Science Rockstars (and destined for greatness)
- Joseph Jaffe—best-selling author on progressive forms of advertising
- John Mescall—executive creative director at McCann, Australia, and creator of the 'Dumb Ways to Die' campaign for Metro Trains Melbourne
- David (Nobby) Nobay—creative chairman at Droga5 and one of the world's most influential creatives
- Michael Norton—Harvard University professor and best-selling author
- Ivan Pollard—a friend and global head of communications strategy for Coca-Cola
- Mark Sherrington—founder of brand consultancy Added Value and former global marketing director of SAB Miller, a most envied marketing job
- Rory Sutherland—inspirational leader of the UK Institute of Practitioners in Advertising, and vice-chairman of the Ogilvy Group, UK

- Simon Thatcher—an old friend and beautifully good psychologist
- Faris Yakob—good mate and advertising visionary; Fast Company called him one of the top 10 modern day Mad Men (how cool is that?).

My commerce professor at university relayed the following quote which, apparently, is written on the wall outside the University of Chicago's library. It made a big impression on me: 'Within these walls contain no wisdom, only the ability to weigh and consider.' It's why I've included insights from many people on how to change the behaviour of others (and, indeed, whether you should try). Most are from people I've met inside the advertising and marketing space, hence the name 'The Insiders'. They have opinions that I believe you'll find useful or at the very least interesting. Each Insider was asked exactly the same question:

Changing the behaviour of others is difficult—yet our ability to do just this dictates how successful we are in various challenges, such as selling our brands, getting people to join our cause, getting our kids to clean up their room, and ensuring people in our office use the recycling bins. Knowing this—what one bit of advice would you give to others about how to change human behaviour?

Their points of view are included at the end of each chapter. I've also taken the liberty of including how I know them (or don't), so that you can understand a little more about their point of view.

ACKNOWLEDGMENTS

I realise now more than ever that writing a book (or achieving just about anything of any significance) is rarely an individual pursuit. It's taken a team of people to make this happen, and I'd like to take the space to thank them all. At weddings—anyone's wedding—I'm the kind of guy who loves hearing the speeches (in my ideal wedding the entire night would be a series of speeches I could listen to), and when buying books I always read the thank-you bit of the book first (in fact, I'll often decide whether to buy a book dependent on the thank-yous). The thank-yous are a little like the groom's speech at a wedding. It's also the bit of the book I've been most excited about writing. So here goes my book's thank-you speech!

Firstly I'd like to thank everyone who buys, reads or even picks up a copy of this book and flicks through it. I thank you because I am pleased you've taken the time to understand a little more how advertising works, and how it works on you. With this knowledge you'll be more in control of your decisions as consumers. This, in turn, will ensure corporations make goods and services that we want, rather than the ones they can sell. I'm hoping you can do me a favour (later in the book you'll understand why I've asked this so blatantly) and recommend this book to your friends and colleagues. Please feel free to tweet it up (@theadeffect) or have a look at the accompanying YouTube page (www.youtube.com/theadvertisingeffect). In fact, any help promoting this book at all will be greatly appreciated.

Next, a massive thank-you to my co-author Jennifer Fleming. Jen is one of Australia's best-selling authors (co-authoring the *Spotless* series) and has been wonderful in helping to structure the book, helping me 'find my voice', and helping with draft after draft. I've known Jen for several years and she has been marvellous to work with. Jen also introduced me to the lovely Virginia Lloyd, who helped Jen and I muddle our way through the book when we were setting everything out.

To Sean Hallahan (a client) and Ian Perrin (a colleague), it was after separate conversations with each of you that I decided to focus on the art and science of behaviour change. I haven't told either of you this yet, so here it is—'thanks guys'. To Brooke Ward (an amazing psychologist) and Mel Barden (super-smart brand strategist—and my ex-girlfriend), thank you respectively for the additional references and research, and help with structuring the action spurs that appear throughout the book. The supremely organised Emma O'Leary must also receive special thanks for helping to make the book happen.

I'd also like to thank the businesses I've worked in while in advertising, and the people who work there (I can't bring myself to thank the Department of Corrective Services—what a rabble of a place!). Added Value, Saatchi & Saatchi, Naked Communications and now The Cummins Partnership have all taught me so much. However, I'd especially like to thank Naked and the clients I've had there, as it's where I've spent the majority of my time in advertising. The case studies I draw upon, although often written in the first person, were always a collaborative effort between the brilliant people who worked at Naked, and in many instances the strong agencies we worked with. Further, part of the structure of the book, and the thinking behind the action spurs, was developed while I was at Naked. To all, thanks.

Thank you to all the clients whose work appears in this book. You've been inspiring and fun to work with. In particular, I'd like to thank two clients: the Coca-Cola Company and Art Series Hotels. Coke was Naked's foundation client in Australia (and always our biggest), and is full of intelligent people who understand the power and positivity of brands. Art Series Hotels were the 'dream' client: smart and keen to innovate. With both we had loads of fun, and did globally renowned work. In no particular order I'd also like to thank the following: Unilever (the makers of Lynx, Dove and Rexona); Transport Accident Commission (TAC); Good Goods (the makers of Who Gives a Crap); Twinings & Co (the makers of Jarrah); FBi Radio; Cancer Council NSW; Cheetham Salt; adidas (with Hawthorn Football Club); WorkSafe; George Weston Foods (makers of the Ministry of Muffins); Mentholatum (makers of the most disgusting ad of all time); and www.realestate.com.au.

Then, of course, I'm deeply thankful to Karen and the team at Oxford University Press for being interested in this area and 'outing' advertising (I've also since found out that in literary circles it's the cool thing to refer to you as OUP, so to OUP—sincere thanks). It was Karen who first identified the value in this book, and she has been completely wonderful to work with. Peter, thank you for doing such a good job at the editing stage.

However, most thanks must go to wife Anna and son Asterix. Deciding to write a book at the same time as you have a newly born bub in the house requires a degree of understanding and patience that stretches the boundaries of what's reasonable. Anna is an amazing woman, wife and mother to Asterix, and her opinions on behaviour change are included in this book. Asterix, I hope the little behavioural experiments I play on you are not the source of some therapist's revenue down the track, and you grow up to be a happy little chap. Behavioural economist Daniel Kahneman says in his book *Thinking, Fast and Slow* (which I reference in a few chapters), the one thing you can wish for a child is that they are born with a sense of optimism. As a near two-year-old, little Asterix, you're demonstrating that in spades. However, when Asterix had climbed up on my leg and banged on my keyboard one too many times, I sometimes had to leave the house and continue writing in the bars and cafés of St Kilda. I'd sit quietly in the corner (very) slowly drinking stout or coffee (which ever was time-appropriate), so to Dr Jekyll, Mr Wolf, the Newmarket, the Local Taphouse and the Woodfrog Bakery—much thanks. I'll drop a copy of this over to you.

Finally, I'd like to thank all the people I've met and learned from in both psychology and advertising. Both are incredibly fun and interesting professions to be a part of. I feel lucky to be in a position where I've been able to pick the eyes out of both, and lay them down in this book. I hope by outing advertising and the role psychology plays in it, I attract more (interesting and kind) people to this profession.

To everyone who's wanted to write a book, 'just do it'—it's an amazingly rewarding experience.

Adam Ferrier

INTRODUCTION

A magazine is simply a device to induce people to read advertising.

James Collins, 1907

WHY THE BOOK?

Hi. I'm Adam and I work in advertising. I've persuaded you to buy a particular brand of soft drink, to stay within the speed limit when driving and to book a room at a particular hotel. How did I do that? Well, you're about to find out. *The Advertising Effect* is an insider's guide to the tips and tricks that advertisers use to convince you to part with your money. It exposes how advertisers use psychology to influence your behaviour. So, why would I want to reveal this, particularly since I want to continue working in advertising? There are a couple of reasons: first, I want to stop *mindless* consumption; and second, I think you might find it useful to know the tricks advertisers use, and how you might apply them to your own needs.

So, the mindless consumption thing. Don't get me wrong—I don't have a problem with consumption per se. According to a report by the World Bank (2013), consumer-driven demand is responsible for approximately 65 per cent of the GDP of most developed countries. Strong consumer spending equals a strong economy, more jobs, progress and a lot of other good stuff. Consumer-driven demand is a good thing and keeps the economy healthy. However, I believe the more we know about how advertising works, the better our choices will be. And hopefully, we will shift from *mindless* consumption to *mindful* consumption.

Advertising attracts brilliant thinkers and arguably some of the most creative minds on the planet. These people are paid large sums of money to change consumer behaviour; that is, to encourage consumers to consume more and more. Thousands of brands pay billions of dollars to influence and change consumer behaviour. The global advertising industry is valued at $557 billion (Nielsen 2012). That's a lot of money telling people not only to eat, drive, drink, shop, wear and holiday more, but also how to behave and how to consume.

When I conduct research or run focus groups, the two most common comments I hear are: a) 'I don't watch TV'; and b) 'Advertising doesn't work on me'. The fact is advertising *does* work and it works really well or why else would corporations spend so much money on it? What's more, advertising is obviously no longer restricted to TV. It permeates every facet of our lives. Our social connections are conducted through brands and advertising. Events we attend are created (or at the very least sponsored) by brands, with commercial messages omnipresent. Even the news we consume is often created, sponsored or (at the very least) influenced by advertising.

When I was growing up, advertising only happened in certain predictable places. It was shown on TV, featured in magazines and newspapers and on large outdoor billboards. That was the 1980s. Since then, brands have dropped off billboards and left the confines of the idiot box. We now live in a marketing-saturated landscape. The ability to discern what is, and what is not, advertising is increasingly difficult.

Within this marketing-saturated landscape, many advertisers and marketers believe today's consumer is marketing savvy. They think consumers know how they're being influenced. I disagree. In fact, nothing could be further from the truth. *Today's consumer is marketing saturated, not marketing savvy.* To prove this point, who do you think is more likely to fall for the latest advertising-driven trend? A 16-year-old girl or an 80-year-old grandfather? It's the former. She's like a cat that's only lived in an apartment and never roamed the streets, and doesn't know there's a whole other world outside. Advertising is an omnipresent, super-powerful force. Those billions of dollars are making an impact. The cumulative power of all that advertising 'hitting' any one individual is scary.

This book aims to even up the ledger. If consumers—that's you and me—are more educated about how advertising works, we'll be able to make informed decisions about the advertising vying for our attention. And then we'll make better consumer decisions. And when this happens, marketers will have to respond and give consumers what they want. When this happens, everyone will win. Advertising is here to stay, so let's learn its secrets.

However, the second motivation for writing this book is because I love advertising and want to share how clever it is, how mischievous it is, and how, on occasion, devious it is (hopefully in a good way). Advertising attracts clever and creative people and puts that clever creativity to work to generate ingenious solutions to everyday problems. These solutions nearly always require that someone somewhere has to change their behaviour. This book aims to codify and share this knowledge in such a way that you understand how advertisers apply their craft—whether you work in advertising or not.

You see, *we are all in the behaviour change business—all of us.* A mother influences the behaviour of her children. A brother wants to negotiate with his older brother to stop hitting him. A teacher convinces students to sit silently. A manager works on keeping her employees engaged. An advertising agency sells ideas to its clients. It's not just advertising that persuades and influences—we're all in the behaviour change game. The better we are at changing the behaviour of others, the happier and more successful we'll be.

Let's peek behind the curtains of advertising and find out which psychological buttons are being pushed. I only ask that you use these powers for good.

WHO AM I TO EXPOSE THE SECRETS OF ADVERTISING?

When I was 17, I was unsure what I wanted to do with my life. I visited a careers counsellor, Kim Soia, who asked about my interests. I talked for some time before he eventually said, 'Well, you like money and you like people. You should become a consumer psychologist.' I have no idea how Kim arrived at this conclusion—but it sounded right.

I went to university and received a Bachelor of Commerce (Marketing) and a Bachelor of Arts (Psychology). To become a registered psychologist, I did three more years of study, completing a Postgraduate Diploma in Psychology as well as a Masters of Psychology (Clinical). I'm still a registered psychologist and Member of the Australian Psychological Society (MAPS).

My early career was in the field of forensic psychology, where I witnessed the extremes of human behaviour. For several years I worked at the Department of Corrective Services with prisoners before moving into a private practice. I made psychological assessments of people appearing before the courts and specialised in assessing sexual offending behaviours (more on that later in the book). I was thrown into the deep, dark pool of humanity, trying to make sense of it all while not drowning. Unravelling sexual dysfunction and harmful behaviour was an ideal training ground to understand human behaviour. In understanding the drivers of such dysfunction, I saw an exaggerated version of how many of us make sense of the world. Many of the principles I learned about human behaviour in these formative years have stayed with me—and helped to shape the thoughts you're about to read.

After some time, I decided to steer my career back to my initial aspiration of 'consumer psychology'. I did some more study and completed my Master's thesis: 'Identifying the Underlying Constructs of Cool People'. I then made the natural leap from understanding criminal behaviour to understanding consumer behaviour, and became a global 'cool hunter' for marketing consultancy Added Value. A cool hunter looks at the components of cool people, and the trends they adopt and ignore around the world. I got to stay at cool hotels and watch people's obsessions with fashion and trends—quite a change from criminal psychology. After Added Value, I worked at one of the world's most respected advertising agencies, Saatchi & Saatchi. There, I learned about the craft of advertising and the power of the brand. I then started my own shop with two friends. We were the founding partners of Naked Communications Asia Pacific.

Naked made a name for itself for avant-garde communications work and a consumer-centric approach to advertising and media. Under our stewardship, Naked won Agency of the Year awards several years in a row. We also won many of the world's top advertising awards, from a coveted Gold Lion to the WARC (World Advertising Resource Centre) World Prize for Innovation (2013). We were one of the hottest agencies in Australia and round the world. The *Wall Street Journal* claimed we were one of 'five agencies to watch worldwide'. According to advertising body, the Communications Council, Naked was the fifth most effective agency in Australia in 2013—despite being significantly smaller than other players on that list. My co-founders and I eventually sold Naked, and I have recently made the move to become a partner and co-owner of another independent agency, The Cummins Partnership. The Cummins Partnership is notable for being both a media and creative agency in one, or a 'creative: media agency', as we like to refer to it. This was how agencies were structured 20 years ago, until media separated from creative agencies. We've 'put the genie back in the bottle'.

During my time in advertising I've been at the forefront of many ideas that have won global acclaim. I've also won numerous Gold Effies, which are awarded for effective advertising, not necessarily creative solutions. To win an Effie, a carefully constructed case study needs to be written. These case studies have, where appropriate, been referenced throughout this book (they are a great source of information for people who want to understand what makes advertising effective). In 2014 I also won the Cannes Chimera, awarded by the Bill and Melinda Gates Foundation for ideas that tackle poverty. We won it for an idea called 'The Act Button'. I've also won awards from just about all the global advertising bodies, including Cannes Lions, Clios, D&ADs, New York Festivals and LIAs, along with Australian awards such as ADMA (Grand Prix, 2012 and 2013), AIMIA and CommsCon (Grand Prix, 2013).

These acronyms may not mean much to some of you, but if you're in advertising, hopefully you're suitably impressed and will continue reading. In 2013, *The Australian* newspaper described me as 'one of Australia's most creative and strategic thinkers in advertising'. Other advertising publications have awarded me:

- *AdNews'* 40 under 40 (2010)
- *Mumbrella's* 7 Top Strategists (2011)
- *Australian Creative's* Power 20 (2012)
- *Encore's* Power 100 (2012)
- *Australian Creative's* Power 20 (2013).

I've been involved in creating many behaviour change models used in advertising and have contributed to several academic studies. I'm a regular panellist on ABC TV's *Gruen Transfer* and *Gruen Planet*, which deconstruct advertising and communications. I'm a regular guest on *Sundays with James O'Loghlin* on ABC Local Radio and I'm often asked to give my opinions and views to the media and at conferences round the world. Somewhat oddly, I also host an interactive permanent exhibit at the Museum of Australian Democracy, Eureka (M.A.D.E) called 'The Power of Influence'. The exhibit covers some of the same issues covered in this book. It's a great museum, and a recommended day trip from Melbourne. It probably goes without saying that I really love advertising, and I really love psychology.

WHAT DO YOU THINK OF PEOPLE WHO RIDE ELECTRIC BIKES?

For the past year, I've been riding the streets of Melbourne on a lime-green electric bike. It looks great, cruises at around 25–35 km/h and I don't even have to pedal. When I get home, I just remove the battery and recharge it overnight. In the morning, I slide the battery back into place and away I go. What do you think about me and my electric bike?

Do you think I'm lazy? In which case, are you comparing me with riders of regular pushbikes? You know the ones—those fit-looking, 'higher moral ground' people in lycra. However, you may not view me as lazy. You might think I'm being very environmentally aware. In which case I'd guess you're comparing me with people who drive cars every day—the ones stuck in traffic and burning fossil fuels.

Humans aren't great at making 'absolute' judgments. Instead, we compare what we are judging against other frames of reference. I make this point because your frame of reference will have a significant impact on how you read this book. To this end I would like to be very clear: although this book is a mix of advertising and psychology, it is very much a practitioner's guide. The knowledge is based on my 11 years working in advertising and five years working in forensic and clinical psychology. I have taken what I've learned as a practitioner and delved into the science behind why and how it has worked. However, this is not a 'scientific' or research-based book, nor am I an academic. *It's a practitioner's book exploring the advertising effect.* My combined expertise in psychology and advertising puts me in the box seat to decode and explain how advertising works. If you'd like to read an academic perspective on behaviour change, I recommend starting with Andrew Darnton's (2008) literature review on various behaviour change methodologies. It's exhaustive and excellent (some of the models Darton refers to are drawn upon in various chapters of this book).

I hope you enjoy this read and find it useful. As a consumer, I hope it opens your eyes, makes you stop and think, and helps to explain why you buy what you buy. Also, as someone in the behaviour-change business (and we are all in the behaviour-change business), I hope you find the applications useful. If there's one key take-home message, it's that *action changes attitude faster than attitude changes action.* If you get people to act towards your goal, you will be far more effective and influential. In advertising this is still a new thought, and one that has not been entirely embraced (many in advertising still like doing big emotional ads). If you want to know more, read on.

REFERENCES

Darnton, A. (2008). *Reference report: An overview of behaviour change models and their uses. GSR behaviour change knowledge review.* London: Government Social Research.

Nielsen (2012). *Global Ad Spend Grows 3.2% in 2012.* Accessed at http://nielsen.com/us/en/newswire/2013/global-ad-spend-grows-3.2-percent-in-2012.html.

World Bank (2013). *Household Final Consumption Expenditure, Etc. (% of GDP).* Accessed at http://data.worldbank.org/indicator/NE.CON.PETC.ZS.

WHICH BEHAVIOUR TO CHANGE?

THE DARK ARTS: AN OVERVIEW OF ADVERTISING

The philosophy behind much advertising is based on the old observation that every man is really two men—the man he is and the man he wants to be.

  William Feather, US author

I have learned that it is far easier to write a speech about good advertising than it is to write a good ad.

  Leo Burnett, founder of Leo Burnett

VOLKSWAGEN 1

Exiting the underground train station in Odenplan, Stockholm, is like exiting most modern train stations. After stepping onto the platform, you walk through a turnstile and along a brightly lit tiled tunnel until you reach stairs and an escalator side-by-side, both of which take you to street level. But one day in October 2009, commuters faced an unexpected choice.

When they arrived at the final part of the exit, the 40 or so stairs rising to the street had been transformed. Instead of brown steps, the entire staircase had been turned into a giant piano. When your foot touched a black or white step, a different note sounded.

When the stairs became a giant piano, something happened to the behaviour of commuters. Instead of opting for the escalator, as usual, more chose to leave the station by climbing the stairs. Some ran up the stairs, producing a frenzied scale. Others lingered over the black notes or tentatively tapped several keys to create a tune. Over the course of a day, every type of person played on the stairs: young, old, male and female. At one point, two dogs bounded up the keys. In fact, when it was a giant piano, 66 per cent more people chose to use the staircase rather than the escalator. You can see the case study on YouTube (www.youtube.com/watch?v=SByymar3bds).

It's not surprising more commuters opted to take the stairs that day. They were presented with an opportunity that influenced their behaviour. How were they influenced? A mundane task became playful and fun. The piano staircase stunt was devised by advertising agency DDB in Sweden for car manufacturer Volkswagen, kick-starting the company's 'The Fun Theory' campaign 'dedicated to the thought that something as simple as fun is the easiest way to change people's behaviour for the better. Be it for yourself, for the environment, or for something entirely different, the only thing that matters is that it's change for the better.'

VOLKSWAGEN II

Would you expect an advertising agency to be behind this piano staircase stunt? Why would they need to do this? When a brand wants our attention, it usually screens advertisements on TV. In the case of Volkswagen, the ad would describe the car's rational features, such as self-parking, in the hope that viewers with think, 'Gosh, that would be handy'. The ad would also find a clever way of appealing at an emotional level through catchy music; for example, a woman bopping away while listening to the music as the car parks itself. The viewer might feel joy and a sense of freedom as they watch the car perfectly manoeuvre itself into its spot. The intention is to make the viewer think and feel differently about Volkswagen and, eventually, when it's time to buy a new car, they'll choose Volkswagen—or so the theory goes.

This is the dominant model of advertising: Attention, Interest, Desire and Action, or AIDA (see Figure 1.1). It was developed in 1896 by door-to-door insurance salesman, E St Elmo Lewis, who used his experiences to formulate the AIDA model for advertising. As he put it (Lewis 1903):

> *The mission of an advertisement is to attract a reader, so that he will look at the advertisement and start to read it; then to interest him, so that he will continue to read it; then to convince him, so that when he has read it he will believe it. If an advertisement contains these three qualities of success, it is a successful advertisement.*

Figure 1.1 The AIDA model

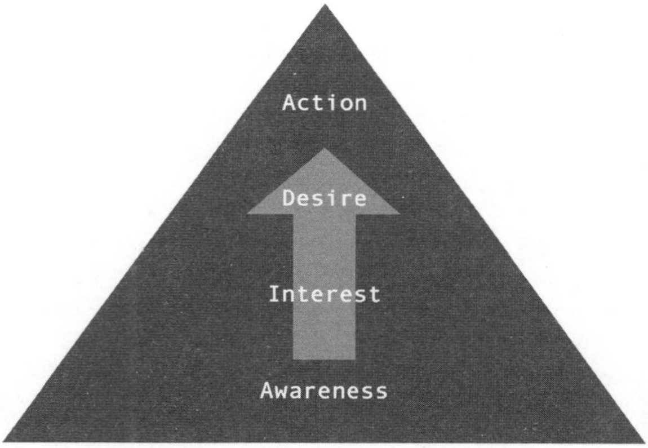

Source: adapted from Lewis (1903).

As unlikely as it seems, this model is still the standard used by many research agencies to measure the health of a brand. It's also the way many marketers talk about brands and communications. Despite the persistence of this outdated model, and the fact that advertising is a bit hit and miss (loads of it really is dreadful), the fact is that advertising works (Sethuraman, Tellis & Briesch 2011). If it didn't, companies wouldn't spend so much money on it every year. It does change behaviour. My issue with the model isn't about its effectiveness but rather that other forms of communication may work better. Second, this model was developed over 100 years ago when advertising was passive—the consumer couldn't be involved. Now, there's an interactive marketing communications landscape that means advertisers can do more than just talk *at* people—they can involve them in the communications. A school teacher doesn't change the behaviour of her class by just talking at them. She involves them in their learning.

VOLKSWAGEN III

Imagine driving home from work and passing three large outdoor ads that you don't pay any attention to—they happen to be for Volkswagen. You get home, read an online news site and fail to notice another ad for Volkswagen on the right-hand side of the news stories. Is Volkswagen wasting its money? Not according to Robert Heath, an influential academic and researcher based in England. Heath's book *The Hidden Power of Advertising* (2001) suggests that advertising works not through depth of message, or from viewers' processing the rational or emotional messaging, but largely through 'low involvement processing'.

Until Heath's work, it was assumed that advertising only worked if people paid conscious attention to an ad, or were at the very least aware they had seen the ad. Heath argues that advertising works whether we are aware of it or not. Every time we see an ad, it makes an impression on the brain. Heath explains that advertising creates enduring brand associations in our minds, even if we don't notice them. These associations build up over time and drive us to change behaviour and choose brand X over brand Y. There is an effect in psychology called the 'mere exposure effect' (Zajonc 2001), which states that we like something more simply because it is more familiar to us. The more familiar the brand becomes, the more we like it. And no, we don't even need to be aware of the ad for it to work. The more we like it, the more likely we'll buy it, with liking and purchasing highly correlated. Does this sound like 'subliminal advertising'?

ADVERTISING IS ABOUT CHANGING BEHAVIOUR

Advertising is really the business of behaviour change. There is not a single brief advertisers receive that does not require someone, somewhere, to change their behaviour. There's not a marketing director in the world that's paid to be happy with the status quo, or an advertiser with a brief that states, 'We don't want your advertising to have any effect'. We are in the behaviour change business. But changing other people's behaviour is extremely complicated. If you were the marketing director of Volkswagen, which of the following three forms of advertising would you choose to change behaviour?

1. something interactive and interesting enough to spread via social media?
2. 'traditional' advertising that speaks to a rational and emotional benefit simultaneously?
3. low-involvement processing, slowing renting mind space in your consumer's head?

This is the current predicament for so many in advertising at the moment. There are many things they could do, but what *should* they do?

Over the last 15 years, advertising has been transformed by the internet, technology advancements, social media, data and smartphones. It's become interactive. However, in a fully interactive media landscape, advertisers can influence and change behaviour more effectively. How? They involve the consumer.

If a teacher wants to influence the behaviour of his students, he can't just talk at them. To quote Confucius: 'Tell me, I forget. Show me, I remember. Involve me, I understand.' Whether it's a teacher in front of a class or a parent teaching a child how to kick a football, learning is more effective when the learner is involved in the learning. In a fully interactive marketing landscape, the same is now true of advertising. All marketing can now be interactive—as consumers, we don't just have to receive it passively. Advertising is starting to understand that action changes attitude faster than attitude changes action.

INFLUENCE AND BEHAVIOUR CHANGE IN EVERYDAY LIFE

It's not just advertisers who want to influence other people. Everything you believe, every choice you make, is in some way influenced by others. Think of the café owner seeking more customers, or the doctor who wants her patient to exercise, or the office manager tasked with reducing the amount of electricity that workers use in the office. It's the politician seeking your vote, the neighbour who wants the street to recycle and the parent trying to convince his child to eat vegetables. They want to influence other people's behaviour.

There's a widely held belief that you can't change other people. When I studied psychology, this joke did the rounds. Question: 'How many psychologists does it take to change a light bulb?' Answer: 'None. The light bulb has to want to change itself.' Although not funny, it reminds me of the advice given by my mother when, as a teenager, I was dumped by a girl I really liked. As I sobbed in my bedroom, heartbroken, mum came in for a chat. 'I just want her to like me,' I cried. My mum said, 'Adam, you can't change other people.'

If this is the case, what about the many professions that aim to change other people's behaviour, including psychology, teaching and advertising? A psychologist helps a patient with new patterns of behaviour. The teacher helps students to learn. The advertiser convinces consumers to buy a particular brand. We are all in the persuasion game. And as the giant piano steps experiment suggests, you can influence others to undertake a behaviour you want.

Learning about influence and behaviour change is very useful. In fact, I'd argue it's one of the most important skills to develop for success and happiness. This is obvious in advertising. If your advertising encourages people to do what you want, you'll be more successful. It's the same with the doctor trying to get her patients to exercise or the person with a noisy neighbour or the mother who wants her kids to eat their vegetables. It's also the case for a CEO of a charity that needs donations, or the police chief who wants to reduce assaults, or the minister for education who wants students to stay in school until Year 12, or a president who wants her country to adopt health-care reforms. It's the same as the mother wanting her daughter to eat breakfast before she leaves the house, or the boyfriend who wants his girlfriend to move in with him. We are all in the behaviour change business. The better we are at it, the happier and more successful we'll be.

PSYCHOLOGY IS SCIENCE—ADVERTISING IS ART

There's a quote in advertising that goes: 'Fifty per cent of my advertising budget is wasted. I just don't know which half.' The quote is attributed to several marketers, including John Wanamaker, a retailer; Henry Ford, the founder of Ford Motor Company; and Lord Leverhulme, one of the founders of Unilever (perhaps they were all a little confused as to how marketing works—how prophetic). It implies that many in advertising don't quite know how or why what they do works—they just know that it does. When I left psychology and started practising in advertising, I was astounded by this. People on the outside think that advertising is practiced as a science, but in large part it's not—in fact, far from it. Mostly it's made up. Michael Schudson, an American sociologist who studied the power of advertising and advertising agencies, said in his book *Advertising, the Uneasy Persuasion* (1984), 'Advertising is much less powerful than advertisers and critics of advertising claim, and advertising agencies are stabbing in the dark much more than they are practicing precision microsurgery on the public consciousness.' In most advertising agencies there is still only one god—the executive creative director—and that one god reveres just one thing: 'creativity'. Injecting science into this thinking has been difficult. Therefore many advertising agencies are very, very good at their craft, while simultaneously not entirely sure why it's effective.

HOW AN AGENCY WORKS

Broadly speaking, there are four roles within an advertising agency:

1. **Account service**—Affectionately known as 'suits' (or less affectionately as 'bag carriers'), they look after the account with the client, and make sure stuff gets done. They also act as general management within the agency.

2. **Strategic planners**—These are the 'thinkers' and pontificators. When I joined Saatchi & Saatchi as a strategic planner, my boss's first words of advice were: 'Adam, don't get in the way.' Planners are paid to be the 'strategic' ones in the agency, but truth is that people are still not sure what to do with them. There is an old joke in advertising. Question: 'What's the difference between a suit and a planner?' Answer: 'A planner knows when they are lying.' The joke is a play on the (mistaken) perception that everyone in an advertising agency just aligns behinds the creative work that is there to be sold and says what they need to say to sell it.

3. **Creatives**—These are the people who normally have the actual creative ideas.

4. **Production**—People in production help to make the creative output, or liaise with people (like film directors) who will make the idea come to life.

In addition to advertising agencies, there is another significant agency in the communications landscape. This is the 'media agency'. The media agency buys and sells media space, and recommends to the client what media channels they should use. Up until the late 1980s these two services (creative and media) were housed in the one agency. It's absurd that this is no longer the case, as advertising and media need to be considered together when trying to change behaviour. A very small number of agencies are now bringing media and creative services back together (where they belong).

THE PITCH

When I worked at Saatchi & Saatchi, we pitched for and won an account to advertise a well-known beer brand. In advertising, people love working on beer campaigns because there are large budgets, meaning they can do really creative things (there's a saying in beer marketing that 'with beer you drink the advertising', meaning whoever has the best ads wins). Many regard winning a beer account as the best thing that can happen to an agency. In recent years, beer companies and ad agencies have sailed a pub from New Zealand to England, bought an entire island off the coast of Australia, and replumbed a man's house so beer flowed from every tap—all done in the name of getting people to buy more beer. So how do agencies typically come up with these ideas? Perhaps the 'cleanest' way to demonstrate this process is to outline how an advertising agency pitches for a piece of business. In this environment the agency has full control of how it develops their ideas. Pitching is the part of an ad agency's work that is the most fun, the most challenging, and potentially the most creative as well. Nothing is left to chance in an effort to win the pitch. Everything goes into a pitch—everything the agency has. As Maurice Saatchi (co-founder of Saatchi & Saatchi) said: 'We don't have to win. We just have to make you lose.' Here's what happens, using the beer account as an example.

1. First comes the brief. This describes the aim of the campaign. It includes a PowerPoint deck of around 40 pages full of trends on beer (mainstream beer is flat; craft beer is growing), some images of the target consumer, and a 'pen portrait'—something like: 'Steve is a typical Aussie bloke—he's a "tradie" and at the end of the day he loves nothing more than jumping into his ute and heading down for a surf with his mates. After his surf he may catch up with a couple of the guys for a beer at the local pub before heading home to his girlfriend. She'll no doubt give him some grief for being late—but Steve promises to get home on time tomorrow ...'

2. A strategic planner in an advertising agency (in this example, that person was me) will take the 40-page brief and boil it down to a one-pager. This will follow a template like that in Figure 1.2, which is similar to an actual brief used by a well-known global agency. Deciding what to take from the client's information to put into this one-page brief is really up to the skill of the strategic planner. Sometimes it operates as a springboard for the creative work—and sometimes it's completely ignored.

3. Once the brief is written, it is shared with the 'creative teams'. To this day creative teams are often made up of the traditional pairing of an art director (a visually oriented creative) and a copywriter (a linguistically oriented creative). So, words and pictures together. Anyway, for this particular pitch I think we briefed around eight teams at once. The brief involved everyone sitting in the agency bar—and over a few beers I walked them through what we required from the creative idea.

4. Next the creative teams go away for a period of time (in this case, two weeks) and develop ideas. The process for developing ideas is very individual. Some are inspired by watching YouTube videos, others read books with old advertising ideas and attempt to repurpose those, and others go for a walk (or to the pub) and let inspiration hit them. In this case most ideas met the brief—but some did not. If an idea was really good but didn't meet the brief, we went with it anyway.

Figure 1.2 The creative agency brief template

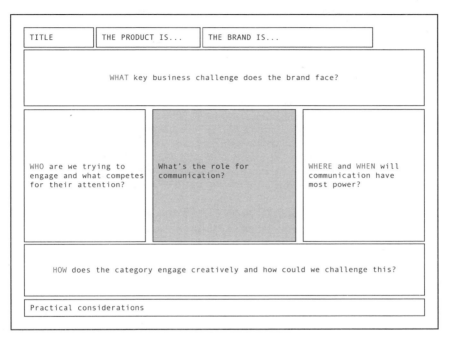

5. After two weeks all of the ideas from all of the creative teams are reviewed, and four or five are selected to work on further. This process takes a few hours. At this stage, it's likely the client will see the ideas and offer their input. With this particular pitch, we gauged opinions on three favourite ideas in focus groups held in pubs across Australia.

6. Having selected one or two favourite ideas, a strategy document is written to justify why these ideas will work. The strategy document will say something about: a) why the consumer will like the idea; and b) why the idea is good for the brand.

7. We then do 'the pitch' to the client, where we first present our strategy and then our favourite ideas. The ideas are presented with lots of different articulations. The idea that won this particular pitch was made into some loose TV scripts, some outdoor examples, a few radio ads and some other more 'stunty' ideas.

8. The client declared this idea was the best—and we won the account. When an agency wins an account like that it is a huge celebration. The CEO put his agency credit card across the bar, and the entire agency went across the road to the pub, and fittingly celebrated with a beer or two.

BRINGING PSYCHOLOGY AND ADVERTISING TOGETHER

In 2005, global CEO of Saatchi & Saatchi, Kevin Roberts, wrote the book *Lovemarks* about how to create a successful brand. When I worked at Saatchi & Saatchi, we shared copies of the book and would talk passionately about it. There was some lovely language in the book, such as 'a brand should create loyalty beyond reason', but little science on how advertising works, or indeed, how to actually create a 'Lovemark'.

My experience in psychology was completely different. Psychology is often referred to as a 'soft science', meaning it's not fact-based (like mathematics or biology), so is seen as less robust, reliable or valid. Many psychologists have a chip on their shoulder about this. They don't believe they are accepted as part of the medical profession—rather, they're seen to be part of 'allied health' that supports the medical profession. At the heart of the medical model is the doctor, and in the world of mental health, the specialist is a psychiatrist. A psychiatrist has medical training, can prescribe drugs and is very well paid. Most psychologists are not medically trained, can't prescribe drugs and don't get paid particularly well. However, psychologists conduct a great deal of research, and in my view are eternally keen to prove themselves to the psychiatry profession. The result is that psychologists take science and research extremely seriously. Most work to the 'scientist practitioner' model, meaning they don't do or recommend anything that isn't validated by science.

While many academic psychologists have studied advertising, but much of this research stays in the world of academia and doesn't flow through to the practitioners. After working in advertising for 14 years, and in psychology for five years, I feel qualified to write about the intersection of advertising and psychology and how to use both to change behaviour.

Now obviously I'm not the first psychologist to work in advertising, and nor am I the first psychologist in advertising to write about how it works. That honour goes to John Watson. His beliefs (and hubris) are clearly articulated in perhaps his best-known quote: 'Anyone, regardless of their nature, can be trained to be anything.' Watson was a behaviouralist and strongly believed in a stimulus-and-response style of learning. According to Watson, we have little free will and our behaviours are simply the manifestation of reward and punishment. Before he got into advertising, Watson and his researcher Rosalie Rayner became famous for the experiments they carried out on an 11-month-old child who would become to be known as 'Little Albert' (Watson & Rayner 1920). In short, they would show Albert a rabbit and pair the showing of the rabbit with a very loud bang to see if Albert would eventually become scared just seeing the rabbit (before the loud bang even happened). It didn't take long before exposure to the little rabbit set poor Albert off, breaking down in tears.

These experiments lay the foundations for classical conditioning, meaning that if we pair something (such as a cute rabbit) with an unconditioned stimulus (that is, something that we have an innate good or bad reaction to; in this case, a loud noise) we can get people to respond to the now 'conditioned stimulus' (the cute rabbit). In advertising it works like this. A beer ad shows a guy sitting next to a good-looking girl on the beach, drinking a beer. Eventually the beer is paired with the unconditioned stimulus (good-looking girl) and becomes a conditioned stimulus—so a viewer goes and buys the conditioned stimulus (beer) as it is strongly associated with the unconditioned stimulus (good-looking girl).

Watson's career as a psychology professor was cut short after a scandal involving him having an affair with Rosalie. He left academia and, like any good psychologist lacking in moral judgment, made his way into advertising, joining JWT (or J Walter Thompson as it was then known). There his career blossomed and he was involved in many very famous advertising campaigns for household brands including Maxwell House.

Around 20 years later, psychology was again exposed as having a key role in advertising by the book *The Hidden Persuaders* (Packard 1957). This best-selling (and often reprinted) book looked at how advertising worked on the subconscious and proffered that advertising, through all manner of manipulation, tapped into our deepest motivations to change our behaviour. Much of the book feels like hyperbole, with its insistence that every minutia of advertising is symbolic of some deep-seated, unexpressed desire, but it still makes for interesting reading.

Recently, however, psychological theories of human behaviour, and the behavioural sciences in general, are making their way back into advertising, economics and consumer understanding. The catalyst for this new body of work was Daniel Kahneman, a psychologist who won the Nobel Prize for Economics for his work into behavioural economics (see Kahneman 2002). This work looks at how we actually make decisions and derive value. Rory Sutherland, head of the IPA (Institute of Practitioners in Advertising), has led the charge in ensuring this work is embraced by the advertising profession—that is, that the industry takes a more scientific approach to what we do. Recently Sutherland commissioned a series of papers summarising where advertising sits with behavioural economics, including *Behavioural Economics: Red Hot or Red Herring* (IPA 2012). Ariely and Norton (2009) also provide an interesting overview, looking at how we consume and derive value from the consumption choices we make. (Norton is one of the 'Insiders' in this book.)

I mention this because sometimes it's a case of *plus ça change, plus c'est la même chose* ('the more things change, the more they stay the same'). For example, the work of both Watson and Packard feels as relevant today as ever. As you read this book, you'll see two key themes emerge. The first is that behavioural psychology is now very much back in vogue, with behavioural campaigns and action-based advertising proving themselves to be very effective (as Watson discovered all those years ago). The second is that much of advertising still operates in ways we, as consumers, are not consciously aware of—as Packard suggests.

The Insider: Rory Sutherland

First of all, to succeed in business, you do not have to be right—you simply have to be less dumb than your competitors. In any case, you can never be perfectly accurate in predicting human behaviour, any more than you can forecast the weather with perfect accuracy—it is simply too complex for that. The trick lies in being wrong less often than anyone else.

I would say there are at least three major assumptions about human behaviour that pervade business thinking, to a point where they are treated as axiomatic. These assumptions are quite often false. And so, by abandoning these assumptions, or at least by testing what happens when you abandon these assumptions, you may make considerable headway in being less wrong than your rivals. The three are as follows:

1 We assume that people can give accurate descriptions of the reasons behind their behaviour, and can explain to you accurately what they will choose in future. This underlies marketing's reliance on research. Yet more and more brain science reveals that we do not have introspective access to large parts of our unconscious mental workings. When we do explain or predict the decisions we make, it is often either a false post-rationalisation—or a false pre-rationalisation—which can offer very little of value and may be woefully misleading.

2 The microeconomic assumptions of mainstream economics are often assumed to be a given—yet more and more evidence contradicts them. Sometimes you can increase demand by increasing the price of some good, for instance.

3 The assumption that human behaviour follows the rules of Newtonian physics. Complex systems are different. The most important thing to realise here is that the size and cost of an intervention need have little or no bearing on the scale of its effect. The butterfly effect can work in marketing too. Think small.

Rory Sutherland is the executive creative director and vice-chairman at OgilvyOne London and vice-chairman at Ogilvy & Mather UK. He is also President of the Institute of Practitioners in Advertising (the UK's advertising industry body). I've been influenced by his passion for behavioural economics, and his desire to create value in the profession of advertising by introducing the behavioural sciences to our craft.

The Insider: Ivan Pollard

As I have become older, I have realised that a big part of our brains is like the chap that played centre-forward in my school football team when I was 9—lazy and selfish. For almost every decision, my brain says, 'How hard is this and what is in it for me?' Now I can work my way round that, but for the small, subconscious decisions (and even some of the big, thoughtful ones) this is my default setting. In that context, getting me to change my behaviour is a challenge—but not an insurmountable one.

My advice—based on my personal experience and experimentation with a 9-year-old, non-passing goal hanger, among others—is that if you want me to change my behaviour, you have to make it really easy for me to do so and really rewarding once I do. Oh, and once I have made the change you desire, you need me to adopt that as my new default and not change back. The trick is in the 'how'... I fall back on the ancient Chinese for that: 'Tell me, I'll forget. Show me, I remember. Involve me, I understand.'

Ivan Pollard leads communications strategy globally for the Coca-Cola Company, based in Atlanta, Georgia, and is considered by many to be one of the world's best communications strategists. I know Ivan after working with him for some years at Naked Communications. He's one of the most interesting people I've ever met, and I feel honoured to count him as a friend.

REFERENCES

Ariely, D. & Norton, M.I. (2009). How concepts affect consumption. *Annual Review of Psychology*, 60(1), 475–99.

Heath, R.G. (2001). *The Hidden Power of Advertising*. Admap Monograph no. 7, Henley-on-Thames: Warc.

IPA (2012). *Behavioural Economics: Red Hot or Red Herring*. London: Institute of Practitioners in Advertising.

Kahneman, R. (2002). Maps of bounded rationality: A perspective on intuitive judgment and choice. *Nobel Prize Lecture*, 8, 351–401.

Lewis, E.S. (1903). Catch-line and argument. *The Book-Keeper*, 15, 124.

Packard, V. (1957). *The Hidden Persuaders*. New York: D. McKay Company.

Roberts, K. (2005). *Lovemarks: The Future Beyond Brands* (expanded ed.). New York: PowerHouse Books.

Schudson, M. (1984). *Advertising, the Uneasy Persuasion: Its Dubious Impact on American Society*. New York: Basic Books.

Sethuraman, R., Tellis, G.J. & Briesch, R.A. (2011). How well does advertising work? Generalizations from meta-analysis of brand advertising elasticities. *Journal of Marketing Research*, 48(3), 457–71.

Watson, J.B. & Rayner, R. (1920). Conditioned emotional reactions. *Journal of Experimental Psychology*, 3(1), 1.

Zajonc, R.B. (2001). Mere exposure: A gateway to the subliminal. *Current Directions in Psychological Science*, 10(6), 224–8.

DEFINITION: IDENTIFYING THE BEHAVIOUR YOU WANT TO CHANGE

When it is obvious that the goals cannot be reached, don't adjust the goals, adjust the action steps.

      Confucius, Chinese philosopher

I've never found a client's business problem that could be solved solely through advertising.

      Lee Clow, Chairman, TBWA Worldwide (creator of Apple's '1984' ad and the 'Think Different' slogan)

DEFINE THE BEHAVIOUR TO CHANGE

To me it's crassly obvious that we need to be experts in changing the behaviour of others to achieve success and happiness—yet there are many messages in society that suggest we simply can't change other people. This may be because it's seen as rude to set out to change the behaviours of others, or that we would all like to think that we have more free will than behaviour change theory suggests: we don't like to think we could easily be the victim of another person's behaviour change program, therefore it must be hard to change the behaviour of others. However, I think the reason the myth persists is because, like all myths, there is a small element of truth in it. And the truth is that it *can* be difficult to change the behaviour of others, therefore, carefully defining what behaviour you really want to change becomes a significant precursor to success.

Getting others to do want you want them to do does not just happen. The first stage in such an everyday Machiavellian pursuit is to **decide on the behaviour that you want to happen**. What is it you want someone else to do? To briefly summarise, we can influence others, and change their behaviour, if: a) they are **motivated** to do what we are asking them to do; and b) what we are asking them to do is relatively **easy**. (The concepts of motivation and ease are central to behaviour change, and are the basis of the action spurs discussed throughout this text.) For example, if I ask my son Asterix to open his mouth to receive some ice cream, there is a high degree of motivation, and it's easy for him to do so. Or to make this even more clear, the less motivated someone is to do a particular behaviour, and the harder it is to do, the lower is the likelihood you'll be able to get them to do it. If I ask Asterix to take out the garbage, he not only lacks the motivation to do such a task, but because he isn't walking yet (at 18 months) it isn't easy for him to do either.

The KISS approach *for Ad Campaign.*

Daniel Kahneman (2012) suggests that if you want people to engage and believe your message, you have to make the message intuitive and easy to understand. This is jocularly known as the KISS approach (Keep It Simple Stupid). It's why I've used the following three techniques throughout the book:

1. Key words and phrases are highlighted in **bold.**

2. The language used has been kept simple because research shows knowledgeable people who use everyday language are more believable than those who use jargon (Oppenheimer 2006, in a paper that won him an Ig Nobel Award).

3. Stories and anecdotes are used to illustrate points because they are more memorable.

The same is true for advertising. In terms of changing someone's behaviour, an advertiser of beer, for example, is most likely to (in descending order):

1. get beer drinkers of a particular brand to try a new line extension of that brand

2. get beer drinkers of a rival brand to try their brand

3. get beer drinkers to buy more beer

4. get a non-beer drinker to start drinking beer.

In each case the task is progressively greater as we are asking the consumer to deviate more and more from their already established patterns of consumption. For the same reason, an advertiser is normally more likely to get people to visit a website than visit a store (it's easier) and an environmentalist is more likely to persuade someone to switch off the lights when leaving a room rather than to embrace a totally 'green' life (there's higher motivation and it's easier).

❯❯ Rule 1

If you want to change someone's behaviour, it will be most likely to happen if the person is motivated to adopt that behaviour, and if it's easy for them to do so.

CHIPS FOR BREAKFAST?

Advertising tends to be more effective when it asks you to change your behaviour ever so slightly, such as switching your breakfast cereal from Corn Flakes to Wheaties. But imagine if an advertiser asked you change from eating cereal for breakfast to instead eating potato chips. So rather than following your morning routine of getting a bowl, pouring in some cereal and then adding milk, they instead asked you to open a pack of chips and eat them on the way to work. This is asking for a much bigger change in behaviour and certainly would be harder to achieve. I know this from experience, as it was a brief I once received from a food manufacturer.

The client had found a way of basically putting cereal through a potato-chip-making machine. The end product was a packet of chips that were made out of, and tasted like, cereal. On paper the brief was interesting. The cereal chips tasted really nice, and they offered consumers a reasonable benefit: they were significantly easier to eat than cereal—just open the pack and start eating! Further, people wouldn't have to eat them at home as they could be eaten on the way to school or work. Sounds promising, no?

The product had spent a few years in what's called 'sensory development' (getting the taste and texture perfect), the name was carefully selected after extensive market research (they conducted 14 focus groups looking at the name and other packaging elements), and at launch the product was heavily advertised. However, it failed, with few people buying these cereal chips (and I doubt anyone can remember them briefly being on supermarket shelves). For despite breakfast chips being easier to eat, the motivation to do so just wasn't there. In part we were asking for too great a change in behaviour.

Now if we'd had more money and more resources, we might have been able to convince people to eat chips for breakfast. We could have:

- advertised all day and every day about the merits of 'cereal chips'
- hired a nutritionist to promote the health of 'cereal chips'
- offered discounts to make 'cereal chips' cheaper than cereal
- offered incredible prizes for people who endorsed 'cereal chips'
- organised an 'amnesty' where people could exchange empty cereal boxes for new packs of 'cereal chips'
- paid celebrities to promote our 'cereal chips', and so on.

I'm not saying you need a big marketing budget to change behaviour. My point is that some behaviour is harder to change than others. If you choose a behaviour that's difficult to change, it's going to take much more resources and effort to change it. This is why Rule 1 is so important. When seeking to influence someone, select a behaviour that is more likely to happen.

So how do we know which behaviours are likely to happen, and which are not? To answer this we need to delve a little more into psychological research.

BEHAVIOURAL PROPENSITY

When I worked in forensic psychology, one of my jobs was to write assessments of men accused of sexual assault that were used by the defence or prosecution to support their arguments and verdicts.[1] Speaking broadly, courts are interested in three aspects of criminal behaviour:

1. Did the accused have a **motivation** to commit the crime?
2. Did they have the **capacity** or skills to commit the crime?
3. Did they have the **opportunity** to commit the crime?

If it can be proved that the accused had the motivation, capacity and opportunity to commit the crime, the more likely they are to be found guilty.

Interestingly, these three components mimic almost exactly the findings of an international behaviour change conference held in Washington DC (Fishbein et al. 2001)—the only one of its kind ever undertaken. The purpose of the meeting was to gather together all of the best social scientists of the time and identify the common elements for understanding, predicting and modifying general human behaviour. To ensure the workshop was all-encompassing, all mainstream behaviour change theories (stages of change/transtheoretical model, health belief model, social learning theory, theory of planned behaviour, etc.) were represented. In other words, this was the first definitive meeting ever undertaken to try to explain why people behave the way they do and how to change behaviour.

After days of discussion by leading psychologists, eight influences on human behaviour were listed. As the authors of the subsequent paper highlight, 'The first three conditions are considered "necessary and sufficient" for adopting a behaviour, and the remaining five affect the intensity and direction of the intention' (Fishbein et al. 2001). The first three conditions were:

1. The person has formed a strong positive intention (or **motivation**) to perform the behaviour.
2. The person has the skills to perform the behaviour (or the **capacity** to perform the behaviour).
3. There are no environmental constraints that make it impossible for the behaviour to occur (the **opportunity** to do the behaviour).

Again, the recurring themes are motivation, capacity and opportunity. Here we can see motivation relates to the individual intent or desire to do something. However, 'ability' and 'opportunity' are somewhat different from motivation—they are objective measures on whether the behaviour can be done or not; that is, the level of difficulty there is to do the behaviour (is it 'easy' or not). Thus, we return to the two main variables when looking at likelihood of a behaviour occurring: motivation and ease (with the latter comprising opportunity and ability).

---

1 I know this is a book on advertising, but just a quick deviation. I enjoyed my time in forensic psychology and being an expert witness for whoever was paying me until I read *Whores of the Court: The Fraud of Psychiatric Testimony and the Rape of American Justice* by Dr Margaret Hagen (1997). Dr Hagen clearly articulates why it's impossible for psychologists and psychiatrists to give independent and neutral advice on an individual when they are being paid by the defence or prosecution (as are the vast majority of all court reports). In short, if you think advertising is unethical, try being an expert witness.

Thinking back to the breakfast chips example: breakfast chips are easier to eat than breakfast cereal, but there is little motivation to make the change from cereal. Had there been high motivation and high ease to do the behaviour it's likely the behaviour would have happened. Let's look at motivation and ease in a little more detail.

MOTIVATION

Motivation is a very complex subject. In psychology, it's about making someone move towards, or make an effort to achieve, a certain goal. It relates to physiology (if I'm hungry, I'm motivated to eat), cognition (I want good marks at school, so I'm motivated to study) and social standing (I want to fit in with a social group, so I'm motivated to like what they like). If you lived alone on a desert island, there would be one determinant of motivation: what's in it for me? The reality is we are social animals and depend on others to survive and thrive. This means there's another determinant of motivation: what are other people doing? Therefore, motivation is composed of two different factors; **individual incentives** and **social norms**.

INDIVIDUAL INCENTIVES

For an individual to undertake a behaviour there are, according to behavioural theorists, two key considerations: pleasure and pain. We chase pleasure (rewards—things that feel good) and avoid pain (punishment—things that feel bad). On the most basic level, humans are driven to find rewards and avoid pain. If there are incentives to undertake a behaviour, then the behaviour is more likely to happen. Incentives can be things such as money, food and prizes, or feelings such as pride, joy or excitement. Incentives also include information that is interesting or entertaining. To work out how much incentive is needed for a behaviour to occur, first consider the rewards and punishments for that particular behaviour. Second, determine the value placed on those outcomes; that is, to what degree does someone care about those rewards and punishments?

With this in mind we are able to approximate the level of incentive there is for a behaviour to occur. The greater the incentive, the greater the motivation. What were the incentives to eat cereal chips over breakfast cereal? Potentially there were not enough clear incentives that made cereal chips a preferred option over cereal.

Perhaps the best-known work on motivation and incentives was carried out by BF Skinner, utilising various behaviour changing gadgets including his 'Skinner box' (Evans 1968). The Skinner box offered incentives to pigeons (the main occupants of the box, although lots of different animals were used) every time they did a certain behaviour. With this basic principle Skinner was able to train various animals to do very complex tasks.

Skinner built on the work of Watson and Pavlov (of 'Pavlov's dog' fame) and believed firmly that humans neither enjoy free will nor clearly decide what we want to do. Instead, he believed that all human action was either reinforced or discouraged by the consequences of that action. If the consequences are good, we'll do it more often. If they are bad, we won't keep doing it. Skinner is possibly the most widely known and influential behavioural psychologist of all time. You can find out more about him and his work via any good introductory psychology text, or read Daniel Bjork's *B. F. Skinner: A Life* (1993).

SOCIAL NORMS

However, we are not pigeons, and nor are we living on a desert island (or in a Skinner box) and we are surrounded by other people. Psychologist Albert Bandura (1977) believed that watching what others do has a far greater impact on human behaviour than internal motivations or individually driven incentives. When deciding how to act, many people ask (subconsciously), 'How will I look if I undertake this behaviour?' 'What are the social norms around this behaviour?' 'Are people I consider to be influential undertaking this behaviour?' Fishbein and Ajzen (1975) are two psychologists who have been studying behaviour change for many years. They articulate the influence of social norms on motivation as being 'the person's perception that most people who are important to him or her think he should or should not perform the behavior in question'.

Coming back to our cereal chips example, what do you think most people would think of someone eating chips for breakfast on their way to work? How would you feel sitting on the train eating a bag of cereal chips as you make your way to work in the mornings? I imagine that the negative social norms associated with eating what looks to be junk food first thing in the morning were the main barriers to cereal chips being a success.

However, we know that motivation is only half the story. Now we look more closely at the concept of 'ease'.

EASE

In the past, most advertisers influenced behaviour by attempting to change people's minds; that is, by increasing motivation. Advertising in the traditional and stereotypical sense is all about increasing motivation to purchase. How do I get people to buy my chocolate bar? I'll make it look delicious on TV, and promise that it provides enough energy to get through the day.

Often when you want to change an aspect of other people's behaviour, motivation is where you will start. Imagine your daughter's homework is messy and you want her to make it neater. You could convince her of the importance of appearances, and how people will value her work more if it's neat. Alternatively, you could ask her to stop doing her homework while lying down on her bed and explain it's *easier* to make it neat if she sits at her desk!

In behaviour change 'ease' has been the missing variable in many disciplines as we've focused incessantly on increasing motivation for something to happen. Just making a behaviour easier to occur can have dramatic results. As previously mentioned, ease has two components:

- ability—does someone have the actual attributes, or 'internal factors', needed to complete a behaviour (Can they do that?)
- opportunity—is the person's environment conducive to that behaviour taking place? (Does the environment or situation allow the person to do that behaviour?).

Consider one of the toughest behavioural challenges of our time: weight loss. Someone might be very motivated to lose weight—they could suffer from Type II Diabetes, for example—but lack the skills to lose weight. They don't know how to do it, and the environment sometimes does not make it easy for people to lose weight.

In 2012, while working with their PR company One Green Bean (no, I've no idea why they are called that), I devised an experiment for weight-loss company Weight Watchers in which 20 food journalists and bloggers were invited to a buffet lunch. As they arrived at the venue, they were randomly sent to one of two rooms, each of which had a variety of foods laid out in a buffet (Buffet A and Buffet B). None of them knew about the existence of the other buffet due to the layout of function centre (see Figure 2.1). The food at both buffets was identical, but there were key differences in how the food was presented:

- In Buffet B, a slender woman continually loaded her plate with food. Research by McFerran (2010) has revealed that people are likely to eat more if a thin person is eating near them.
- Buffet B had larger-sized plates and serving utensils than Buffet A. Wansink (2006) found that people put less food on their plates if the plates and utensils are smaller. Wansink also found people consume more food when the food is the same colour as the plate.
- Buffet B had images of plates piled high with food. Madzharov and Block (2010) discovered that people eat more if they see an image of larger serving sizes.
- Buffet B had healthier food at the back of the buffet and less healthy food at the front. People are more likely to choose unhealthy food when it's easier to reach. In a study by Painter, Wansink and Hieggelke (2002), workers ate 5.6 more chocolates per day if the chocolates were placed in a bowl on their desks rather than 2 metres away on a table.

Figure 2.1 The layout for the Weight Watchers food experiment

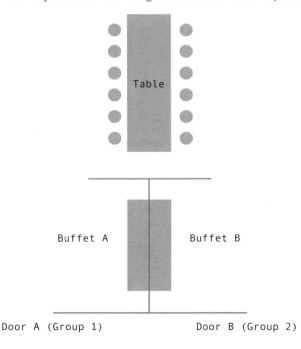

osing their food from either Buffet A or Buffet B, the two groups were brought on table and their selections analysed. The differences were quite astounding. Buffett B had, on average, 50 per cent more food on their plate than those who ᴣlections at Buffet A. Not only that, the food choices by those in Buffet B tended to ʋ less healthy, with more people selecting fattening foods and very little salad. The behaviour changed not because of motivation but because of opportunity. People at Buffet A made better food choices because it was easier for them to do so.

Google is a company renowned for the special way it treats its staff, offering free food buffets in every office, along with many other perks. In 2011, Google's head chef Scott Giambastiani embraced the above principles and redesigned their buffet to 'make it really easy for people to make healthy choices' (Nestle 2011). Google's buffet changed to display healthy food at the front and hide the bad stuff. They also scaled down the size of their servingware, colour-coded the food from healthy to unhealthy, and put scales at the end of the buffet so employees could weigh their food. By all accounts, the Googlers (the slightly cringe-worthy name Google calls its employees) are now eating more healthily—because it's easier for them to do so. Notice that all of these changes made it easier for people to eat healthier food by changing the environment—creating the opportunity for people to more easily choose healthier food.

Another way to encourage behaviour is by increasing someone's ability to undertake the behaviour. Again, this is related not to motivation but to ease. When people attend Weight Watchers, they are given information on healthy eating and tips on how to manage their food intake. They learn why it's better to eat a banana than banana bread. Further, Weight Watchers uses a points system for keeping track of kilojoules consumed. The points system increases people's ability to track and manage their kilojoule intake, thus making it easier for them to lose weight.

So to make it easier for someone to change their behaviour, you can increase the *opportunity* of making something happening and increase their *ability* to do it. Ease is a function of **ability** and **opportunity**.

PUTTING MOTIVATION AND EASE TOGETHER

BJ Fogg is one of the most interesting thought leaders in the world on behaviour change. He founded the Persuasive Technology Lab at Stanford University and created a way of looking at behaviour change through three factors: motivation, ability and triggers. The model in this book draws on some of BJ's thinking in that I want to clearly delineate between motivation and ease. Roughly speaking, motivation is an internal measure ('Is the person actually motivated to do something?'), whereas ease is a slightly more objective measure ('Looking at this situation and the person's ability, can this behaviour be easily achieved?'). However, using Fishbein and Ajzen's 'theory of reasoned action approach' (2010), motivation can be split into individual incentives and social norms, as discussed earlier. So we can now put motivation (and its constituent parts) and ease (and its constituent parts) together to form a framework that allows us to assess the likelihood of a behaviour being changed (see Figure 2.2).

Figure 2.2 The behaviour framing grid

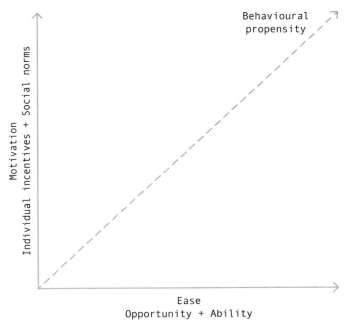

Roughly speaking there are four areas on the behaviour framing grid. For example, imagine the behaviour we wanted to change was to get someone to eat a Mars bar. Getting someone to do this behaviour would depend on their motivation to eat the Mars bar (such as hunger levels) and where the Mars bar was (close or far away). Have a look at the following situations:

1. Behaviours that are high in motivation and high in ease—these behaviours *are likely* to happen (for example, asking a hungry person to eat a Mars bar that's right in front of them).

2. Behaviours that are high in motivation but low in ease—these behaviours *might* happen (for example, asking a hungry person to eat a Mars bar that they have to walk down the street to get).

3. Behaviours that are low in motivation but high in ease—these behaviours also *might* happen (for example, asking a person who's not that hungry to eat a Mars bar that is right in front of them).

4. Behaviours that are low in motivation and low in ease. These behaviours are *unlikely* to happen (for example, asking a person who is not hungry to eat a Mars bar that they have to walk down the street to get).

With this map we can plot where any behaviour we want to change sits, and the likelihood of it occurring. If we return to the example of cereal chips, where do you think 'Get people to eat cereal chips for breakfast' would sit? As discussed, there is only moderate motivation to carry out this activity. The incentives may be there, but motivation to conform with social norms is extremely low. By contrast, it feels like a relatively high 'ease' proposition as people have both the ability and (assuming good distribution of the product through supermarkets) the opportunity to consume these chips. Hence we would map the behaviour to change in the bottom right of the behaviour framing grid, as illustrated in Figure 2.3.

Figure 2.3 Mapping people's likelihood to eat cereal chips for breakfast

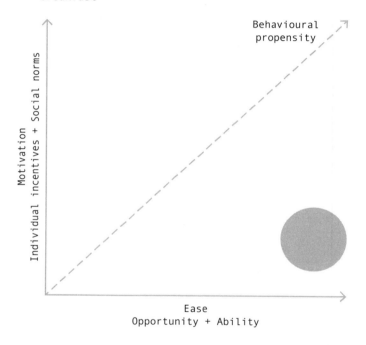

Using this grid should always the first step in deciding which behaviour to change. To change someone's behaviour, ask these four questions.

Motivation:

1. Individual incentives: What's in it for them? Will they be rewarded and to what extent?

2. Social norms: What will others think of them if they undertake that behaviour?

Ease:

3. Ability: Do they have the resources, competency and skills to do the behaviour?

4. Opportunity: Does the environment allow the behaviour to happen?

These four questions will help you understand how susceptible the behaviour is to change or influence. As we will see later, they also act as a diagnostic tool to help people see where the potential triggers and barriers are to behaviour change. For example, is it a motivation or ease issue? Is it a social norming or individual incentive issue? Now, there's one final step to take into account: does the behaviour you want to change contribute to your overall goal?

CHANGING THE RIGHT BEHAVIOUR

A friend of mine owns a microbrewery that makes a lovely premium pale ale beer. After investing a significant amount of money to create his beer, he needed to generate some sales and asked for my help. Who should he sell to? Or more specifically, what behaviours should he change to sell more of his beer? I told him there were at least four behaviours he could influence:

1. Get friends and family who already love his beer to recommend it to others.

2. Ask family and friends who don't like beer to try it.

3. Ask existing beer drinkers to try his beer.

4. Ask friends and family who love his beer to purchase more of it.

I mapped these four behaviours against ease and motivation (see Figure 2.4). In my estimation, the behaviour that is most likely to occur—and therefore make happen—is behaviour number 1: 'Get friends and family who already love his beer to recommend it to others.'

Figure 2.4 The potential behaviours to change to sell beer

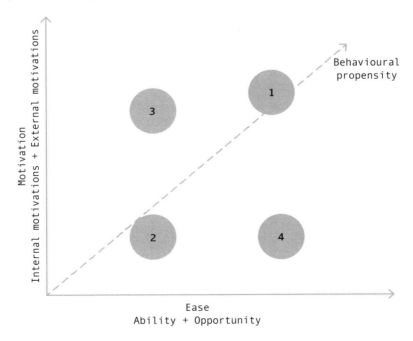

25

However, this is fine if my friend only wants to sell 10,000 cases of beer. But it's another story if he wants to sell a million cases of beer. And that's when '**sizing a behaviour**' comes into play. This simply means choosing a strategy that matches your goal. There are five key questions when sizing a behaviour.

1. How many people am I influencing?
2. How many people are they influencing? And how influential will that group be?
3. What is the frequency of the behaviour?
4. What is the likely penetration? How many people are likely to change?
5. What is the importance of that behaviour in meeting my goal? Is having people talk positively about my brand as important as generating a sale?

Taking these questions into account, I then revisited each of the four original behaviours and approximately sized them. In Figure 2.5 the behaviours are not only mapped but also now sized (the larger the circle, the greater the potential contribution to overall beer sales). You can now see that will be better for my friend to target the behaviour of the third group: beer lovers who haven't yet tried the beer. They are more likely to try his beer because they're already beer drinkers. Let's work through why.

Figure 2.5 Approximate sizing of the behaviours to change as a contribution to sales

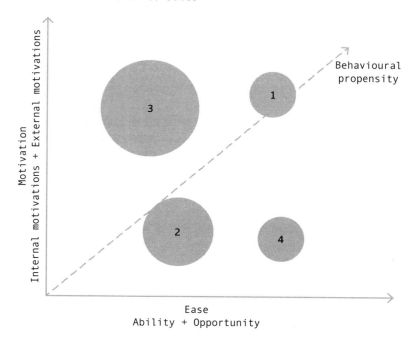

First, many people can be influenced because while there are many beer lovers, few are already familiar with my friend's beer. Second, we can assume the beer lovers who are prepared to sample my mate's beer are early adopters who will in turn influence others. Third, our beer lovers love beer. Fourth, if we assume the frequency of beer drinking is quite high, then the motivation to try the new beer is also high. If our beer is good, then I predict 'penetration' will be reasonable; that is, if we get them to try the beer, then a number will convert. Finally, we can trial the behaviour by giving samples. It's better for people to try the beer, rather than just talk positively about it. My friend opted for this behaviour.

The only marketing my friend did was mass sampling at venues where the beer was distributed. It meant people could sample the beer and then buy it. The beer got traction thanks to the trial and has become a successful beer brand.

Rule 2

Change the behaviour that will help you achieve your goals.

SUMMARY

There's no question that influencing behaviour is challenging, but you make the task much easier by following a couple of simple rules. The first is to choose a behaviour that has a greater likelihood of occurring. To work that out, examine how motivated someone is to undertake a behaviour and how easy it is to do the behaviour. Next work out which behaviour best matches your overall goal. Once you've worked this out, it's then a matter of using techniques to increase motivation and ease, of which there are many. I'll give you a sneak peek—it's about making people act towards your goal.

1. It's difficult to change behaviour, so choose one that's more likely to be changed.

2. A behaviour is more likely to be changed if there's a high degree of both motivation and ease to do the desired behaviour.

3. Motivation is comprised of individual incentives and social norms.

4. Ease comprises ability (the person's skills and resources) and opportunity (how the environment allows the behaviour to happen).

5. Size the behaviour you want to change, and choose to change the behaviour that is both susceptible to change and helps you achieve your business goals.

The Insider: Claudiu Dimofte

To induce behaviour change it is useful to first define its parameters. Two important dimensions are (1) the degree to which the behaviour is altered (i.e., slightly or radically) and (2) the desired time frame for the change (i.e., short or long lasting). If the intent is that decisions, choices, and actions be altered to a small degree or over short periods of time, situational cues can be manipulated in ways that may not be consciously perceived but can be very effective. On the other hand, long-lasting or dramatic behaviour changes are much more difficult to induce. They generally require a shift in terms of personal characteristics (i.e., what academics term individual difference variables) or that powerful motivators be at work. In today's interconnected, social media based world, it is often the case that the need to obtain others' acceptance, interest, or respect can be the critical motivator to drive significant behavioural change. Framing the desired new behaviour (e.g., the conspicuous adoption of a marketed product, idea, or cause) as a self-efficacy enhancing opportunity to reach these other, related goals can be a successful strategy. After all, most Toyota Prius owners drive their hybrid cars not to conserve the environment, but to be perceived as doing so by others ...

Claudiu Dimofte is an associate professor at San Diego State University, where he teaches the core marketing course in the MBA and EMBA programs. He also serves on the Editorial Board of the *Journal of Consumer Psychology*. I met Claudiu when I presented at the annual consumer psychology conference in San Diego, California, in 2013.

REFERENCES

Bandura, A. (1977). *Social learning theory.* Englewood Cliffs: Prentice Hall.

Bjork, D.W. (1993). *B. F. Skinner: A Life.* New York: HarperCollins.

Evans, R.I. (1968). *B.F. Skinner: The man and his ideas.* New York: E.P. Dutton.

Fishbein, M. & Ajzen, I. (1975). *Belief, Attitude, Intention, and Behavior: An Introduction to Theory and Research.* Reading: Addison-Wesley.

Fishbein, M. & Ajzen, I. (2010). *Predicting and Changing Behavior: The Reasoned Action Approach.* New York: Taylor & Francis.

Fishbein, M., Triandis, H., Kanfer, F., Becker, M., Middlestadt, S. & Eichler, A. (2001). Factors influencing behaviour and behaviour change. In A. Baum, T. Revenson, J. Singer J. (eds), *Handbook of Health Psychology* (pp. 3–17). Imahwah: Lawrence Erlbaum Associates.

Fogg, B.J. (2011). *BJ Fogg's Behavior Model.* Accessed at www.behaviormodel.org.

Hagen, M. (1997). *Whores of the Court: The Fraud of Psychiatric Testimony and the Rape of American Justice.* New York: HarperCollins.

Kahneman, D. (2012). *Thinking, Fast and Slow.* New York: Macmillan.

Madzharov, A.V. & Block, L.G. (2010). Effects of product unit image on consumption of snack foods. *Journal of Consumer Psychology,* 20(4), 398–409.

McFerran, B., Dahl, D.W., Fitzsimons, G.J. & Morales, A.C. (2010). Might an overweight waitress make you eat more? How the body type of others is sufficient to alter our food consumption. *Journal of Consumer Psychology,* 20(2), 146–151.

Nestle, M. (2011). What Google's famous cafeterias can teach us about health. *The Atlantic,* 13 July. Accessed at www.theatlantic.com/health/archive/2011/07/what-googles-famous-cafeterias-can-teach-us-about-health/241876.

Oppenheimer, D.M. (2006). Consequences of erudite vernacular utilized irrespective of necessity: Problems with using long words needlessly. *Applied Cognitive Psychology.* 20(2), 139–56.

Painter, J.E., Wansink, B. & Hieggelke, J.B. (2002). How visibility and convenience influence candy consumption. *Appetite,* 18(3), 237–8.

Wansink, B. (2006). *Mindless Eating: Why We Eat More than We Think.* New York: Bantam-Dell.

3

THOUGHTS, FEELINGS AND ACTIONS: USING ACTION TO CHANGE BEHAVIOUR

Action is the foundational key to all success.

Pablo Picasso

Before we go any further, I was wondering if you could do me a favour. If you do, *it'll help me to help you to get the most out of this book.* And it's easy. I promise. I really want you to do this favour for me. Will you do it? Just turn to the last page of this book and read the message in the box. I'll wait here.

Thanks again for doing that. Pretty surprising, don't you think? I hope it gives a small demonstration of the importance of encouraging someone to act towards your goal. (Note: if you didn't do it, please go to the last page and read it now. If you already have, just read on—I don't want you caught in some weird *Groundhog Day* loop or anything!)

When I worked as a psychologist, one of my main tasks was to help patients 'act' towards a goal. Inside my modest office, with its desk, bookshelves and two chairs placed on a fluffy white rug, clients shared their deepest issues with me. On the wall was a quote: 'Success in life cannot be measured in heights achieved, but only in obstacles overcome.' The quote was adapted from Booker T Washington, who wrote about slavery in America. I love that quote—it takes the pressure off. My office also had a small whiteboard placed to my left. If you came to see me, I'd welcome you into the room, ask you to sit down and tell you a bit about my approach to therapy, using drawings on the whiteboard.

The first diagram I'd invariably show you appears in Figure 3.1 (over the page).

The diagram is adapted from the work of two of the most influential psychologists of the last 30 years, Albert Ellis and Aaron T Beck. I had the good fortune to meet Albert Ellis when I attended one of his group therapy sessions at the Albert Ellis Institute in New York City's Upper West Side. Even though Albert died in 2007, the Institute still runs group therapy sessions and they are a must to attend if you are even vaguely interested in people and behaviour change. Albert was famous for his extreme dogmatism and was overbearing with his patients—sometimes bullying them into change. There is a wonderful video of him with a patient called Gloria you can watch on YouTube (www.youtube.com/watch?v=odnoF8V3g6g) though you'll have to ignore the politically incorrect language of the day. You can get a good understanding on his work in *The Albert Ellis Reader by* Ellis and Blau (2001).

Albert was in his nineties when I met him. The first thing he said to me was, 'Well, what do you want to see me for?' I was a little taken aback, but told him how his ideas had made a deep impression on me both professionally and personally. Then I asked if the story

Figure 3.1 The interrelationship between thoughts, feelings and actions

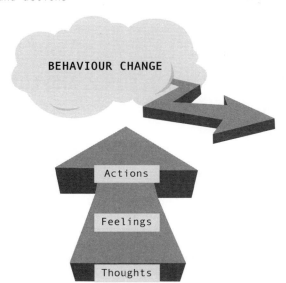

about how he dealt with shyness towards women was indeed true. When Ellis was 19, he read the work of behavioural psychologist John Watson (who we met in Chapter 1). After reading his books, Ellis set himself the task of talking to 100 women and asking them on a date. The story was true and had a significant impact on his life. He told me that every day he would wander around the Bronx Botanical Gardens and approach women sitting alone on a park bench. He said in total he approached 130 women and talked to around 100 of them, asking each out on a date. He wasn't successful with any of them. One date was arranged, but she never turned up. But there was a bigger impact: he overcame his fear and shyness of women, and did okay with the next 100 women he asked. Thus Albert overcame his shyness of women by setting himself the action orientated task of actually speaking to them. His actions changed his attitudes.

But I digress. Let's return to my consulting room with the whiteboard. If you were my patient, I'd explain that 'thoughts' influence 'feelings', which in turn influence 'actions', the sum of which equals behaviour. It's called cognitive behavioural therapy (CBT), and seeks to change behaviour using three triggers: thoughts, feelings and actions. Imagine you're driving a car and someone swerves in front of you. You might **think** to yourself, 'They did that on purpose.' How does it make you **feel**? You probably feel angry. Your **action** might be to shake your fist at the driver. This influences your **behaviour** of becoming an aggressive driver. Your thoughts, feelings and actions are intertwined.

CBT asks you to imagine a different scenario, one in which the other driver has just learned some awful news. They've just been told their child has been in an accident and is now in hospital, which explains why they're driving so erratically. What are your feelings towards the other driver now? Instead of anger, you might feel concern. In considering an alternative rationalisation, you've had a different response. Your interpretation of the behaviour affects how you feel and behave.

Back in my consulting room, I would help you understand the interrelationship between thoughts, feelings and actions. Then we could work on changing your behaviour.

WE LIKE OUR THOUGHTS, FEELINGS AND ACTIONS TO BE ALIGNED

Thoughts, feelings and actions are part of a powerful psychological loop. Unless the three are aligned, we feel uncomfortable and suffer what psychologists call **cognitive dissonance** (Festinger, Riecken & Schachter 1957). It's how I imagine an environmentalist would feel if she worked for a tree-logging company—her thoughts and feelings would not be aligned with their actions. Contradictions make us feel uncomfortable and this internal discomfort motivates us to change. To alleviate her cognitive dissonance, the environmentalist would be motivated to either take action (for example, change her job) or change her thoughts and feelings about the environment (for example, by recognising that we need timber for furniture and construction). We change our actions to follow our thoughts and feelings, but interestingly, we also change our thoughts and feelings to make sense of our actions. Take the case of Albert Ellis in the park. He felt shy about talking to girls, so he acted differently, approaching 100 of them until his thoughts and feelings about girls changed—he was no longer shy when talking to them. For me, behaviour change is certainly about influencing thoughts and feelings, but most of all it's about influencing actions.

There's growing evidence that action is the most important lever to pull when changing behaviour. However, to explain its importance we need to go back in time and look at the work of psychologist Leon Festinger, author of *A Theory of Cognitive Dissonance* (1957). Although he studied cognitive dissonance his entire career, he is best known for his initial experiments that demonstrate the effect. This is what he did (note that it's a little counterintuitive, so please read carefully because it's an important principle). Seventy-one people were recruited for a study called 'Measures of Performance' in which the subjects were asked to do two extremely boring tasks. In the first task, for 30 minutes they had to place 12 cotton spools onto a tray, empty the tray and refill the tray—over and over again. In the second task, they were given a board with 48 square pegs and told each peg had to be turned one after the other by a quarter clockwise, again for 30 minutes non-stop. On completion of their task, the subjects believed that the experiment was over, and it was at this point the researcher asked them for a favour. They were told the researcher's colleague hadn't turned up for work. Would they mind stepping in? They were informed that the experiment they had just done was about mental preparedness and its relationship with task performance, and all they had to do was tell the following subjects about the experiment and to say that the experiment was really interesting and fun to do. They'd be paid for doing this.

Half of the unwitting subjects were paid $1 to lie about how interesting the tasks were and half were paid $20. At the end of the day—after lying to a number of people about how interesting and fun the tasks were—the subjects were interviewed. They were asked how interesting or fun they found their original spool-turning or peg-turning tasks (which were obviously very dull and boring). Who do you think reported the task as more fun? Those who were paid $1 or $20? (Please think about the question and answer it now before moving on.)

Who reported the task as more fun and interesting?

A Those paid $1

B Those paid $20

Why?

The actual task was designed to be mundane and boring. You would be lying if you said it was otherwise. So it was the act of lying to others that was expected to create cognitive dissonance in the participants (because they lied to others saying it was interesting, whereas they actually did a very boring task for an hour). You would expect that those paid $20 would more easily change their opinion than those paid $1 saying that they too enjoyed the actual task. However, Festinger predicted the opposite to be the case. He thought the $20 group would have less justification to change their opinions because they were paid a larger sum and felt less internal conflict. That is, they lied but they were paid $20 so there was less dissonance. Those who received only $1 would feel more dissonance and justify their lie by changing their opinion of the boring task to match the lie they told others. Festinger was right. Participants who only received $1 to lie resolved the dissonance by rating the boring experiment as significantly more fun and interesting. Participants who received $20 didn't experience as much dissonance because the money justified their actions.

Learning about this study was a game-changer for me. I realised just how powerful the alignment of thoughts, feelings and action is. And here's the thing: if you disturb that alignment, you can influence behaviour. You can see the original experiment on YouTube (https://www.youtube.com/watch?v=1kmVy1QPXn0).

As discussed, cognitive dissonance occurs when there's a discrepancy between beliefs and behaviours—and something has to change to eliminate or reduce the dissonance (Cherry 2006). If you do something you don't want to, there's a gap between your thoughts ('I don't want to do this') and your actions ('I just did this'). How do you reconcile this contradiction? Well, you can't change the action—it's already happened. What you can change are your thoughts or your feelings about the action. If you get people to act, they will change their thoughts and feelings to make sense of their actions (to ensure there is alignment and minimise any cognitive dissonance). This leads to the third rule of behaviour change.

⊗ Rule 3
Action changes attitude faster than attitude changes action.

When I made psychological assessments of paedophiles, I witnessed the power of cognitive dissonance in action. These sexual offenders are not as you might imagine.

Most are not born with a desire to destroy lives and cause harm. In many instances, they themselves were abused as children or grew up in very dysfunctional homes. The majority didn't learn how to have loving, consensual sexual relationships with adults. I don't say this to excuse their actions or reattribute blame but to explain that, in my experience, sexual offenders aren't born evil and most don't like the idea that they have caused significant harm to someone else.

I was stunned at the justifications they came up with to make sense of their behaviour. They would sit in front of me and say, 'I loved that child. It was important that child learned about sex from someone who truly loved them.' Others would say, 'It was consensual. They asked me for sex.' These men knew my assessment of them would be used in a court of law and believed their rationalisations were perfectly reasonable. In their mind, the thoughts made sense. But to anyone else, they were obviously distorted and wrong. They had spent years making their thoughts and feelings align with their heinous actions—in a way that was acceptable to them.

There are many examples of cognitive dissonance influencing behaviour. It can happen when you're offered a job by a rival firm. They were once considered the opposition, and associated with negative thoughts and feelings, but you might now think of them more favourably (they can't be that bad if they want you to work for them). Maybe you hated a TV show until you discovered that a friend watches it, so you begin to watch it, too. The more you watch it, the more you start to like it. You change your thoughts and feelings to make sense of the action to avoid cognitive dissonance.

Again, once an action has taken place, the only way to reduce cognitive dissonance is to change your thoughts or feelings about the action. The action can't be undone. Philosopher William James (1884) wrote that it isn't our feelings that guide our actions—it's our actions that guide feelings. 'If you want a quality, act as if you already have it,' he wrote. Fast forward 117 years and nothing has changed. If you act as if you're happy and put a smile on your face, you will feel happier as a consequence (an example of actions changing attitudes) (Duclos & Laird 2001). Psychologist Richard Wiseman picks up on this theme in his book *The As If Principle* (2013) and offers these examples:

- If you ask older people to act younger, their memories and cognitions improve.
- If you ask someone to squeeze their fist, their willpower improves.
- If you ask a procrastinator to spend three minutes pretending they find a task more interesting, they're more likely to complete the task.

Amy Cuddy, a US social psychologist, has spent much of her career looking at how actions change the way you feel. In particular, she's looked at how acting out certain 'stereotypical' body stances changes the way people feel about themselves. Amy has quickly achieved worldwide fame for her startling discoveries. *Time* magazine named her as one of the Global Game Changers in 2012.

For many years researchers have known that if you adopt a 'powerful pose' (for example, legs apart, arms outstretched and leaning forwards, or placing your hands behind a desk or your feet on a table—think alpha male in a boardroom), people will think you are more powerful and influential. Our body language says a lot about us. However, Amy and her colleagues found that even if you're actually *faking* these poses, you'll still feel more powerful, be more powerful and take more risks (Carney, Cuddy & Yap 2010). If people adopt postures of dominance and power, even for as little as two minutes, they'll experience significant increases in testosterone and decreases in cortisol. This is the neuroendocrinal profile of dominance and leadership ability.

Amy's research shows that if you act more dominantly, then you'll actual *be* more dominant. This is a powerful example of feelings following actions.

Why not try it now? Adopt a pose of power for a couple of minutes and assess how you feel. Perhaps do it in the next meeting you have (or indeed when dealing with your unruly teenage son). Remember, **action changes attitude faster than attitude changes action**.

INSIGHT OR ACTION?

If you work in advertising, you'll know the reverence given to the process of discovering 'insight'. Insight is that piece of human understanding that you hope unlocks an opportunity for brand growth. I think this process is outmoded. It's like a therapist sitting behind someone lying on a couch asking them to recount stories about their mother. The stories might be full of wonderful insights and occasionally the therapist will go 'Ah ha', and the journey into the 'subconscious' continues. This style of psychology (Freudian, psychodynamic or whatever you want to call it) has been largely dismissed by the scientific community (Webster 2005). Lying on the couch talking about your past doesn't change a thing. Insight and action are very distant cousins.

Psychologist Paul Watzlawick (1997) wrote a wonderful paper titled 'Insight may cause blindness'. In the paper, he recounts a fictitious patient who walks into a therapist's office. Every twenty seconds, the patient claps his hands loudly. When the therapist asks, 'Why are you clapping so loudly all the time?' the patient replies, 'To keep the elephants away.' When the therapist says there are no elephants around him, the patient replies, 'See, it's working.'

There are four treatment options for this patient:

1. establish a relationship of trust over a period of time and eventually convince him there are no elephants

2. analyse the man's past, find the unconscious reasons for the behaviour and bring them to a conscious level

3. introduce elephants into the session and show that his clapping won't make them go away

4. hold the man's wrists so that he can't clap any more and keep holding them until he notices that elephants don't come into the room.

The most effective treatment option is the fourth one. Often the answer is behavioural, and just getting someone to act in the manner you want will create the necessary behaviour change. Insight does not need to come before action to change behaviour.

SHORTER SHOWERS PLEASE

In 1992, Chris Anne Dickerson at the University of California conducted an experiment to see if cognitive dissonance would encourage people to take shorter showers. The study involved 80 women at a swimming pool. After the women got out of the pool and went to the change room, some were asked questions about whether they supported water conservation, whether they turned the water off when soaping up or shampooing, if they always tried to have short showers and how long they believed a shower should be. Others were asked to sign a flyer that read: 'Please conserve water. Take short showers. Turn showers off while soaping. If I can do it, so can you.' A third group both answered questions and signed the flyer. The women believed that was the end of their survey. What they didn't know was that another experimenter was in the showers secretly timing the length of their showers and noting whether they turned the water off while soaping up or shampooing.

The group that took the shortest showers was the third group. The reason being was that they had both a) spoken about their own showering habits, and b) signed a pledge asking others to shower less. This dual action (bring into consciousness their own behaviour whilst also asking others to take shorter showers) created cognitive dissonance leading to this group taking shorter showers than the other groups. To publicly declare that you support water conservation, and to sign a flyer that encourages others to do so, was the most effective way to change behaviour. The desired behaviour change (shorter showers) happened because people acted towards that proposition and aligned their thoughts and feelings to that action. Creating cognitive dissonance is a powerful tool of influence—especially if you can make people act towards the desired behaviour.

WHAT YOU CAN LEARN FROM CULTS

In 1959, psychologist Elliot Aronson looked at how cults use cognitive dissonance to maintain a powerful hold over their followers. In perhaps his most famous experiment, women were asked to do an embarrassing task in order to join a group. Aronson theorised the more embarrassing the task, the more effort someone would put into it and the more they would want to be part of the group (Aronson & Mills 1959).

In the experiment, the women were asked to join a group that discussed the psychology of sex. The embarrassing task was to read out explicitly sexual words and a paragraph of graphically described sex in front of the group. A second group had to read out a toned-down version. The third group, the control group, didn't talk about sex at all. Each group was played an audio recording of a meeting of the group they wanted to join and were asked to rate how enjoyable it was to listen to the group. Those in the first group rated that group as most enjoyable, followed by the mildly embarrassed group, and finally the control group. The more effort we put into an achievement, the more we feel obliged to like the group. Even though the experiment seems quaint in its execution, it appears to provide good supporting evidence that the effort we put into joining a cult or group means that we, in turn, like the group more, and feel a stronger affiliation with it (Lodewijkx & Syroit 2001).

Many cults and cult-like organisations have initiation nights in which newcomers spend time with the group to see what it's like. The first thing most cults do is to ask new members to stand up and tell the group why they've come along. I've been interested in the operation of cults for many years and have witnessed several initiation nights and the techniques used to bind people to the group. Curiously, I met my wife, Anna, at one of these initiation events. She mistakenly believed she was attending a 'meditation weekend', but it was a cover for a cult.

At this particular meeting, the 'retreat' was lovely and peaceful. The cult members wore white robes, and the newcomers were a mixed bag of people. Some giggled because it was a bit weird and others earnestly adopted the ways of the white robed disciples. During the seminar where I met Anna, the presenter shared this information: that there was only room for seven billion souls on the planet, and if there was one soul over that number, the world would end—except for everyone who was part of this cult. Someone in the room challenged this assertion, pointing out there were already more than seven billion people on Earth. The presenter became defensive, and went on to justify the statement, claiming that there were lots of inaccurate statisticians in the world! Anna and I made eye contact, we both smirked, and from that smirk we fell in love. But that's another story.

I've also observed and written about the techniques used by the Church of Scientology to recruit members (Ferrier 2010). A public 'initiation' is part of the process of recruitment, with newcomers told to share why they've come along. They are told this act of self-disclosure, which can be embarrassing and difficult at the time, will help to set them free from their distress. Some people say, 'I want to find happiness.' Others share the fact that they were abused as a child and still feel angry. Unfortunately, self-disclosure doesn't set the person free but rather has the opposite effect. Sharing inner turmoil starts to bind the individual to the group or cult. The positive action of sharing their troubles leads them to have positive thoughts and feelings about the group. As we've seen, thoughts and feelings follow actions.

One cult, the Oak Park Study Group, predicted the end of the world. When the world didn't end, rather than feeling embarrassment, cult members had an even stronger bind to the cult, rationalising that their strong belief in the cult had somehow saved the Earth. As Festinger (1956) wrote, 'Tell him you disagree and he turns away. Show him facts or figures and he questions your sources. Appeal to logic and he fails to see your point.'

DONATIONS FOLLOW ACTION

Here's a test of my contention that action changes attitude faster than attitude changes action—in a 'brand' setting. In our experiment, conducted with Deakin University and global children's charity Save the Children, we tested different donation models for charities (Ferrier, Ward & Palermo 2012).

Traditionally, charities use two methods to unlock people's wallets. The first is through rational messages, with statistics showing how important the charity is, the lives that are at risk, how many people have died, how many degrees the Earth has warmed and so on. The second is through an emotive message, with evocative images of the cause (scenes of devastation, or flies in the eyes of starving African children) or the effect (scenes of happy, smiling people) of the charity. Fear, hope and joy are all obvious emotions to tap into. However, a third technique has emerged. It asks the donor not only for money, but also to actually do something for the charity. For example, Movember asks people to raise and donate money, but also asks men to grow a moustache during the month of November to show their commitment to the cause.

Our subjects were divided into four groups. One group received a rational message (facts and figures), the second an emotive message (smiling happy kids, with an inspiring music track), the third group was asked to create an advertising campaign for the charity, and finally there was a control group (that solved unrelated puzzles). Each of the four groups was then asked for money.

As you can see in Figure 3.2, the group that gave the most money was the third one—the one that had the action approach of writing an ad for Save the Children.

Figure 3.2 Type of message received and donation level

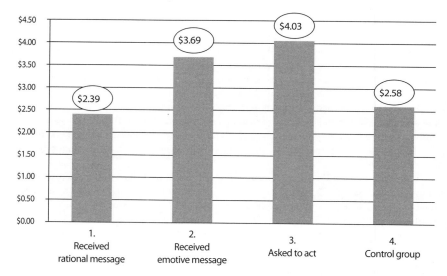

Why did they donate more than the others? First, they had a 'sense of ownership' of the charity, which made them feel more engaged with the message. Second, 'cognitive dissonance' kicked in. The positive action of creating an ad was aligned to thoughts and feelings. Third, people felt a sense of 'autonomy'; that is, they were invited to interact with a message on their own terms rather than it being forced on them. This circumnavigates resistance to the message and makes it more likely they will give.

If charities involve donors in their cause, rather than just asking for money, they'll have a much greater likelihood of success. The lesson? Involve people in your mission through action and they will match their thoughts and feelings to make sense of the action. If you're still not convinced by the power of action, can you do me another favour? Please read about Benjamin Franklin, the man who discovered the impact of asking for a favour. It's one of the most interesting things I know.

THE BENJAMIN FRANKLIN EFFECT

Benjamin Franklin was one of the Founding Fathers of the USA, and had a ridiculously impressive résumé. His accomplishments include inventor, scientist, publisher, politician, musician, postmaster, diplomat—the list goes on. When he ran for a second term as clerk of the Pennsylvania Assembly, one of his opponents delivered a long speech, much if it attacking him. In his autobiography, Franklin (1791/1998) describes the unnamed man as 'a gentleman of fortune and education' and thought he would one day become a person of influence in the government.

Franklin was angry about the speech—who wouldn't be? But there was another reason he was upset. Franklin had never even met or spoken to the guy. Now, I'm not sure if his first instinct was to return serve and deliver a stinging rebuttal of his opponent. He didn't. Instead, he took a very different course of action—one that was ultimately more effective. Franklin sat down at his large, wooden desk and wrote a letter to his opponent asking for a favour. Could he borrow one of his books? It's the last thing you'd expect.

The surprised opponent agreed to the request and sent the rare book to Franklin's office. A week later, it was returned with a thank-you note. It wasn't long before the two bumped into each other. How do you think the exchange went? In his biography, Franklin writes that his opponent spoke to him 'with great civility'. Not only that, they became lifelong friends.

How did Franklin explain the opponent's change of heart? 'This is another instance of the truth of an old maxim I had learned, which says, 'He that has once done you a kindness will be more ready to do you another than he whom you yourself has obliged.' (Franklin 1791/1988). In other words, if you want someone to like you, as Benjamin Franklin did, ask that person for a favour. It sounds counterintuitive, I know. But people find it more difficult to dislike you once they've done something to help you. The positive action of lending Franklin a book was converted into positive thoughts and feelings towards Franklin. Once again, action changes attitude faster than attitude changes action.

Think about the last time you were asked for a favour. You might have felt both a sense of flattery that your opinion had been sought as well as a sense of accomplishment that you had been able to help someone out. You become invested in that person and change your feelings to match the action.

The Benjamin Franklin effect can be summed up as, '**the most efficient way to get someone to like you is to ask them to do you a favour**'. This is true for individuals, but also for brands and organisations. If you can get others to invest something of themselves into you, they will like you more. This is probably the single most interesting thing I ever learned at university, and a key theme of this book. If you are a brand owner, or in advertising, then I would suggest you stop asking what you can do for your consumer, and instead ask 'what can my consumer do for me?'. If you are a consumer, be careful about doing favours for brands—it will just make you like them more.

ACTION ADVERTISING

Consumer involvement works in the same way. If you want to influence someone else's actions, get them involved in your mission. This is a fundamental mind shift for many advertisers. Historically, advertisers focused on informing or entertaining consumers, and

1emselves to the consumer through advertising. Advertisers have been 1 making funny ads and trying to entertain and amuse. Now, advertisers no at can we do for consumers?' but 'What can our consumers do for us?' Take 1d's Facebook page. How many brands have they 'liked'? This is effectively brand pic. ion. How many times have you completed 'research' for a brand without being paid? Brands ask for favours and consumers willingly invest in them.

Advertising's new frontier is to make people act first and think and feel later. It's also easier to achieve through interactive technology such as smartphones and social media. Previously, advertising changed behaviour by attempting to influence 'thoughts' or 'feelings'. In the 1980s, Nike encouraged you to buy their shoes by:

1. influencing your thoughts about the product through rational advertising. The advertising might say 'Available now' or 'Only $59.95' or 'The most comfortable shoes ever'.

2. influencing your emotions about the product through emotive advertising. The ads used anthemic music and people achieving against the odds.

As you can see in Figure 3.3, these approaches fulfil the first two steps of my whiteboard drawing, with the hope that it would translate into action.

Figure 3.3 Messaging alternatives with passive advertising

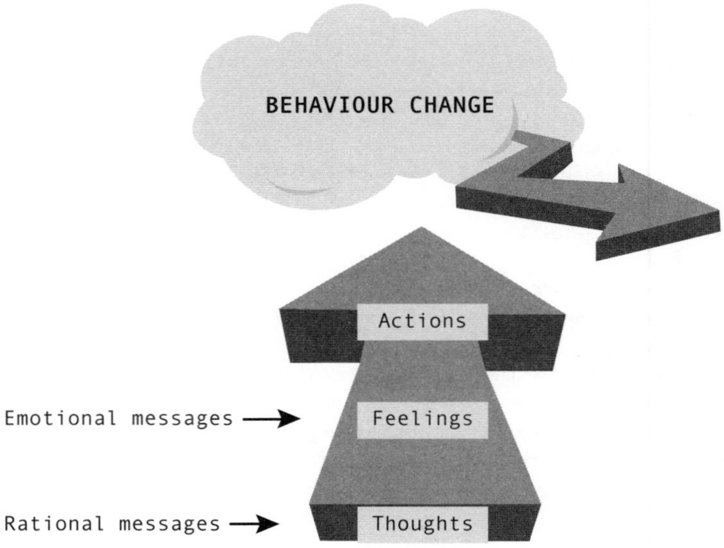

BEHAVIOUR CHANGE

Emotional messages ⟶ Feelings

Rational messages ⟶ Thoughts

Actions

Both strategies are effective at influencing behaviour, but these days advertising is no longer passive but interactive. Today, 77 per cent of TV viewing happens with a smartphone in your hand or a laptop or tablet on viewers' laps (Google, Sterling Brands &

Ipsos 2013). It's the era of multi-screening and interaction. Just as with behaviour change, if an advertiser makes you act, you'll change your thoughts and feelings to justify your actions and like the brand more. How does Nike influence behaviour? It gets users involved in the marketing. More than five million people monitor their running prowess through the Nike+ app or wristband Nike FuelBand, which tracks energy expenditure. Many users talk about both gadgets with friends and online. Nike no longer needs to spend so much of its marketing budget on advertisements as 'in their place is a whole new repertoire of interactive elements' (Cendrowski 2013). For example, interactive billboards pump out Twitter messages from consumers. There are fun runs, events created exclusively for women, and interesting content made for and shared on Facebook. Even though Nike was a champion of persuasion through old media, it has established itself as a champion of interactive media. Cendrowski (2013) continues: 'After a decade of growth, [Nike's] sales have reached $21 billion, making it the world's largest sports company, a full 30 per cent bigger than closest rival adidas.' Brands like Nike are now asking consumers to act with their brands first, and the thoughts and feelings will follow. Why? Because action changes attitude faster than attitude changes action.

SUMMARY

The most effective way to influence behaviour is through action—by making someone act towards your goal. The reason it works is through psychological principles including cognitive dissonance—we like our thoughts, feelings and actions to be aligned or we feel uncomfortable. When you involve people in your mission through action, they adapt their thoughts and feelings to make sense of the action. It's the quickest way to achieve change.

1. There are three ways to change behaviour: thoughts, feelings and actions.

2. The creation and minimisation of cognitive dissonance is a strong behavioural change ally.

3. If people act, they will align their thoughts and feelings to that action.

4. Advertising has previously focused on thoughts and feelings.

5. Advertising now exists in an interactive landscape and can make people act, thereby creating cognitive dissonance and leading to feelings and thoughts that are more favourable to the brand.

The Insider: Simon Thatcher

Our resistance to behaviour change represents a resistance to something deeper. And that immediately makes this resistance worth honouring. Like all defences, resistance can be a way that we protect ourselves from difficult feelings associated with the unknown. And attempting behaviour change, regardless of context, will often trigger such a defence because it implies that we must behave differently and in a way that we are not yet familiar with.

So my one bit of advice about behaviour change is this: instead of criticising, challenging or reframing this resistance against such change, welcome it in and move with its inertia—even if it comes in the form of a tantrum. And love it like a small child because that's essentially what it is. It's a younger part of you. And like all small children, our fears deserve to be held and heard. Perhaps from time to time that was something that was missing from your own childhood. But, most importantly, the feelings need to be felt.

And once the feelings behind your resistance have had an opportunity to be acknowledged, watch what happens. I'm not suggesting that such fears will never return. I'm suggesting that by being more aware of your deeper emotional realms, you'll be ready when they do! Your resistance to changing your behaviour is just as beautiful and mysteriously wise as your openness to such change.

Simon Thatcher is a psychologist in private practice. I've known him for a long time. We went to university together and lived together for a short while. He's the best clinical psychologist I know and has been a fantastic friend. He knows more about the psychology of Batman than any reasonable man should!

REFERENCES

Aronson, E. & Mills, J. (1959). The effect of severity of initiation on liking for a group. *Journal of Abnormal and Social Psychology*, 59(2), 177–81.

Beck, A.T. (1975). *Cognitive Therapy and the Emotional Disorders*. Madison, CT: International Universities Press.

Carney, D., Cuddy, A.J.C. & Yap, A. (2010). Power posing: Brief nonverbal displays affect neuroendocrine levels and risk tolerance. *Psychological Science*, 21(10), 1363–8.

Cendrowski, S. (2013). Nike's new marketing mojo. *Fortune*, 13 February. Accessed at http://management.fortune.cnn.com/2012/02/13/nike-digital-marketing.

Cherry, K. (2006). What is cognitive dissonance? *About.com Psychology*. Accessed at http://psychology.about.com/od/cognitivepsychology/f/dissonance.htm.

Dickerson, C.D. (1992). Using cognitive dissonance to encourage water conservation. *Journal of Applied Psychology*, 22 (11), 841–54.

Duclos, S.E. & Laird, J.D. (2001). The deliberate control of emotional experience through control of expressions. *Cognition & Emotion*, 15(1), 27–56.

Ellis, A. & Blau, S. (2001). *The Albert Ellis Reader: A Guide to Well-being Using Rational Emotive Behavior Therapy*. New York: Citadel.

Ferrier, A. (2010). Forensic shopping investigation II: Shopping for religion. *The Consumer Psychologist*. Accessed at www.theconsumerpsychologist.com/2009/08/12/forensic-shopping-investigation-ii-shopping-for-religion.

Ferrier, A., Ward, B. & Palermo, J. (2012). *Behavior Change: Why Action Advertising Works Harder than Passive Advertising*. Presented at Society for Consumer Psychology: Proceedings of the 2012 Annual Conference, Las Vegas, 16–18 February.

Festinger, L. (1957). *A Theory of Cognitive Dissonance*. Stanford: Stanford University Press.

Festinger, L., Riecken, H.W. & Schachter, S. (1957). *When Prophecy Fails*. Minneapolis: University of Minnesota Press.

Franklin, B. (1791/1998). *Autobiography of Benjamin Franklin* (J. Manis, ed.). University Park: Penn State University Press.

Google, Sterling Brands & Ipsos (2012). *The New Multi-Screen World: Understanding Cross-Platform Consumer Behaviour*. Accessed at www.google.com.au/think/research-studies/the-new-multi-screen-world-study.html.

James, W. (1884). What is an emotion? *Mind*, 9, 188–205.

Lodewijkx, H.F.M. & Syroit, J.E.M.M. (2001). Affiliation during naturalistic severe and mild initiations: Some further evidence against the severity-attraction hypothesis. *Current Research in Social Psychology*, 4(7), 90–107.

Watzlawick, P. (1997). Insight may cause blindness. In J.K. Zeig (ed.), *The Evolution of Psychotherapy: The Third Conference* (pp. 309–21). New York: Brunner/Mazel.

Webster, R. (2005). *Why Freud Was Wrong: Sin, Science and Psychoanalysis.* Oxford: The Orwell Press.

Wiseman, R. (2013). *The As If Principle: The Radically New Approach to Changing Your Life.* New York: Free Press.

ACTION SPURS: SOMETIMES WE NEED A LITTLE KICK

Human behavior is incredibly pliable, plastic.

> *Philip G Zimbardo, psychologist notorious for the Stanford prison experiment*

A good horse should be seldom spurred.

> *Thomas Fuller, English author from the 1600s*

LET'S GO FOR A RIDE

Ever been for a ride on a horse? Even if you haven't hoisted yourself over a saddle and taken a ride, I'm sure you'll be able to picture this scenario. I'd like you to imagine the person you seek to influence is a horse and you are a rider. You've been for a ride on this horse several times and enjoy a lovely rapport. Your horse is well fed and groomed. It's a beautiful day and you're ready to head off. There's just one problem. Your horse won't budge. What do you do?

It's a situation most of us face when seeking to influence others. We select the behaviour to influence—one that meets our goals. We understand that action, rather than thoughts and feelings, is the most powerful trigger to pull. But despite creating an ideal environment for the action we seek, our horse won't move. I have a solution for you: give your horse a little kick.

I'm sure you've seen a spur—the metal device that horse riders attach to their ankles to nudge or jolt the horse into action. And indeed a horse's spur is the inspiration behind the 10 techniques I use to encourage action in others. In fact, these 10 action spurs are the foundation for the ideas created during my career in advertising. The following chapters outline how each spur was developed, why they work (the psychology behind it) and how each has been applied. Of the 10 action spurs, the first seven work on increasing someone's motivation to perform an action, and the remaining three work on making the behaviour easier to perform.

SPURRING ACTION

How were these 10 action spurs devised? They are distilled from academic experiments and real-life applications in the areas of persuasion; cognitive, behavioural and social psychology; advertising; and behavioural economics. Some references, especially those relating to social psychology, date back to the 1950s and 1960s, when many theories of human behaviour were first articulated. This was a time when ethics committees within universities didn't exist, so the experiments conducted then wouldn't be permitted today. Other references come from the relatively new study of human behaviour—behavioural economics—that you'll read about in later chapters. Further, some other chapters hardly have references at all, such the chapter on the utility spur, which is one of the more recent and exciting developments in advertising.

Influencing behaviour is both an art and a science. While science is inexact and incomplete, ignoring its insights is a wasted opportunity for advertising. I've found these insights to be invaluable in my work in advertising, as you'll discover throughout the book.

>> Rule 4

There are (at least) 10 spurs to get someone to act.

THE TWO TYPES OF SPURS

As outlined earlier, I believe behaviour change has two main drivers: **motivation** and **ease**. If the motivation to perform a behaviour is low, there are seven action spurs to boost them. It's the same with ease—if this is low, there are three action spurs to encourage the behaviour (see Figure 4.1). Discussion of these different spurs take up the bulk of the remaining text in this book, with a chapter devoted to each. Following is a quick overview of each of the spurs.

Figure 4.1 The behaviour framing grid and spurs

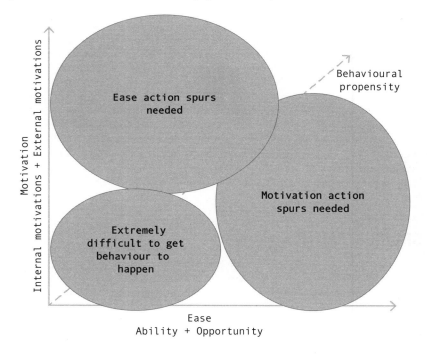

MOTIVATION ACTION SPURS

Spur 1   Reframing (Chapter 5)

What is it? Reframing takes the existing behaviour and frames it in a different, more appealing way. It focuses on benefits rather than features and taps into the assumptive and implicit ways we make decisions.

When to use it: To boost individual incentive (or 'What's in it for me?').

Example: Menu design that frames expensive, high-margin meals as more appealing than lower-cost items. The whole menu is framed to ensure you spend as much as possible.

+ Spur 2   Evocation (Chapter 6)

What is it? Evocation stirs powerful emotions to motivate behaviour. When you stir strong emotions, people are more likely to act.

When to use it: When behaviour has become ingrained and when people are no longer conscious they perform the behaviour. It's the equivalent of a 'slap in the face'.

Example: Scary and graphic quit smoking campaigns.

+ Spur 3   Collectivism (Chapter 7)

What is it? We often decide how to behave by looking at what other people do. If it feels as though the rest of the tribe is doing that behaviour, you're more likely to as well. It's based on 'social norms'—those written and unwritten rules of appropriate behaviour.

When to use it: To boost social norms (or 'What will others think of me?').

Example: Wearing a pink ribbon in support of finding a cure for breast cancer.

Spur 4   Ownership (Chapter 8)

What is it? Rather than tell people what to do, ownership asks people what they think should be done. It asks them to be involved in the solution to your problem. When they become involved, they're more likely to exhibit the behaviour you seek because they are co-creators.

When to use it: When it's advantageous to give a person a sense of control and efficacy over an issue.

Example: McDonald's asking for help to name a new burger.

Spur 5   Play (Chapter 9)

What is it? Play makes the desired behaviour enjoyable by embracing the principles of structured play or gamification.

When to use it: When you have control over the environment within which the behaviour occurs.

Example: Rewarding drivers who obey the speed limit by using the fines levied on speeding drivers.

Spur 6   Utility (Chapter 10)

What is it? Utility is about offering additional benefits and services to encourage the behaviour.

When to use it: To increase individual incentive (or 'What's in it for me?').

Example: An app that connects football fans during away games or an app that offers statistics on running.

Spur 7   Modelling (Chapter 11)

What is it? When we watch certain behaviour, we copy it. We work out how to behave by watching how other people behave. Modelling uses a high-profile, credible person to inspire or inform behaviour.

When to use it: When the model is relevant and when there's positive reinforcement for the behaviour.

Example: George Clooney promoting Nespresso.

EASE ACTION SPURS

Spur 8   Skill up (Chapter 12)

What is it? Skill up shows someone how to do the behaviour. You might be highly motivated to undertake behaviour, but simply lack the skills or ability to do it. Skilling up is about making it easier for people to do the behaviour you want.

When to use it: If someone says they don't know how to do something.

Example: Whisky-tasting nights that make novices feel comfortable ordering and drinking whisky.

Spur 9   Eliminate complexity (Chapter 13)

What is it? Eliminating complexity is about removing as many barriers as possible to undertake behaviour. We generally use the least amount of effort and energy to do a task, so the idea is to anticipate barriers and remove them.

When to use it: When you control the environment and are able to remove impediments to make a behaviour happen.

Example: Poker machines designed with big buttons to press, minimal time between rounds, and a screen with optimal tilt to prevent fatigue, which combine to make the machine easier to use.

Spur 10   Commitment (Chapter 14)

What is it? Commitment is a powerful tool of influence. It's an important first step to behaviour change. Asking for a small favour first increases the likelihood of securing a bigger agreement later.

When to use it: When the behaviour change is significant and you can't change the entire behaviour in one go.

Example: Asking people for a pledge to vote in the US presidential election.

SELECTING WHAT SPURS TO USE

As outlined in previous chapters, you'll be more successful influencing others if you select a behaviour that's more likely to be influenced. For example, you're more likely to convince someone who drinks beer to drink more beer, than you are to get a non-beer drinker to start drinking beer. You can plot these behaviours on a behaviour framing grid, which allows you to see which action spur to use to influence the behaviour. To help you with this task, ask these questions:

Motivation:

1. **Individual incentives**: What's in it for them? Will they be rewarded and to what extent?

2. **Social norms**: What will others think of them if they undertake that behaviour?

Ease:

3. **Ability**: Do they have the resources, competency and skills to do the behaviour?

4. **Opportunity**: Does the environment allow the behaviour to happen?

In answering these questions, you'll be able to see the barriers to the behaviour change and select an action spur that reduces these barriers. For example, in Chapter 2, we looked at the introduction of a new breakfast option—cereal chips. Let's look at how that behaviour stacks up against these questions.

Motivation:

1 *Individual incentives: What's in it for them? Will they be rewarded and to what extent?*

Moderate incentive—the product could save time and is convenient.

2 *Social norms: What will others think of them if they undertake that behaviour?*

Low social norms—chips are viewed as unhealthy and consumers may feel negatively judged by others if they eat them.

Ease:

3 *Ability: Do they have the resources, competency and skills to do the behaviour?*

High ability—nearly all people have the ability and it's easier to eat chips than cereal.

4 *Opportunity: Does the environment allow the behaviour to happen?*

High opportunity—the environment doesn't prevent people from eating cereal chips.

This quick analysis suggests that getting people to eat cereal chips for breakfast has high ease, but relatively low motivation, as can be seen in Figure 4.2 (over the page). Having assessed the four key barriers, we can see that social norms is the key barrier to overcome in this case (that is, people will feel funny if others see them eating chips first thing in the morning).

Figure 4.2 Mapping people's likelihood to eat cereal chips for breakfast

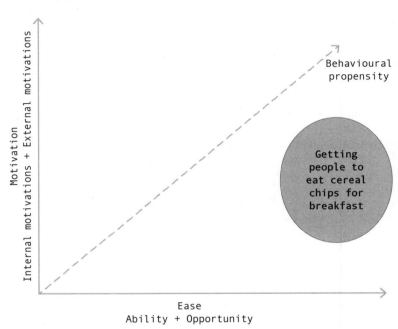

The action spur selection matrix (see Figure 4.3) gives an overview of which spurs are likely to be useful in overcoming particular barriers. For example, if the behaviour you want to influence, such as getting people to eat chips for breakfast, has high ease (there is the opportunity and ability), but only average motivation (there is something in it for them, but no one else is doing it), then look at social norming to influence the behaviour. We can see in the cereal chip example that this would lead to using the Action Spurs of Collectivism and/or Modelling. Perhaps the Framing Spur, or Play Spur could be useful too (as these Spurs straddle both the Individual Incentive and Social Norms barriers).

The other variable to consider when selecting an action spur is the level of control you have over the environment. Imagine you are a prison officer and want inmates to reduce the incidence of violence. You have complete control over the environment. One option is to reward inmates for pro-social behaviour using a points system. At the end of each week, the points can be used to obtain privileges. The action spur in this case is 'play'. Other examples of control over the environment include classrooms where teachers reward diligent students or workplaces where bosses reward employees for exhibiting the desired behaviour. It's a different situation when you don't have control of the environment, such as charities seeking donations on street corners or someone selling door-to-door. Use Figure 4.3 to help you choose the action spur that best applies in high-control and low-control environments.

Figure 4.3 The action spur selection matrix

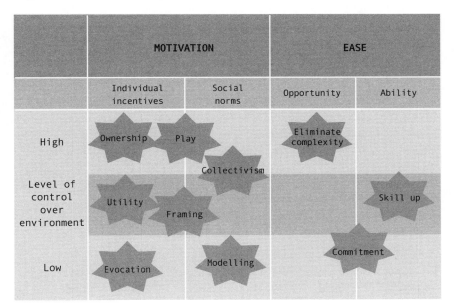

HOW ACTION SPURS LEAD TO BEHAVIOUR CHANGE

Here's a story you'll find either disgusting or funny. I'll risk telling it on the assumption you'll find it funny. In 2012, my business partner, Jon Wilkins, and I were invited to speak at the Cannes Lions, the pre-eminent international awards show for the advertising industry held in France every year. Needless to say, we were really excited about it. The venue was the exclusive Palais Theatre and some of the other speakers that year were former US President Bill Clinton, Facebook founder Mark Zuckerberg and British philosopher (and one of the 'Insiders' in this book) Alain de Botton. Not bad, huh?

On the night before our speech, Jon and I caught up for dinner at a beachside restaurant to go over the final details of the talk. I ordered the prawn pasta, a decision I would come to rue a few hours later. You can probably guess what happened. Not long after eating the meal I became sick. Very sick. I developed an acute case of food poisoning with one symptom being violent diarrhoea. After a sleepless night spent mostly on the toilet, I managed to crawl down to breakfast to meet Jon. He took one look at me and told me to go straight back to bed and assured me I would be okay by the time our 2 p.m. talk came round.

I returned to bed but spent most of the time using the toilet. At around 1 p.m., we were both worried. The diarrhoea showed no signs of abating. The problem was I was the only one who knew my bit of the presentation. It wouldn't make sense without my part. Jon suggested we ring the organisers to see if we could change the time of our talk. It wasn't possible. He suggested taking more Imodium or just risking it. I said I didn't want to risk public humiliation—it would be better to cancel the speech than embarrass myself. And then inspiration arrived. Jon came up with a solution: a way for me to appear on stage, risk-free. The solution was to wear an adult nappy.

And so, on the way give a presentation to my international peers at the Palais in Cannes, I bought a box of adult nappies and put one on. Crisis averted. If you want to see a clip of the talk, you can watch it on YouTube (https://www.youtube.com/watch?v=RbJCR01WHhA).

The reason I share this story is to demonstrate that, despite the best-laid plans, if people are involved then so is uncertainty. My point is that action spurs are just the starting point for ideas. You still need creativity and fresh thinking, such as Jon's nappy idea.

In the following chapters, you'll read about the application of each action spur and their creative and psychological underpinnings. Creativity is a wonderful and mysterious process and there's no single switch to flick. There are several. I can't tell you the one creative idea that will help you influence someone. That's up to you. But I hope the descriptions of several advertising campaigns will offer insights into the process. This process is shown in Figure 4.4:

1. Establish your goal.

2. Select the behaviour to change.

3. Select the action spur.

4. Develop a creative way to apply the spur.

Figure 4.4 The relationship between goals, behaviour change, action spurs and creative ideas

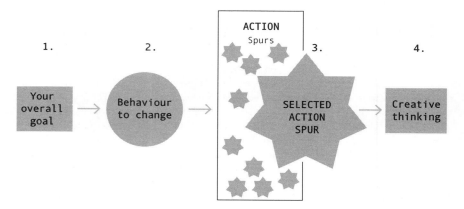

THE COMPLEXITY OF BEHAVIOUR CHANGE

You'll quickly realise that not all behaviour change is created equal. Some changes are relatively easy while others are extremely complex. Some goals can be achieved quickly, while others can take years. With more complex behaviour change, you might need a series action spurs to get the behaviour you seek.

In 1982, James Prochaska and Carlo DiClemente developed the five stages of change model. While this model was developed in relation to problematic health behaviours (such as alcohol abuse), the stages apply equally to behavioural change in buying habits. The stages are (Prochaska & Norcross 2013):

- *Precontemplation (not ready)*—'People are not intending to take action in the foreseeable future, and can be unaware that their behaviour is problematic.'

- *Contemplation (getting ready)*—'People are beginning to recognize that their behaviour is problematic, and start to look at the pros and cons of their continued actions.'

- *Preparation (ready)*—'People are intending to take action in the immediate future, and may begin taking small steps towards behaviour change.'

- *Action*—'People have made specific overt modifications in modifying their problem behaviour or in acquiring new healthy behaviours.'

- *Maintenance*—'People have been able to sustain action for a while and are working to prevent relapse.'

Action spurs can be integrated into this model (see Figure 4.5). If there is a degree of complexity in the behaviour you are trying to change you may need to develop one overall action spur—the large spur in Figure 4.5—and this will guide the overall idea development. You can then use smaller spurs to continue to promote the behaviour change desired, depending on where the person is in their behaviour change lifecycle.

Figure 4.5 The stages of change model and the use of spurs

THE SIX STEPS TO BEHAVIOUR CHANGE

Here is the overall six-step behaviour change process as it relates to a real-world example of mine: raising money for my son's daycare centre.

STEP 1: SET YOUR GOAL—WHAT DO YOU WANT TO ACHIEVE?

Ensure your goal is **specific** and **measurable**. Set a **timeline** to achieve the goal. Keep your goal **outcome focused** and don't make it behavioural—it's what you want to achieve as a consequence of changing someone else's behaviour.

For example, my son goes to daycare two days a week. The centre is always raising funds to improve its services. I would set this goal: 'Raise $20,000 for my son's daycare centre within three months.'

STEP 2: CHOOSE A BEHAVIOUR TO CHANGE THAT IMPACTS YOUR GOAL

This step is where the heavy lifting happens. Firstly, generate a list of all the different behaviours that could be changed to meet the goal. Then map these behaviours against motivation and ease, and assess their likelihood to meet the goal. Finally, select a behaviour to change.

In my example, the behaviours I could influence include:

1. Ask my family and friends to donate money to the centre.
2. Ask all the mums and dads at the centre to ask their friends and family for money to donate.
3. Ask all the mums and dads of the centre to donate themselves (notice the subtle but important difference between behaviours 2 and 3).
4. Ask the children who stay at the centre to ask their parents for more money (which is somewhat more radical).
5. Ask the local community to donate to 'their' childcare centre.

   This list isn't exhaustive list but gives an idea of different options available.

   Now, map these behaviours against motivation and ease, as described earlier in this chapter:

   Motivation:

   • Individual incentives: What's in it for them? Will they be rewarded and to what extent?

   • Social norms: What will others think of them if they undertake that behaviour?

   Ease:

   • Ability: Do they have the resources, competency and skills to do the behaviour?

   • Opportunity: Does the environment allow the behaviour to happen?

Now we need to know to what extent will the behaviour meet the goal? This is when we 'size the behaviour', a process I explained in Chapter 2 (where a small circle means we are having a small impact on the goal, and a large circle means a larger impact). Let's plot these options on a behaviour framing grid (see Figure 4.6).

Figure 4.6 Mapping potential behaviours to change to raise money for the daycare centre

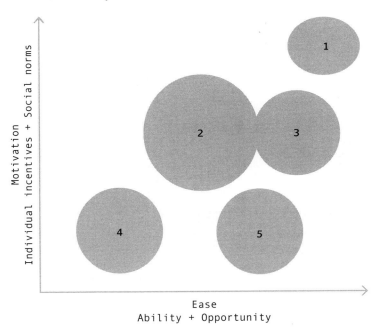

After this assessment, we can see that the behaviour seek to influence is number 2: get all the mums and dads at the centre to ask their friends and family for money to donate. Although this behaviour is slightly harder to change than behaviour 1, it will have a greater impact on our goal if we change it.

STEP 3: SELECT THE ACTION SPUR

Once you have identified the behaviour to influence, assess where and why you've mapped the behaviour. This understanding will help you select the most effective action spur. For example, do you need to increase motivation or ease? If you have to boost motivation, do you need to influence individual incentives or social norming? If you have to boost ease, do you need to increase ability or opportunity?

In my example, the motivation of parents to ask family and friends for money is already high. The sticking point is ease—particularly the opportunity to pay. I need to find ways to make payment easy. The best action spur in this case is 'eliminate complexity'.

STEP 4: DEVELOP AN IDEA TO INFLUENCE BEHAVIOUR

Eliminating complexity is about identifying barriers to the desired behaviour. In this case, what are the barriers to people donating money to the daycare centre? They could be payment methods (Can they use electronic banking?), communicating the message with family and friends (How will the money will be used?) or donation amounts (What's the expected donation?).

In my example, we could use a crowd-sourcing website to make it easy for friends and family to donate.

STEP 5: DEVELOP A PLAN AND EXECUTE THE IDEA

Make it happen. It's important to write your plan with details of each stage of the process. In advertising, this happens when formulating 'the pitch', as outlined in Chapter 1. When you have a plan, you're more likely to achieve your goal.

STEP 6: MEASURE AND EVALUATE

Did you change behaviour? Did it help you achieve your objectives? If it didn't work, what other strategy could you adopt?

Yes, the process is complicated, but influencing behaviour is a complex process. Don't expect it to be easy. But as you'll read in subsequent chapters, behaviour change is achievable. It's time to get on that horse again and give it a kick.

⊗ The four rules of behaviour change

- Rule 1: If you want to change someone's behaviour, it will most likely happen if the person is motivated to adopt that behaviour, and if it's easy for them to do so.
- Rule 2: Change the behaviour that will help you achieve your goals.
- Rule 3: Action changes attitude faster than attitude changes action.
- Rule 4: There are (at least) 10 ways to get someone to act.

SUMMARY

The field of behaviour change and our ability to build effective behaviour change strategies have always been limited due to the complexity of human behaviour. In response, I prefer to use action spurs, a series of 10 strategies that can be applied to different behaviour change challenges. Although there are guidelines for which spur to use in which situation, it's not an exact science—sometimes you have trial a few spurs to see what works best. Equally, don't always rely on a single spur to change behaviour—it may take a combination of spurs to get the change you want.

The Insider: Bob Garfield

What, is this a trick question?

The only way to influence behaviour change is to provide a motivating reason for doing so. It comes down to naked self-interest. That, of course, is where the psychology and artistry come in, locating and communicating that self-interest. Marketers typically default to vanity, fear-mongering, problem resolution and outright bribery. But in a post-mass, digitally connected media environment, the wisest, most sustainable path is to be so admired and trusted that being associated with you allows the individual to feel better about himself or herself. Not in an Axe Body Spray way, as a matter of self-delusion, but in a Prius way, as a matter of pride.

No greenwashing, please, or 'charitable' efforts that are really sales promotions in disguise; those are dishonest and manipulative and transparently untransparent. The key for brands in a socially connected world is simply to be respected; to offer quality goods and services without being a total dick to anyone along the way.

I met Bob Garfield in 2013 when I was speaking at Cannes. He was hosting the session and halfway through my talk he got my attention and impulsively mouthed, 'I want to interview you.' So he did, and we got on very well. Bob has been the editor of US advertising bible *Adage* and is co-host of TV show *On the Media*. In 1997, Garfield's 'Ad Review' won a Jesse H. Neal Award for best column in its classification.

REFERENCE

Prochaska, J.O. & Norcross, J.C. (2013). *Systems of Psychotherapy: A Transtheoretical Analysis*. Belmont: Brooks/Cole.

FURTHER READING

Below are is series of texts that I explored when developing action spurs. The list is by no means exhaustive, but is a good start to understanding the world of behaviour change.

Psychology

Coon, D. & Mitterer, J.O. (2010). *Introduction to Psychology: Gateways to Mind and Behavior*. Belmont: Wadsworth/Cengage Learning.

Edelman, S. (2002). *Change Your Thinking: Positive and Practical Ways to Overcome Stress, Negative Emotions and Self-defeating Behaviour Using CBT*. Sydney: Harper Collins.

Montgomery, B. (2006). The keys to successful behaviour change. *InPsych*. Accessed at www.psychology.org.au/publications/inpsych/behaviour.

Seligman, M.E.P. (1990). *Learned Optimism*. New York: Knopf.

Behaviour change

Bregman, P. (2009). The easiest way to change people's behaviour. *Harvard Business Review*, 11 March. Accessed at http://blogs.hbr.org/2009/03/the-easiest-way-to.

Central Information Office (2009). *COI Reveals New Five Step Plan for Behaviour Change*. UK Government. Accessed at www.mynewsdesk.com/uk/view/pressrelease/central-office-of-information-coi-reveals-new-five-step-plan-for-behaviour-change-347692.

Goldstein, N.J., Martin, S.J. & Cialdini, R.B. (2008). *Yes! 50 Scientifically Proven Ways to be Persuasive*. New York: Free Press.

Behavioural economics

Ariely, D. (2008). *Predictably Irrational: The Hidden Forces that Shape our Decisions*. New York: HarperCollins.

Kahneman, R. (2011). *Thinking, Fast and Slow*. New York: Farrar, Straus and Giroux.

Thaler, R.H. & Sunstein, C.R. (2008). *Nudge: Improving Decisions about Health, Wealth, and Happiness*. New Haven: Yale University Press.

Advertising

Barden, P. (2013). *Decoded: The Science behind Why We Buy*. London: John Wiley & Sons.

Grant, J. (1999). *The New Marketing Manifesto*. London: Orion.

Ogilvy, D. (1983). *Ogilvy on Advertising*. Toronto: John Wiley & Sons.

Oldham, M. (ed.) (2013). Advertising Works 21: IPA Effectiveness Awards 2012. London: Warc.

Steel, J. (1998). *Truth, Lies, and Advertising: The Art of Account Planning*. London: John Wiley & Sons.

Trott, D. (2009). *Creative Mischief*. London: LOAF Marketing.

MOTIVATION ACTION SPURS

MOTIVATION ACTION SPURS	The following seven motivation action spurs all increase people's motivation to do a certain behaviour: reframing, evocation, collectivism, ownership, play, utility and modelling. If you want to change a behaviour and the main issue is that there is not enough motivation to undertake that behaviour, then consider using one of these spurs.
>>	

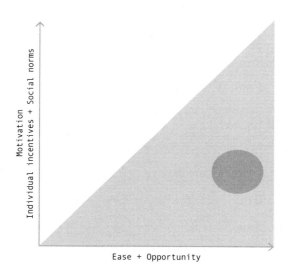

REFRAMING: IT'S NOT WHAT YOU SAY—IT'S HOW YOU SAY IT

I am impressed with what happens when someone stays in the same place and you take the same picture over and over and it would be different, every single frame.

Annie Leibovitz, US photographer

Ads are carefully designed by the Madison Avenue frog-men-of-the-mind for semiconscious exposure.

Marshall McLuhan, US communication theorist

THE ICE CREAM EFFECT

When I was a kid, ice cream came in a plain white plastic container with limited flavours to choose from. Neapolitan was as exciting as it got—the strawberry flavour would always go first, then the chocolate, while the remaining vanilla strip could remain untouched in the freezer for months—with Hokey Pokey reserved for rare treats. In those days, ice cream was a simple dessert mainly for children. But around fifteen years ago, someone decided that ice cream isn't just frozen milk. Rather, it's about indulgence, care and comfort. People eat ice cream when they feel alone or miss their loved ones, or just want a little treat. In the blink of an eye, ice cream was no longer simply a child's dessert but a premium adult indulgence. And the packaging changed to reflect its new status. The containers were smaller but more stylish in design, standard ingredients were given premium names and the price went up (and up). Ice cream had a new identity. It had been **reframed**.

Reframing is a popular tool in advertising and perhaps the most subtly manipulative. Our brains can't process every little detail we perceive. If we did, what would you be paying attention to right now? Look at the words on this page. Look at the word 'word'. How are the letters shaped? Which letter is most important? What's the colour of the print? What's the weave of the paper? Or glow from the computer screen? Now look at your hands holding the book or screen. Do your fingernails need a cut? What about what you are sitting on? Is it comfortable? I could go on. My point is that it's impossible to think about or cognitively process every single piece of information—and nor would you want to. You couldn't make it through the day. Instead, your mind does something very neat. It frames chunks of information in the same way a frame holds a picture. It uses stereotypes, assumptions and rules of thumb to make judgments; it clusters information and takes leaps of logic. Psychologists call these 'schemas': templates our brain uses as shortcuts for processing information. If the information seems to fit the template then our brain fills in the rest of the detail for us. So when our brain sees ice cream in a smaller but more sumptuous-looking container, with fancy fonts and more descriptive ingredients, it grabs the template marked 'premium' and accepts the higher price tag.

To give you an insight into how clever and surreptitious reframing ice cream can be, consider the following. Say there are two types of ice cream available for sale. One is called Frish the other is called Frosh—which one do you want to buy? Please answer this question now.

Okay, I'm willing to bet you chose 'Frosh' and here's why. Eric Yorkston and his doctoral supervisor Greta Menon (2004) conducted a most interesting experiment where they created two fictitious brands of ice cream similar in every way except their names: Frosh and Frish. Eric and Greta wanted to test if the name or sound of a product had an impact on purchasing decisions. In their experiment, the vast majority of the participants wanted to try Frosh. Why? Because they expected the ice cream to be creamier, and better quality than Frish. Apparently, 'ih' vowel sounds convey impressions such as small, light and fast (these are 'front vowels'). 'Back vowels' (such as the 'oh' sound in Frosh), convey qualities such as slowness and being large. Hence, an ice cream that used a back vowel was perceived to be creamier, since it subconsciously sounds as though it will feel slower (thicker) and more substantial in your mouth. This is just a small demonstration of how the brain frames information and makes decisions. What's in a name? A lot.

So there you go, and that's just the name! When marketing a product, all elements of a brand will be deconstructed to ensure the product is framed in such a way that we (the consumers) will make assumptions about its quality.

IS POOL SALT BORING?

In 1888, just outside of Geelong, Victoria, Richard Cheetham cleared some land and started producing salt. The company he founded on the site would become Cheetham Salt, Australia's largest salt producer. No matter the type of salt you need—from table to industrial—Cheetham Salt supplies it. Salt is normally a low-margin business. Companies make a lot of it and sell a lot of it, but make very little profit—industrial salt can be sold for as little as $50 per tonne. Some years ago, Naked Communications formed a partnership with management consultancy Edgar Dunn. The CEO of Edgar Dunn, Lance Blockley, was a wealthy, very English gentleman. He spoke the Queen's English, religiously drove a Jaguar and had a wonderfully cutting dry wit. Over the years we've become somewhat unlikely friends.

Cheetham Salt approached Lance and shared their issue: they wanted to extract more profit from the salt they were selling. Lance and his team ran some numbers on the size of various salt markets in Australia (I hope you're still reading this riveting story about salt—it gets better, I promise) and decided that 'pool salt' was worth a look. The category was growing as many new houses in the ever-growing urban fringes of our cities were being built with pools. Historically most pool owners use chlorine to kill algae and bacteria, but many pool owners were now starting to use salt water. And to achieve that crystal clear, bacteria-free state, you need pool salt.

In marketing, it's much easier to kill an idea than an opportunity. **Identifying the opportunity is crucial**. If you get that right, you can fire ideas until one sticks. To identify the opportunity in pool salt, we went back to basics and talked with people who knew a lot about pools—pool owners. In marketing, the standard way to get information from 'consumers' is to run focus groups; that is, putting eight strangers in a room, usually under bad fluorescent lighting, and asking them a battery of questions.

As the peak-hour traffic made its way home, the first group of eight people stepped into a brightly lit room in the geographical heart of Sydney, Parramatta. I had organised a series of focus groups with pool owners to garner their thoughts and feelings. Seated around a large table, participants snacked on cheese and crackers and drank concentrated orange juice. I was also seated at the table and asked questions such as, 'What characteristics do you look for when choosing pool salt?'

The standard response was: 'I just buy whatever the local pool store stocks.'

When I asked, 'Do you prefer any brand in particular?' I was met with overwhelming ambivalence. No one cared about the brand of pool salt. In fact, no one could even name a brand of salt. I was told, repeatedly, that pool salt cost around $10 (they guessed) and came in a hessian bag. The crunch of crackers was sometimes the only sound in the room.

Each night, two groups met back-to-back so I was talking about pool salt for four straight hours a night. If that sounds boring, it was. After two days—or eight hours— asking questions about pool salt, the only new information I uncovered was that moisture sometimes got into the bag, which hardened the salt, making it heavy to carry. Also, it was difficult to carry the bag from the store to the car and sometimes the salt stung their eyes. Needless to say I was very bored running these groups, while the clients, sitting on the other side of a one-way mirror, were almost falling asleep.

As I drove home that night (at 10.30 p.m., after another four hours of talking about pool salt), I wondered what could be done. I felt a responsibility to the client to get some understanding from these people that might help. We were being paid, after all. I am fond of saying, 'There are no low-involvement categories, just low-involvement marketers.' To honour this I was determined to find out something about pool salt that got these people excited.

Four more groups were booked, but rather than endure more torturous sessions, I did something different. At the beginning of the next session, I placed butcher's paper and coloured pens on the table and asked participants to draw a picture of how it felt to own a pool. If we couldn't uncover anything interesting about pool salt, perhaps we could discover the 'opportunity' in the pool itself.

After initially expressing concern about their drawing skills, the group began scribbling pictures of pools. I turned to a burly looking man aged in his fifties and asked if he would share his picture of a proud-looking man standing next to a pool filled with smiling children.

'It's not just my kids but other kids from the street who use our pool,' he explained. 'When it's hot, they all come over after school. It's like you're the community babysitter.'

I asked about the figure standing at the side of the pool with his chest puffed out. 'That's me. I'm proud as punch to see all the kids at our house happy and playing together.'

I'd flicked a switch. The group now talked enthusiastically about their pools and shared a sense of pride about being pool owners. Because of their pool, they met and interacted with neighbours. Most talked about the care they put into maintaining their pools. One man described in detail his process of delicately spreading the salt across the entire pool and stirring it in with a brush to make sure it dissolved completely.

We had discovered the opportunity. Despite the perception that all pool salt was the same, users showed a high degree of emotion about looking after a pool. How could we use this opportunity to frame pool salt differently?

HOW *YOUR* FRAME DICTATES WHAT *OTHERS* DECIDE

If you've grown up watching alarmist Hollywood films, what I'm about to ask shouldn't be too difficult to do. Imagine the USA is preparing for the outbreak of an unusual Asian disease, which is expected to kill 600 people. Let's set our film in the White House Situation Room. There's Denzel Washington, Matt Damon, Claire Danes and a host of people in military attire looking concerned. And there's you. Denzel announces there are two different programs to combat the disease and you must choose one.

- Option 1: 200 people will be saved.
- Option 2: There is a 33 per cent chance that all 600 people will be saved and a 66 per cent chance that no one will be saved.

What's your choice?

The camera pans across the room until it stops at you. What's your decision? When these options were put in a study conducted by psychologists Amos Tversky and Daniel Kahneman in 1986, 72 per cent chose option 1 and 28 per cent chose option 2.

Denzel speaks again: there are another 600 people in a different area at risk. Again Denzel is asking you to choose between two more options. They are:

- Option 3: 400 people will die.
- Option 4: There is a 33 per cent chance that no one will die and a 66 per cent chance that all 600 people will die.

In the 1986 study, 22 per cent chose option 3 and 78 per cent chose option 4.

Now, a feisty but fragile Claire Danes pushes her chair back and heads to a whiteboard. She explains that options 1 and 3 are, in fact, exactly the same. Saving 200 of 600 people is the same as losing 400 of 600 people—200 remain alive. But it doesn't end there. Options 2 and 4 are also the same, although the maths is a bit more complicated to explain. The only difference is the language. When the options are presented as lives saved, people preferred to go with the safe option—option 1. When the options are expressed in terms of deaths (or losses), people chose the gamble (option 4). This is the classic study of the framing effect—the way a problem is presented affects choices. The reason is partially explained by Kahneman and Tversky (1984) and their work on loss aversion.

Colin Camerer is a rather smart behavioural economist (he had an arts degree, MBA and doctorate, all by the age of 21!) who looked at how New York taxi drivers behaved to demonstrate the real world implications of loss aversion (Camerer et al. 1997). At the time, taxi drivers had to rent a vehicle and paid a flat 12-hour rental fee, regardless of how long they actually drove it. Most had a daily revenue target they were happy with. Camerer found the taxi drivers generally worked until they made their daily pay level and then stopped. So on busy days, they tended to clock off early, but on slower days, when there were fewer fares available, they had to work more hours to make the same amount of money. Does this make sense to you?

Now on the surface, this seems reasonable—you work until you make your pay. But actually, wouldn't it make more sense to generate more money when it's busy (that is, work longer hours) and give up on your losses on quieter days (that is, work fewer hours)? Following this pattern, the taxi drivers would make considerably more money. The cabbies' work patterns might seem 'irrational', but can be understood as 'loss aversion'—they would rather work harder, longer hours (on quieter days) to ensure they did not lose money than they would for a potential gain by working longer hours on the busy days.

Advertising also frames messages in terms of 'loss aversion'. It's expressed as 'Don't miss out', 'Only two left' or 'Hurry before they're all sold'. Advertising appeals to our desire to avoid a loss. It's a well-established frame in advertising, and the reason why you'd rather save 200 people than risk losing them all. Loss aversion is just one of the ways the brain makes systematic, predictable and seemingly irrational biases. Others are 'observation selection bias', in which you notice something more often and assume its frequency has increased—such as the number of red cars on the road—and the 'well travelled road effect', in which you underestimate the time taken to travel somewhere because you travel it all the time, and overestimate how long it takes on new routes because they're unfamiliar. Cognitive bias explains why we can be manipulated. Interestingly, as the list is still being developed, and constantly added to, it appears that Wikipedia is currently the global hub for this information.

HOW WE COPE WITH A COMPLEX WORLD

As mentioned previously, we cannot process all the information that we perceive. To do so would be exhausting and debilitating. Further, we like to conserve cognitive energy. Thinking is hard work, and we are programmed to reserve effortful thinking for when it really matters. We can thank Daniel Kahneman, who I mentioned earlier, for uncovering and describing how the brain processes information.

Kahneman is a Jewish American, and became interested in the complexity of human behaviour after his family's experiences during the Second World War. He partnered with another cognitive psychologist, Amos Tversky, and together they published many papers in behavioural sciences, and in particular on how humans make decisions. In 1980, while professors at Stanford University, they met and befriended a young up-and-coming economist called Richard Thaler. As a team, they brought together economic theory and psychological theory and a new behavioural science was created—behavioural economics. Thaler (1980) published a paper called 'Toward a Positive Theory of Consumer Choice', which Kahneman believes was the founding paper of behavioural economics (Kahneman 2003). However, it wasn't until Kahneman won the Nobel Prize for Economics (called the Nobel Memorial Prize in Economics) in 2002 that behavioural economics really began to be embraced by the world's academic community, and it was some years before institutions and corporations interested in behaviour change began to take note.

Kahneman (2011) explained in his influential book *Thinking, Fast and Slow* that the brain operates in two main modes: System 1 and System 2. System 1 is fast, intuitive and emotional, and is connected to the world through the five senses. It processes roughly eleven million bits of information a second, and to cope with all of this information it makes snap judgments, generalisations, stereotypes and rules of thumb (a similar concept to what psychologists called schemas, as discussed above). It makes educated guesses throughout the day and is how we get by. Kahneman contends that System 1 is the autopilot, and we spend nearly all our time with the autopilot guiding us through the journey of the day.

System 2, on the other hand, is the slower, reasoning and rational part of the brain. It's the part that actually stops and thinks. However, because processing information in such an involved way is difficult, it can only process around forty bits of information a second; it requires more effort and can be tiring. We use it when learning new tasks, such as driving a car. After a while, a task such as driving becomes familiar enough to slip into System 1. Kahneman describes System 2 as the pilot; however, as pilots go this one is incredibly lazy, and doesn't like to be called upon—so for most of the time, autopilot it is. You can learn more about Kahneman on YouTube (www.youtube.com/watch?v=KyM3d4gQGhM).

Marketing often appeals to System 1 thinking, and this is where we get back to the cognitive biases list. Because our brain is operating in System 1 most of the time, making assumptions and leaps of logic, it is open to making mistakes based on the information it sees. That's why we can give a brain scant information (such as our ice cream with its higher price, smaller size, cursive writing and black packaging) and it will jump to assumptions (that the ice cream must be of premium quality).

THE FRAMING EFFECT

Think about how different words and phrases elicit very different feelings in you. Consider 'troop escalation' versus 'troop surge'. Which proposition do you think people would be more likely to agree to? I'm guessing 'troop surge'. An escalation feels more permanent and serious, while a surge sounds like a short-term commitment. In fact, 'troop surge' was the expression used by the US government when making the argument to invade Iraq. Consider the following propositions:

- Counter terrorism versus war on terror.
- Tax cuts versus tax relief
- Newstart versus the dole
- Global warming versus climate change
- 75 per cent lean meat versus 25 per cent fat meat
- Muffin versus cake.

Each describes the same concept, but we think and feel differently about each term depending on the words—or the '**frame**'. Try this. Imagine it's 7.30 a.m. and you've decided to take your dog Charlie for a walk. On your way home from a walk around the lake, you stop at the local bakery to pick up a take-away coffee. As you wait for your coffee to be made, you see and smell some nice-looking, freshly baked goods. The baker behind the counter asks, 'Would you like a carrot and banana muffin? Freshly baked this morning.' Would you buy one? Now imagine exactly the same scenario, but this time the guy behind the counter asks, 'Would you like a carrot and banana cake? It's delicious.' I'm guessing you'll be more tempted by the muffin than the cake. As the saying goes, 'Muffins made it okay to eat cake for breakfast.' It's the same product, but framed differently.

Figure 5.1 depicts a visual representation of 'framing' from Kahneman.

Figure 5.1 Kahneman's demonstration of the power of framing

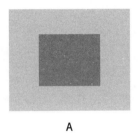

A   B

The square at the centre of each box appears to be a different shade of grey. In diagram A, it appears to be darker than in diagram B. But when you look at the centre square without the frame, you see both are exactly the same colour. According to Kahneman and Tversky, 'perception is reference dependent' (1984). This is why the traditional view, 'buy the worst house in the best street' makes economic sense. However, you'll feel better if you live in the best house in the worst street, as you'll compare it favourably to your neighbours' houses. Our perception is dependent on the frame or context it's in.

IS IT A CAKE OR A MUFFIN?

Let's return to our cakes versus muffins example. Both have similar ingredients: butter, flour, water, eggs and, in this case, carrot and banana. (I may have missed some ingredients. I'm not a great cook.) But for some reason, muffins are framed as a better, healthier option than a cake, as illustrated in Figure 5.2 (over the page).

I witnessed this effect when working with George Weston Foods, makers of Little Bites, whose sales were in decline. I hope you are in the mood for a bit of marketing jargon, as I'm going to have to explain something before taking you through how we changed the frame for Little Bites. As you can see in Table 5.1, there are three levels of branding marketers use when creating a brand that you might purchase. The first is called the **endorsement brand**. This brand is a signifier of quality and endorses a number of **purchase brands**, which sit underneath this endorsement brand. Often the endorsement brand is the name of a company (like Kellogg's or Ford). It's important that the endorsement brand says the right things about your purchase brand—or it can be a liability (for example, Ford now makes Jaguars but Ford doesn't put the Ford brand anywhere near their Jaguar cars, as it does not act as a stamp of quality). Purchase brands are the brands you reach for on a shelf, and the

Figure 5.2 How framing baking ingredients changes perception

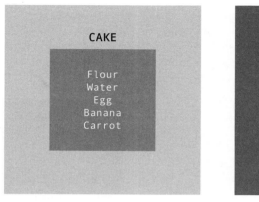

CAKE

Flour
Water
Egg
Banana
Carrot

MUFFIN

Flour
Water
Egg
Orange
Carrot

A   B

brand that you have a 'relationship' with. It's the brand you buy. In this instance you might buy a packet of 'Corn Flakes' or a 'Focus'. The final level of branding is called **navigation**, which simply helps consumers choose which version of the purchase brand they'll select (for example, the 500 g or the 750 g pack, or the five-door hatch or the four-door sedan).

Table 5.1 Levels of branding

LEVEL OF BRANDING	WHAT IS IT?	EXAMPLE A	EXAMPLE B
Endorsement brand	A brand that is an endorsement of quality, and normally sits above a number of purchase brands. Serves to give the consumer confidence in the purchase brand they buy.	Kellogg's	Ford
Purchase brand	The name of the brand with which the consumer has a relationship. It's the brand the consumer reaches for on shelf.	Corn Flakes	Focus
Navigation brand	Descriptors of various options of the brand to help the consumer decide which variation of the purchase brand they will buy.	500 g	Four-door sedan

When we took the brief, Little Bites featured the endorsement brand Top Taste on its packaging. Top Taste has a reputation for pre-packaged 'shelf stable' cakes (that is, they use preservatives to give the products a longer shelf life). The endorsement brand was in effect framing Little Bites as being 'little bites of cake full of preservatives'. We came to the conclusion that no amount of advertising would save Little Bites from this negative Top Taste frame. So before we did anything, we worked with our no-nonsense, extremely quick client, Bronwyn Heys, and innovative packaging agency Landor to change the endorsement brand. Over several weeks, and a number of design iterations, we developed a new endorsement brand for Little Bites called The Ministry of Muffins. We still had the same purchase brand ('Little Bites') but now with an endorsement brand called 'Ministry of Muffins'. This new name for our endorsement brand now framed our ingredients for 'Little Bites' as being muffins not cakes.

Figure 5.3 The same product framed differently

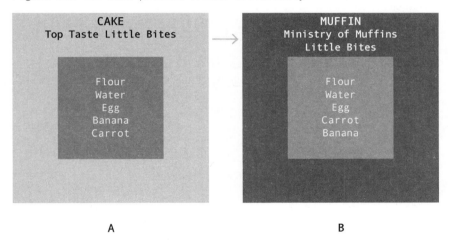

A   B

In addition to TV ads (you can watch them on YouTube: www.youtube.com/watch?v=A7ryhvkREy4), we worked with Landor to create new packaging showing 'The Ministry of Muffins.' The results were remarkable. Sales increased by 11 per cent and now people are enjoying muffins for a snack instead of cake (Ferrier 2010). A new name and packaging reframed the product.

THE ROLE OF PRICE

It sounds odd, but it's much easier to raise the price of an item than it is to lower it. Let me show you why. What would you think if a product you like to buy was suddenly lower in price? You might think the quality has gone down, or it's not selling well. If the same product has a price rise, it suggests it's popular and in demand. This is known as the '**the price placebo**' and it's an incredibly strong effect.

At Stanford University, Baba Shiv (Shiv, Carmon & Ariely 2005) tested the effect on people's brains when they believed they were drinking a more expensive glass of wine. Using an MRI scan, he watched what happened to the brains of drinkers who believed their wine cost $5 compared with another group who were told the same wine was worth $45. The wine was exactly the same, but the brains of the people who believed they were drinking the expensive drop lit up like a Christmas tree in the area that shows pleasure. They not only believed the wine was superior, but their brains also reinforced this belief. So **if you want to communicate a premium product, increase its price**. The more they pay—the better people will think it is.

Another way pricing can help frame something is '**price anchoring**'. This is the point at which you judge an item to be cheap or expensive; that is, good value or bad. But how do you determine an appropriate anchor price? In most cases, it's not very easy. Imagine you visit a store and you see a jacket you love. You try it on and it fits perfectly. You then look at the price and see it's $1200. The salesperson asks if you'd like to buy it, but you say it's too expensive. They tell you that you're in luck because the jacket is 60 per cent off today and only costs $500. Although it's still more than you wanted to pay, you're more likely to buy it because your anchor has been set at $1200. The interesting thing about anchors is they are often set arbitrarily. What's a reasonable price for a barbecue? $100? $500? When you visit a specialty barbecue shop, the first barbecue you see will most likely be the most expensive one—at about $5000. This becomes the anchor, so $500 doesn't seem so expensive in comparison. Your choice has been influenced.

REFRAMING POOL SALT

So how did we reframe pool salt? We suggested the company treat pool salt in the same way as premium ice cream. Until now, pool salt was marketed in terms of its size, weight and price—its physical features. No effort had been made to create positive imagery or to frame the salt in a particular way. Our frame would appeal to the opportunity identified in the focus groups—the pride that pool owners feel. The frame would quickly communicate that this pool salt represented a pool owner's best opportunity to let children swim in the pool safely. This is what we did.

We changed the name from 'Mermaid' to 'Mermaid Finest' with 'finest' communicating both a premium product and the finer quality of the crystals—salt that dissolves quickly when it enters the pool. The packaging changed from a hessian bag to plastic to keep out moisture and make it easier to carry. It communicated that the manufacturer cared about the salt inside. The side of the packaging featured a photo of a happy child in a red swimming costume suspended in crystal clear water with her eyes open—there's no need for goggles when you use Mermaid Finest. We recommended that a clear window be inserted on the front of the bag so you could see the salt—something premium brands often do. The packaging was changed but its contents—the salt—was exactly the same. And here's the surprising element. We reduced the size of the packaging by approximately 30 per cent (to make it easier to carry) and increased its price by 20 per cent to communicate a better quality pool salt (see Figure 5.4).

Figure 5.4 The different frames put on pool salt: a 'regular' frame (A) and a premium frame (B)

CHEETHAM
POOL SALT

Pool salt

Simple name, hessian bag, ugly printing, larger size, lower price

A

MERMAIDS
FINEST

Pool salt

Premium name, plastic bag, cursive writing and photo of girl swimming, smaller size, higher price

B

We decided that Mermaid Finest should only be available in pool supply stores. A brand that's only available in a premium outlet reinforces its premium frame. It also allows the pool supply store to differentiate itself from supermarkets or department stores—supporting the higher price tag of the product. Because Mermaid Finest was more expensive, there was a bigger profit margin. This is what Snow and Benford (1988) refer to as '**frame alignment**'. They argue that the 'robustness, completeness, and thoroughness of the framing effort' will largely dictate whether it is successful. Every little thing you do has to reinforce the same story. In my view, this is why the Occupy Wall Street movement failed. There was no unified, complete frame for the movement.

Mermaid Salt became a premium brand despite the actual salt used remaining exactly the same. It allowed busy shoppers to use System 1 thinking and register: 'This brand is the best pool salt available.' It continues to sell well today.

ADAM, HOW CAN YOU BE SO EVIL?

You might be thinking: Adam, that's horrible. You've reduced the size of an item and put up the price and you're selling the same thing but implying it's something different. How manipulative. But I don't think there's anything wrong in asking people to pay more for the

Figure 5.5 Distribution strategy supporting the brand frame

A   B

same item in different packaging. There's nothing wrong in rebranding a 'cake' as a 'muffin'. That's the role of advertising and marketing. As marketing guru Seth Godin (2005) says in his book *All Marketers Are Liars*:

> *The reason all successful marketers tell stories is that consumers insist on it. Consumers are used to telling stories to themselves, and telling stories to each other, and it's just natural to buy stuff from someone who's telling us a story. People can't handle the truth.*

Godin goes on to use Riedel glassware as an example of a marketer telling us a lie because we want it. Scientific tests, he says, prove that wine does not taste any better when served in Reidel glassware as opposed to any other vessel, even though Reidel glasses can cost 10 times as much. However, as consumers we are prepared to believe that the wine tastes better, because we want the wine to taste better.

Advertising is about changing behaviour. It involves framing products in both a compelling way and one that communicates value. Consider beer. How beer is framed creates differentiation and desire. A mainstream beer framed for a working-class bloke appeals to 'a hard-earned thirst', while an upmarket beer made by the same manufacturer is framed with gold leaf labels, cursive writing and so on. How different are these beers to drink?

When attempting to influence the behaviour of others, this is worth remembering: you're not the only person asking them to act. For example:

- Charities: there are many charities asking for donations.
- Dating: there are lots of people with your attributes.
- Employment: lots of people have your skills.
- Books: there are plenty to choose from. (You've chosen well, by the way.)

The behaviour you seek may not be that different from your competitors. The difference will lie in how you frame your argument, product or request.

FRAMING TO INFLUENCE OTHERS

Framing seems like a nebulous gas. Research in the area is continually expanding with new ways to elicit action. It's endless. What we do know is that in order to effectively frame a message you need to:

- appeal to autopilot System 1 thinking. Ensure your message has complete frame alignment.
- build a frame that takes advantage of cognitive biases. People react differently depending on whether a choice is presented as a loss or a gain. We avoid risk when a positive frame is presented, but seek risk when a negative frame is presented.

Levin, Schneider and Gaeth (1988) looked at the impact of different appeals to behaviour, such as wearing a seatbelt when in a car, applying sunscreen or paying taxes. They found that emphasising the disadvantages of not complying with a request, rather than the advantages of complying with a request, was a more effective frame. For example, rather than claiming you'll be safer in a car if you wear a seatbelt, it's more effective to claim you could be injured in a car accident if you don't wear a seatbelt. Again, this is because of loss aversion—we don't like losing things, and we have an inbuilt negativity bias.[1]

FRAMING IN ACTION

Want your children to eat their vegies? Many parents ask their children to comply by highlighting the positives (for example, 'Please eat the vegetables. You'll grow up big and strong.') Although true, it hasn't framed the argument in a particularly compelling way for the child. Most children don't have a grasp of nutrition and don't really care. Using Levin's research, the best way to get children to eat vegetables is to highlight negative consequences of not complying. 'If you don't eat your vegetables, you'll get sick or be weak or unattractive to others.' However, if you're not convinced you could take a radically different approach. Frame vegetables as unhealthy junk food. And the kids won't be able to resist them!

This was the approach of US advertising agency Crispin Porter + Bogusky. It had the brief to market baby carrots for Bolthouse Farms (whose CEO used to work for Coca-Cola). Its strategy? Treat carrots like junk food. It used crinkly plastic packaging like chips and had the packets placed in specially designed vending machines. Then there were over-the-top advertisements as part of the campaign, which was called 'Baby Carrots: Eat 'Em Like Junk Food'. The campaign mimicked many of the marketing approaches used

---

1 One of the most interesting (and used by advertisers) cognitive biases is negativity bias. This bias means we pay more attention to negative messages than positive ones (Baumeister et al. 2001). There are good evolutionary reasons for this. A negative stimulus (such as a sabre-tooth tiger in a tree) is likely to be far more important to notice than a positive stimulus (such as pretty cloud patterns forming in the sky). This instinct is still with us, and is part of the reason why politicians use so much negative advertising, and so much scare-mongering in their language.

by junk food manufacturers. You can see the case study on YouTube (www.youtube.com/watch?v=sDewR2jM138).

This $25 million campaign transformed the carrot business, reversed record declines in this category (sales in Bolthouse Farms' test markets were up 10–12 per cent from the year before) and ignited a cultural conversation around healthy snacking. For these reasons it won a Gold Effie (as well as a Silver and a Bronze) at the North America Effie Awards.

SUMMARY

We do not have the ability (and nor do we need it) to process all of the information that our five senses receive about the world. To manage all of this information we think in two different ways: System 1 and System 2. System 1 is implicit and makes decisions based on the information to hand, using assumptions and rules of thumb—it's our auto-pilot. System 2, on the other hand, is the slower, reasoning and rational part of the brain. It's the part that actually stops and thinks. However, our default setting is System 1, and it leaves us open to thinking very differently about the same thing if it is framed differently. It allows us to view the same base ingredients as either an unhealthy cake or a healthier muffin, depending on how it's framed.

All elements of marketing and advertising can be used to reframe brands. The more consistently and coherently they are adhered to, the more believable the frame will be This approach to behaviour change can be just as easily applied to getting kids to eat their vegetables as it can to increasing profit or market share of a product.

The Insider: Andrew Denton

I find the most effective way to change the behaviour of others is to appeal to their intelligence. Find a quiet time to lay out all the facts, as you know them, explain why you think it would be best for them to take a particular course of action, then let the other person know that you genuinely respect their capacity to make the smart choice once they've had a chance to think it through.

This only works if you are calm and have made the time to be patient.

Andrew Denton is one of Australia's best-known TV personalities, and producer of many of Australia's top TV shows. His interviews on TV show *Enough Rope*, on which he was producer and host, were notable for the way he employed a mix of candour and empathy to get interviewees to reveal much more than they might have intended.

I've known Andrew for around five years. I knew I liked Andrew when I explained to him that as a child I used to fantasise about a TV show called *Land of the Giants*, where I was a giant and kept half a dozen or so 'little people' in a shoe box. Halfway through this story, he said, 'Oh my, so did I. I am fascinated by that, too. I always ask people if they had that shoebox full of little people, would they: a) shake the box vigorously, or b) take off all the little people's clothes?'

I knew then that I had met a kindred spirit!

REFERENCES

Baumeister, R.F., Bratslavsky, E., Finkenauer, C. & Vohs, K.D. (2001). Bad is stronger than good. *Review of General Psychology*, 5(4), 323–70.

Camerer, C., Babcock, L., Loewenstein, G. & Thaler, R. (1997). Labor supply of New York City cabdrivers: One day at a time. *Quarterly Journal of Economics*, 112(2), 407–41.

Ferrier, A. (2010). *How the Ministry of Muffins Revved the Fortunes of Little Bites of Cake*. Australian Effie Awards. Accessed at www.effies.com.au/attachments/bb07b0e8-5398-4c1f-9fc0-59241fe071ac.pdf.

Godin, S. (2005). *All Marketers are Liars: The Power of Telling Authentic Stories in a Low Trust World*. London: Penguin Books.

Kahneman, D. (2003). A perspective on judgment and choice: Mapping bounded rationality. *American Psychologist*, 58(9), 697–720.

Kahneman, D. (2011). *Thinking, Fast and Slow*. New York: Macmillan.

Kahneman, D. & Tversky, A. (1984). Choices, values, and frames. *American Psychologist*, 39(4), 341–50.

Levin, I.P., Schneider, S.L. & Gaeth, G.J. (1998). All frames are not created equal: A typology and critical analysis of framing effects. *Organizational Behavior and Human Decision Processes*, 76(2), 149–88.

Shiv, B., Carmon, Z. & Ariely, D. (2005). Placebo effects of marketing actions: Consumers may get what they pay for. *Journal of Marketing Research*, 42, 383–93.

Snow, D.A. & Benford, R.D. (1988). Ideology, frame resonance, and participant mobilization. *International Social Movement Research*, 1(1), 197–217.

Thaler, R. (1980). Toward a positive theory of consumer choice. *Journal of Economic Behavior & Organization*. 1(1), 39–60.

Tversky, A. & Kahneman, D. (1986). Rational choice and the framing of decisions. *The Journal of Business*. 59(4), S251–78.

Wikipedia (n.d.). *List of Cognitive Biases*. Accessed at http://en.wikipedia.org/wiki/List_of_cognitive_biases.

Yorkston, E. & Menon, G. (2004). A sound idea: Phonetic effects of brand names on consumer judgments. *Journal of Consumer Research*, 31(1), 43–51.

EVOCATION: CAN YOU FEEL IT?

Emotions are a runaway train.

Paul Ekman, US psychologist

People screen out a lot of commercials because they open with something dull ... When you advertise fire-extinguishers, open with the fire.

David Ogilvy, founder of Ogilvy

APPEALING TO EMOTION

The advertisement begins with a young woman kneeling on a striped black-and-white towel as she prepares to spend a day sunbaking at the beach. As the camera moves towards her shoulders, we hear:

```
Tanning is skin cells in trauma, trying to
protect themselves from cancer.
```

We see beyond the girl's skin and into her cells. Suddenly, a white cell turns black.

```
But one damaged cell can start a melanoma
growing. And just 1 millimetre deep, it can get
into your blood stream and spread out.
```

We see the single black cell multiply, oozing like lava.

```
So even if a melanoma is cut out, the cancer can
reappear months or years later, often in your
lung, liver or brain.
```

A blob of black secretes into the bloodstream to circulate to who knows where. We return to our sunbaker, innocently lying on her towel reading a book.

```
And you haven't even started to burn yet.
```

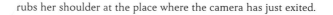
rubs her shoulder at the place where the camera has just exited.

There's nothing healthy about a tan.

This is one advertisement in the 'Dark Side of Tanning' campaign (which you can see on YouTube: www.youtube.com/watch?v=6Giv9lopemY) that aims to change the behaviour of young people who believe tanning is safe. Targeted at 13–24-year-olds, it's graphic and shocking. Since it aired in 2007, 62 per cent of people surveyed claimed they are less likely to get a suntan and 58 per cent have (or are thinking about) increasing their level of sun protection (Cancer Institute 2010). The shock advertisement works because it generates a strong emotional response—fear.

Advertisements draw on positive emotions as well, such as this one called 'Dear Sophie' promoting Google Chrome (see it on YouTube: www.youtube.com/watch?v=R4vkVHijdQk). In it, Daniel Lee types a series of messages to his baby daughter, Sophie, creating a snapshot of her early life using photos and videos. It's a composite electronic love letter from a father to his daughter, using the emotions of joy and pride. Watch the ad now if you can— it's beautiful. Many advertising agencies enjoy creating content that takes viewers on an emotional journey. There's a lot of skill involved in evoking an emotional response in just one minute; and even more in achieving that in just 30 seconds.

THE POWER OF EMOTIVE ADVERTISING

According to the Institute of Practitioners in Advertising (IPA), advertisements that use emotion to move or persuade the viewer are more effective at changing behaviour than those with a more rational, information-based approach. Drawing on 1400 successful case studies, the IPA has an extensive databank of effective advertising—the ones that work. One analysis by Pringle and Field (2012) compared the boost in profits from campaigns that relied primarily on emotional appeals (or **'evocation'**) with those that used rational persuasion and information. Campaigns with purely emotional content were nearly twice as effective—31 per cent to 16 per cent—as those with only rational content. If there was a mix of rational and emotional content, profit boosts were 26 per cent. In this analysis, the use of emotion certainly trumps a rational approach.

The authors of the study attribute the higher profits from emotional advertising to two factors. First, **the brain is able to process emotions without cognition**; that is, the ad will work even if we don't pay attention to it. Pringle and Field call this 'low attention branding' (2012), a concept similar to Robert Heath's 'low involvement processing' (2001). We absorb the message even when we're not aware of the information, and this argument is especially true of emotional stimuli. Second, **our brain is more attracted to powerful emotional stimuli** and is more likely to 'record' and remember such stimuli. This probably has its origins in evolutionary psychology. If something triggered an emotion (fear, disgust, surprise and so on), rather than cognitive interest, it was worth paying attention to for reasons of survival. Evocation gets our attention, and the messages are quickly encoded into our brain. However, this is not as straightforward as it might sound, for two reasons.

First, emotional ads are harder to create than rational ones. It's much easier to generate and communicate a killer fact about a brand than it is to build emotion into the brand through advertising. This takes a clever idea and time. Pringle and Field (2012) say it's easier for Nike to use emotion because it's always used emotion in its branding—it doesn't need to say anything rational. Further, the brand is well known and well recognised round the world. Its entire advertising budget can be spent on building an emotional connection with its customers, with the brand name playing a small supporting role (everyone is aware of Nike and knows what it does). By contrast, how might the new 'Chop Master Pro'—with twice the chopping power of other choppers—employ emotion? I'm not saying it can't be done: it's just more difficult to do. Further, once an emotional territory is carved out for a brand, it's reinforced over the years, allowing the brand to maintain that emotional connection. This takes discipline and time, and is especially difficult when the average tenure for a marketing director is 18 months (and the first thing the new marketing director often wants to do is create a new brand platform).

Second, most of the IPA studies compared rational with emotional advertising—but did not pay attention to the effect of interactivity. This book suggests that interactivity with a message is more influential than passively receiving a message, whether that be rational or emotional. The IPA studies have not taken the interactivity of communications into account.

Nike and its long-time advertising agency Wieden + Kennedy have a history of creating some of the best emotional advertising of all time. But you'd be hard-pressed to recall any epic Nike advertising from recent years. As mentioned earlier, Nike has moved the majority of its media budget into the interactive space. Although its marketing budget has been steadily climbing (to $2.4 billion in 2011), Scott Cendrowski (2012) reveals that Nike is spending 40 per cent less on TV and print media than it did just three years ago—and the move away from TV started well before this. One can only assume it is doing this because it is finding more interactive forms of communications more effective than passive 'emotive' advertising. On the advertising agency side, Nike's long-term love affair with Wieden + Kennedy (one of the most celebrated client–agency relationships in the world) has had to make way for new agency friends including AKQA and RG/A. Both are digital agencies that help the company create technology products such as Nike's Fuel Band, and manage the data from these products.

I want to emphasise this because 'emotional advertising' is often the first thing people associate with advertising. But it's not its most important element—nor its future. Perhaps the reason many people in advertising inflate the role of 'emotional advertising' is because of the 'availability bias' (Tversky & Kahneman 1973).[1]

---

1 Answer this question: Do you think there are more words starting with the letter K or more that have K as the third letter of the word? Answer it now. Most of you would have started trying to list the number of words you know starting with K, as this is a much easier task than thinking of words with the third letter as K. Consequently, you probably said there are more words beginning with K. But just because information is easily available doesn't make it right, important or representative. There are approximately twice as many words with K as the third letter than words starting with K. Concluding otherwise is the 'availability bias' in action, and availability bias could be why advertisers consider 'emotional advertising' to be more important than action-based advertising—because there is more of it around.

SO EMOTIONS ARE NOT IMPORTANT IN MARKETING?

Nothing could be further from the truth, as ensuring a brand connects emotionally is vital due to 'perceived value'. For example, if two cars are exactly the same, I'll pay more for the one that's imbued with status and makes me feel successful. It's the same with beer or even water. If I'm on a date and one water brand makes me appear more successful and sophisticated, I'll buy it, and probably pay more for it.

However, there are many brands that rarely employ advertising yet elicit a strong emotional connection from consumers. For example, my family has strong connections with Twitter, ASOS, ZARA, Google, Skip Hop, Headly, HBO and Carmen's Museli—none of which advertises to any significant degree. The emotional connection is important, but in these examples the connection has been built through a positive experience with the brand, not via the advertising. As indicated in Figure 6.1, both the experience with the brand and the advertising itself can contribute to the overall emotional connection the consumer has with the brand. However, sometimes the best way to build an emotional connection is simply by delivering on your promises; that is, doing what you do well.

Many advertising agencies also try to convince clients that they should do 'emotional' advertising for no other reason than it's what the agency enjoys creating, despite the fact that emotional connections are often more effective through actions. (Again, action changes attitude faster than attitude changes action.) Having said that, I'll get off my soapbox and acknowledge that 'emotional advertising' still has a role to play.

Figure 6.1 Contributions to emotional connection

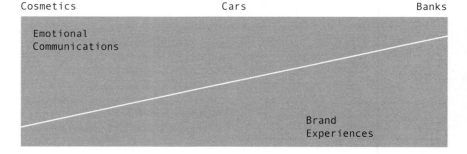

MAKING DEODORANT EMOTIONAL

If you're in New Zealand when the All Blacks are playing, you'll witness a nation totally absorbed. New Zealand's passion for its world-beating rugby union team is obsessive, and a special reverence is reserved for those who pull on the black jersey with the silver fern. When New Zealand was selected to host the 2011 Rugby World Cup, there were big expectations for the team. Despite its dominance of the code, the All Blacks had choked in many critical World Cup encounters over the years, and New Zealanders took it personally. When the team lost during the semi-finals in 1999, the players' luggage was scrawled with the word 'Losers' (presumably written by a disgruntled baggage handler).

Deodorant brand Rexona had sponsored the All Blacks for many years, but 2011 represented an important opportunity. A limited edition product range was created especially for the Rugby World Cup, with a healthy amount of money spent on sponsoring the team. It was our task at Naked Communications to promote Rexona using the All Blacks team. Because of the special relationship between the nation and its rugby team, we knew we had to tread with extreme care. We wanted to leverage, but not to exploit, this emotional connection. If we got the pitch wrong, we could seriously damage the brand.

We made contact with colleagues in Naked's New Zealand office and asked for insights into the All Blacks team. The first things we learned were 'Don't mess with them' and 'Don't joke about the All Blacks'. We wanted to understand what made these guys tick and how they psyched themselves up for the big games. All Blacks coach Graham Henry was very obliging, allowing us to watch the elite rugby union players at gruelling training sessions. I witnessed several players doing push-ups on top of two other players who were also doing push-ups. I'm not sure if this was a regular part of training or the players were showing off, but it was quite a sight.

We also interviewed the players, asking them to describe how they got into the zone before a match. For the All Blacks, confidence meant sticking to their game plan—preparing properly and building routine and control. We also heard about the pre-game rituals that each player uses. When Mils Muliaina showed us the hospital bracelet of his baby that he looks at before a game, an idea crystallised. Pre-game rituals give you confidence. We thought if we could demonstrate how the All Blacks boost their confidence, it would endear them to New Zealanders and show the human side of elite athletes. We return to this campaign later in the chapter, but first we need to look more closely at emotions and how they affect us so deeply.

A LITTLE MORE ON HOW EMOTION WORKS

Emotions are feelings that move us. The word emotion comes from the Latin 'emovere' (to move). Emotions are one of the most powerful ways to cut through and connect with someone. Psychologist Dr Robert Plutchik, an influential researcher into emotions, believed their evolutionary purpose is to make you take action to keep safe—the fight or flight response (1980). Say you're walking in the bush and you see a snake. How would you feel? I'd guess you'd notice your heart beating faster, your muscles tensing up and you might sweat. You'd likely experience the emotion of fear (or at least anxiety) and your response would be to move (or run!) away to safety. The emotion (fear) produces an action (running away) that protects you.

You could describes scores of different emotions, but Plutchik (1980) believed there are only eight primary emotions:

1. joy
2. sadness
3. trust
4. disgust
5. fear
6. anger
7. surprise
8. anticipation.

These are our most basic emotions free of cognitive influence. When you place rotten milk under someone's nose, how do they react? With disgust. What if you sneak up on someone before screaming loudly into their ears? They might feel surprise (that could quickly become anger). What about a child on Christmas Eve? That's anticipation.

Take another look at the list of emotions. Of the eight, at least five are negative,[2] two are neutral (surprise and anticipation) and only one is positive: 'joy'. According to evolutionary psychology, negative emotions are more important for survival than positive ones (it was more important for survival to pay attention to the sabre-tooth tiger in the tree than the pretty cloud patterns forming in the sky). This is the reason for negativity bias and means we pay more attention to negative messages than positive ones (Baumeister et al. 2001).

In his book, *Descartes Error* (1996), Antonio Damasio, Professor of Neuroscience at the University of Southern California, believes emotions play a big part in our decision making. What's more, he says that our previous emotional experiences influence our choices and preferences. He believes the rational–emotional dichotomy is largely fictitious and that emotional experiences are more powerful in guiding our decision making than rational information. I like this thought—instead of thinking about the information available to make a decision, we feel the information available to make a decision.

The importance of emotions in decision making is well documented (Rick & Loewenstein 2008). A study conducted in Pakistan by Niazi et al. (2012) found the emotions evoked in advertising were more influential to the consumer than the advertisement's information. It's a similar story with politics. In his book *The Role of Emotion in Deciding the Fate of the Nation* (2007), psychologist and political strategist Drew Westen (2007) writes:

> Voters tend to ask four questions that determine who they will vote for, which provide a hierarchy of influence on their decisions about whether and how to vote: How do I feel about the individual's party and its principles? How does this candidate make me feel? How do I feel about their candidates' personal characteristics? And How do I feel about this candidate's stand on issues that matter to me? Candidates who focus their campaigns towards the top of this hierarchy and work their way down generally win.

It's how people feel about the parties and candidates that matters, not what they think.

Primary emotions make us act because of cognitive dissonance. As explained in Chapter 3, we like our thoughts, feelings and actions to be aligned or we feel uncomfortable. When our feelings are negatively aroused, we feel discomfort and either change the feeling or change the thoughts or actions. It's why advertisers play on people's fears—or even generate fears—to persuade people to buy products. It's true. Advertisers know they 'dial up' new fears.

One example is anti-bacterial wipes. Playing on the fear of germs, advertisers created a new market in which consumers buy hand-sanitisers and other antibacterial products in the belief it will keep the germs at bay. Ten years ago, these products didn't exist and I doubt germ levels have dropped dramatically since these new products became available. Advertisers created a demand using fear as the driver.

---

2 We've all heard of the term retail therapy. Well, it's not just a myth—we do consume more when we are sad. Not only that, but when we are sad we make worse consumption choices: we'll pay more for products and make more unhealthy food choices (Gard & Lerner 2013). In short, try to avoid shopping when you're not feeling great.

I believe emotion is the equivalent of grabbing someone by the shoulders and telling them to 'stop and listen'. Or of giving them a light slap across the face and a loud 'snap out of it'. It can get people's attention. However, it's what you *do* with that attention that counts if you want to change behaviour. Joanna Flint is a senior executive at Google and co-author of a study looking at the effectiveness of what she calls the 'Zero Moment of Truth' (ZMOT) (Flint & Lecinski 2013). The first moment of truth is the point of purchase and the second moment of truth is when you use a brand. The ZMOT is the moment you decide to find out more about a product or brand on your way to purchase. After passively ignoring information, something happens (a stimulus) that makes you think, 'Actually, I think I want that', and you're motivated to find out more. I spoke to Joanna about the ZMOT when I was Google's guest at a conference in Singapore. Joanna said advertising agencies spend so much time getting the TV commercial right, and create a great stimulus, but they don't do anything with it. They need to get people to act, and investigate that their online activity supports the ZMOT. I strongly agree with Joanna—that many advertisers are missing an opportunity. Around 70 per cent of TV viewing is done using a second screen, such as a laptop or mobile device within arm's reach. If using evocation to change behaviour, advertisers should make sure they close the loop with their online activity and take advantage of any action they motivate.

INTERACTIVE EVOCATION

And then there is this. In 2010, with the help of Google, Canadian indie-rock band Arcade Fire created a music video for their song 'The Wilderness Downtown' using the HTML5 coding language . HTML5 allows coders to create content for the World Wide Web that takes advantage of many multimedia and interactive solutions. The anthemic and beautiful song is about a child growing up, and is rather 'emotional' in a nostalgic kind of way. But there's a kicker: before the music video plays, you enter the address of your childhood home. The video then collects all the Google street view and Google Earth images of the house, the street and the suburb where you grew up. As the video plays, a screen pops up with an aerial shot of the street you grew up in. It zooms along the rooftops of the street and pauses over your home, before rising up for a suburb view. The video shows a young kid cruising around a suburb, but it's actually your suburb. He's growing up in your house and running around your neighbourhood. The child is you. It's an evocative piece of content that won the Cyber Grand Prix at Cannes Lions in 2011. Have a look at it here: http://thewildernessdowntown.com.

WE LIKE TO SHARE EMOTIONAL EXPERIENCES

What was the most recent video you shared with friends or family? Was it funny or surprising, or did it contain interesting factual information? I'm guessing it was funny or surprising. Humans are social and like to share, which is easy to do online. For many advertisers, the Holy Grail is **creating content that's so engaging it's shared and goes viral**. In fact, it's called viral marketing because it acts like a virus. When people share content, they become the media channel. Because there's no fee for sharing, it's free and there's a level of endorsement. A friend is saying 'this is good'. Advertisers call this **'earned media'**—the content is good enough to have 'earned' additional media. This type of endorsement can be further leveraged. When people share content peer-to-peer, it's likely that traditional media will highlight the content as well. Because the content is good enough for people to choose to watch it, if the content appears in 'paid' media like TV ads people will likely choose to watch it. We call this **'paid for media'**. Further, if a brand or company has any assets—such as a website, or in-store screens—then people will likely choose to watch it there as well. This is **'owned media'**.

Emotions are a powerful determinant of content and article sharing online. Whether it's a cute cat or a personal story of protest, an article that taps into emotion is more likely to be shared than one based on facts. This is supported by research company, Brainjuicer, whose digital culture officer, Tom Ewing, conducted a study into viral advertising based on ads shown during the 2013 US Superbowl. The ads included Volkswagen's 'The Bark Side', Coca-Cola's 'Catch' and Chrysler's 'Halftime in America'. The advertisements were shown to people watching online who were asked to describe which emotion the ad elicited. In advertising, this is done through a projective technique where the subject is shown eight faces that each depict a different emotion. People are asked to pick a face that best matches how they feel when watching the ad. This is more effective than describing an emotion. Tom then looked at the emotional content of ads that were shared and compared them with those that weren't shared. The research concluded that three ingredients are needed for viral advertising:

1. surprise
2. a fair degree of intensity
3. a bit of happiness.

There are other ways to create viral messages, but this emotional mix proved to be a winning strategy for these diverse clients. For the record, Volkswagen's 'The Bark Side' was the most shared ad during the 2013 Superbowl. Take a look to see if it successfully uses surprise, intensity and happiness (www.youtube.com/watch?v=KqBfZ6vXPS8). You can see a summary of Brainjuicer's research at http://www.brainjuicer.com/html/stream/webinars.

'REXONA: RITUALS OF CONFIDENCE'

This is how we used emotion to promote Rexona and the All Blacks in New Zealand. In our advertisement, the All Blacks walk in formation down a brightly lit corridor towards the playing field. As atmospheric music plays, a deep voice intones, 'Rituals of Confidence'. In the change room we see the tattooed back of Ma'a Nonu depicting Jesus Christ on the cross. 'For some, it's believing', continues the voice over as Nonu smells his jersey before lifting his deep black eyes to the camera. He appears hypnotised. There's the faint roar of a crowd as the players walk closer to the field. Mils Muliaina holds a plastic hospital bracelet before placing it on the photograph of a baby: 'Reflecting on tough times'. Another player places the team's icon—a silver fern—into his playing boot: 'It can be holding on to tradition.' Another writes the name of a family member on his wrist: 'Keeping family close'. Another picks up a school pin: 'Or remembering where it all began'. The noise of the crowd grows louder: 'It can be anything yet everything.' A bare-chested Dan Carter lifts his arm to apply Rexona: 'Some may say it's superstition. We think not.'

The ad, which you can see on YouTube (www.youtube.com/watch?v=QNlhkUZOnMM) features the main ingredients for a strong emotive ad:

1. an anthemic sound-track
2. nothing jarring to distract viewers from the emotion (including the brand—which is nicely integrated)

3. high-end production values

4. rational benefits that are entwined in (and help to build) the emotional story.

As Antonio Damasio (1996) argues, somewhere along the way advertising became confused and separated rational and emotional advertising. One does not preclude the other. The image of players spraying deodorant under their armpits conveys the message that deodorant prevents smelly armpits.

It's a fairly straightforward advertisement and could be viewed as overly earnest, but when you spend time in New Zealand, you learn pretty quickly that the All Blacks team is not to be toyed with. We wanted people to put their trust in the All Blacks in the same way the All Blacks had put their trust in Rexona. The advertisement used anticipation to emotionally connect viewers to the All Blacks, showing their vulnerability before a game. We wanted New Zealanders to feel that emotion as they stood in front of the deodorant shelves at the supermarket and then act by buying Rexona. Increased sales, and interaction from New Zealanders with the campaign, suggested they did.

HOW AN ADVERTISER WOULD SELL WEIGHT LOSS

If I were a doctor persuading a patient to lose weight, I would consider using emotion to jolt them into action over rational argument. Let's imagine our patient has diabetes as a result of their weight, but they can get off medication if they lose weight. The case I would make is this: 'If you lose X number kilos, you can reduce your diabetes medication. And if you lose Y number of kilos, you can stop taking the medication altogether.' Once the incentive is established, the patient has to take responsibility and decide what changes they're going to make to achieve this outcome. Ask them to agree to three achievable goals. This might include walking for 30 minutes each day, changing what they eat for breakfast and cutting out soft drinks, with regular appointments to monitor their progress. Emotion is the spur to action.

I might ask my theoretical diabetes patient to read the obituary notice of another diabetes sufferer. Or I could make a recording of their children imagining what life would be like if my patient was dead. They could talk about how sad they are that Mum or Dad is no longer around. Use emotion to jolt them into action.

This is something health insurance company Bupa is tapping into, with its series of ads called 'The Moment'. A woman sits at a restaurant nervously playing with a serviette. When her dining companion passes outside the window, she turns and waves. The screen reads: 'These people have not seen each other for many years.' The two women greet each other. 'Nice to see you. How have you been?' one asks. 'Good,' replies the other. We're now outside on a busy street. A man walks towards another man who appears to be his brother and both are smiling. In another scene, a man using a walking stick gets into a car that's driven by a mate, or so it seems. As the advertisement continues, we realise these people aren't siblings or friends. They are the healthy and unhealthy versions of themselves. 'What would you do if you met a healthier version of yourself? We can help you find them.' The ad, which you can see on YouTube (www.youtube.com/watch?v=XnSJ-2i2Jm0), uses the emotion of lost potential to motivate action.

The emotional shock also could be something visual. A very effective advertisement to shock smokers into quitting portrays lungs as sponges that have become black from cancer-producing tar. The black tar from the sponge is wrung out into a glass beaker that measures just how much gunk is produced in your lungs from smoking. It's a visual shock and evokes both disgust and fear.

Don't use evocation by halves. If you decide to use this spur, put some effort into it and do it well. Scare, shock and surprise the bejesus out of your target audience. A great example is an ad to discourage drink driving. Filmed in North London, a series of men wash their hands after visiting the bathroom at a pub. As the water runs over their hands, the mirror in front of them suddenly and loudly shatters and a face dripping in blood is seen through the broken shards of the mirror. The men—and viewers—jump back in shock. It's a campaign to stop drink driving. Again, see it on YouTube (www.youtube.com/watch?feature=player_embedded&v=YJDsH64sqNY).

SUMMARY

Emotion (or evocation) is a powerful tool to influence behaviour. It works because we are hard-wired to protect ourselves from danger, with strong emotions being the warning signal to act. When the All Blacks shared the emotional tension they feel before a game and what they do to give them confidence, it connected viewers with the Rexona brand. Just remember: emotion only opens the door to behaviour change—other tools are needed to effect change. Emotion offers the initial shock to act. It's most effective when complacency has set in and rational arguments no longer work. In advertising the goal of creating an 'emotional connection' via advertising often goes unchallenged. There can be many more effective ways to change behaviour and build brands. Changing behaviour through emotional persuasion can be quite cumbersome, and any effects are often short term. Hence, if you don't keep persuading, people don't keep buying.

The Insider: David (Nobby) Nobay

There's a common misconception that selling—be it an idea or a fridge—is all about confidence. In my experience, it has more to do with the opposite. On some level, most of us, with the possible exception of the odd despot or sociopath, harbour weaknesses and insecurities: *my nose is a funny shape, my accent isn't quite right, I don't read enough, I'm shit at telling jokes.* The point is that flaws make us human. The rough edges give our character its distinct shape. So, my advice when attempting to convince someone to do something is, firstly, convince them that you're (at least in some small way) like them. Empathy is a great seducer. Admit you're a tragically bad presenter. Confess that you had insomnia the night before. Reveal that your hand shakes when you try to control the mousepad in large rooms. Then watch as something strangely human happens ... they lean in and smile.

Nobby is the creative chairman at Droga5 and one of the world's most influential creative directors. I worked closely with Nobby at Saatchi & Saatchi. He's one of the more charismatic and creative people I've ever met.

REFERENCES

Baumeister, R.F., Bratslavsky, E., Finkenauer, C. & Vohs, K.D. (2001). Bad is stronger than good. *Review of General Psychology*, 5(4), 323–70.

Cancer Institute of NSW. (2010). Melanoma awareness campaign 2009–2010, Dark side of tanning. Accessed at http://www.cancerinstitute.org.au/media/77557/web10-259_dark-side-tanning_summary-report.pdf

Cendrowski, S. (2012). Nike's new marketing mojo. *Fortune*, 13 February. Accessed at http://management.fortune.cnn.com/2012/02/13/nike-digital-marketing.

Damasio, A.R. (1996). *Descartes' Error*. London: Penguin Books.

Ewing, R. (2013). *What Makes Ads Go Viral ... And How to Test for It!* Accessed at http://media.brainjuicer.com/media/files/BrainJuicer_Virality_Webinar.pdf.

Flint, J. & Lecinski, L. (2013). *Winning the Zero Moment of Truth in Asia: Women, Consumer Packaged Goods and the Digital Marketplace*. Forthcoming.

Gard, N. & Lerner, J.S. (2013). Sadness and consumption. *Journal of Consumer Psychology*, 23(1), 106–13.

Heath, R. (2001). Low involvement processing: A new model of brand communications. *Journal of Marketing Communications*, 7(1), 27–33.

Niazi, G.S.K., Siddiqui, J., Shah, B.A. & Hunjra, A.I. (2012). Effective advertising and its influence on consumer buying behavior. *Information Management and Business Review*, 4(3), 114–19.

Plutchik, R. (1980). *Emotion: Theory, Research, and Experience: Vol. 1. Theories of Emotion*. New York: Academic.

Pringle, H. & Field, P. (2012). *Brand Immortality: How Brands Can Live Long and Prosper*. London and Philadelphia: Kogan Page.

Rick, S. & Loewenstein, G. (2008). The role of emotion in economic behavior. In M. Lewis, J.M. Haviland-Jones & L.F. Barrett (eds), *Handbook of Emotions*, 3rd edn. New York and London: The Guilford Press.

Tversky, A. & Kahneman, D. (1973). Availability: A heuristic for judging frequency and probability. *Cognitive Psychology*, 5(1), 207–33.

Westen, D. (2007). *The Role of Emotion in Deciding the Fate of the Nation*. New York: Public Affairs.

COLLECTIVISM: EVERYONE ELSE IS DOING IT

What's great about this country is America started the tradition where the richest consumers buy essentially the same things as the poorest ... A Coke is a Coke and no amount of money can get you a better Coke than the one the bum on the corner is drinking.

Andy Warhol, US artist

Like the herd animals we are, we sniff warily at the strange one among us.

Loren Eiseley, US anthropologist

ADAM, WE HAVE A PROBLEM

With her dyed, bright-red hair set in a retro bob, radio program director Meagan Loader exudes cool. I knew her through her brother Duane. 'I'm calling you in a professional capacity,' she said when she contacted me out of the blue. 'Could you come to our office for a meeting? It's kind of urgent.'

Sydney's radio market is very competitive. Before digital radio, frequencies were limited and costly. When the Australian government released Sydney's last three FM licences in the mid-1990s, Meagan and a couple of music-loving friends threw in their well-paid executive jobs to live their dream of running an agenda-setting independent radio station—FBi. Dissatisfied with Top 40-style, high-rotation formats that are the norm on commercial radio, the group believed Australian artists weren't getting the exposure to launch their careers. After a fierce battle for the permanent licence, the Australian Broadcasting Authority granted the 94.5 FM frequency to FBi (Free Broadcasting incorporated) in 2002. With their permanent licence in place, they wrote a business plan and took an unsecured loan for $1 million.

From studios in Redfern, a downtrodden but gentrifying inner-city Sydney suburb, FBi began broadcasting in 2003 with a charter to play 50 per cent Australian music, with half of that by Sydney artists. Staffed by volunteers, mostly in their late teens and early twenties, the vibe in the early days was very raw but the station quickly discovered an audience passionate about Australian music. The station survives on memberships and some sponsorships.

I arrived for the meeting at FBi's studios. After walking past band posters along the wall and mismatched second-hand furniture, I sat down in a cramped office. Meagan's mood could be summed up in one word: glum. In 2008, the Global Financial Crisis rippled across the globe and some of the station's key sponsors withdrew funding. The station faced growing financial pressures—and unless it raised $500,000 in three months, FBi would close down.

Each year, FBi asked listeners for money in its annual drive for funds. These listeners are mostly young university students or at the beginning of their careers—they don't have a lot of spare cash. The most successful FBi fundraiser in 10 years had only raised $80,000. It needed more than six times that amount to keep the station running, and they needed it quickly. Meagan and Evan Kaldor, the ex-investment banker and now supremely likeable station manager of FBi, realised what they had been doing wasn't going to help, so they approached us to see if we could think of a way FBi could raise $500,000 within a few months. At the end of the meeting we discussed a few alternatives: they could ask their current listeners for the money or they could seek big corporate sponsors. But what about a totally different approach: harness the passion and creativity of current listeners to do the money-raising. It was the germ of an idea built around the action spur called collectivism.

WHAT IS COLLECTIVISM?

Humans copy and mimic each other—we are herd-like. We do this to keep the peace and also to fit in. It's a primal drive. Why do so many people like the same music or TV shows? Why does one group of people passionately follow a particular football club, while another group follows a different club? Why do teenage girls like Justin Bieber one year and One Direction the next? Collectivism is based on 'social norms'—those written and unwritten rules of appropriate behaviour. **If you break a social norm, you face exclusion from the group.** It's a very powerful tool of influence, and one often used by advertisers. Advertisers will often make it *appear as though* everyone is already acting in a particular manner, to get everyone to *actually* act in that particular manner! I'd go as far as to say that for a certain type of marketer, collectivism is the gold standard for an idea. Nothing gives the client and their agency more joy than watching the world, a country or a state join in on an idea that they created.

Psychologist Robert Cialdini (2005) revealed the power of social norms in a study of towel use. Imagine you're staying at a five-star hotel. After taking a luxurious bath, you wrap yourself in an oversized bath towel and feel the soft fibres against your skin. Standing at the basin, you see a sign that reads: 'Please reuse your towel to protect the environment.' What do you do? Do you place the towel over the railing ready for another use, or leave it on the floor? Now, imagine it's the same hotel room, the same bath and the same towel. But this time, when standing at the basin, the sign asks you to reuse your towel, adding that: 'A majority of people who stayed in this room reused their towel.' Are you hanging or dumping your towel?

When guests at several hotels in Phoenix, Arizona, were given these options, 33 per cent more people reused their towels when the second sign was placed in their bathroom. The reason? We often make decisions based on what we believe other people would do. Consciously or unconsciously, we look to our peers, neighbours and friends to help us work out how to behave. We are not aware we are doing this, and are unlikely to admit to it when we do.[1]

Collectivism is about creating new perceived norms. A child who wants to stay out late might claim that their friends' parents let their friends stay out late. Although parents would not like to admit they are influenced by this persuasive technique, the evidence suggests they would be. If the parents believe that staying out late is the norm, they'll be much more likely to let their own child stay out later. The behaviour of others can be more influential than a rational argument, information or even an emotional pull.

THE BUILDING BLOCKS OF COLLECTIVISM

There are four building blocks of collectivism. If you leverage all four, you'll create collective action. The first is **obedience**. Sometimes all you need to do to get action is to tell someone to perform an action. People are surprisingly obedient—to the point that many will carry out orders even if it means harming someone else. This was exposed by social psychologist Stanley Milgram (1974). In Milgram's well-known experiments, subjects were asked to administer a powerful electric shock to someone who answered a question incorrectly. Many performed the electric shock because they were asked to. In fact people shocked the poor person even though they were warned that the shock could be fatal. In case you're concerned, the person receiving the shock was an actor who pretended to be zapped. Have a look at the original experiments on YouTube (https://www.youtube.com/watch?v=W147ybOdgpE).

If you're thinking, 'People have changed. That wouldn't happen today', or 'I wouldn't do that', I recreated this experiment in Melbourne for a client, WorkSafe, the state government body responsible for safety at work. We wanted to show employers why they should never ask employees to do dangerous things at work, because employees are likely to follow orders even if it endangers themselves or others.

We set up a fake worksite on a busy city street with two actors pretending to be electricians doing street works. One of the workers tried to pass a dangerous live electrical cable to another worker who was just out of reach. During the busy lunch time rush, random people passing by the site were asked to assist and take possession of a very dangerous looking cable from Worker A and pass the cable to Worker B. The passer-by was told to be very careful as, 'The wire is live, and he [the co-worker] may receive a strong electrical shock.' What do think happened? Do you think they refused to pass the wire? Did they ignore the request and walk on? How do you think you would have behaved in this context?

---

1 In advertising, many ideas are put into market research to help the marketer decide which idea to go with. This market research normally involves a series of focus groups (you may have been to them as a participant. If you have, you'll know how unscientific they are). Normally groups are attended by people with time on their hands who need extra cash. Many of the participants lie just to get their $70–$100 for turning up. 'Do you like Soy milk?' 'Oh, I love it!'—and you're in. Many participants make a second living out of attending these groups, going to one or two a week. The industry calls them (unimaginatively) 'groupies'. Anyway, assessing social norms in a focus group is nearly impossible. Imagine asking people, 'Are you more likely to go along with brand X or cause X if we say lots of other people will go along with it, too?' It's one of the many limitations of the current state of market research.

The results were alarming if not surprising. Ninety per cent of people passed the dangerous cable from one worker to the other, even though it was supposedly 'very dangerous' to do so. They did something that put themselves and others in danger just because someone in authority (Worker A) asked them to. Again, you can see a case study of this 'experiment' on YouTube (www.youtube.com/watch?v=diRwtr-pq4U); note the person using a leaf to pick up a very dangerous electrical cable! We are obedient by nature, as this experiment revealed.

The second building block to collectivism is **conformity**. In the 1950s, psychologist Solomon Asch devised a fascinating experiment to test the power of conformity (1956). Since he was a young child Asch had been interested in social conformity and expectations of behaviour. He devoted his life to understanding this phenomenon and is best known for a series of deviously clever experiments that demonstrate just how conformist we are.

In Asch's experiments, several recruits were seated in a line at a long table and shown two cards. Card 1 had a straight vertical line printed on it. Card 2 had three vertical lines next to one another of varying lengths (see Figure 7.1), with one of these lines matching the length of the line on the first card. The recruits were asked which of the three lines on card 2 matched the length of the line on card 1. It sounds straightforward, I know. But Asch did something very interesting.

Figure 7.1 Cards that approximate the stimulus people were exposed to in Asche's experiments

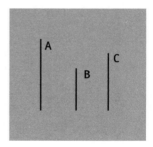

CARD 1   CARD 2

Only one person in the line of recruits was a genuine subject. The others were co-conspirators who were all instructed to give the wrong answer. One after another they said 'Line A', when the correct answer was (in this instance) 'Line C'. In this situation, the genuine subject was much more likely to go along with the stooge recruits and give the wrong answer—even when his own eyes were telling him something different. Approximately seventy per cent of us (depending on a number of variables) will conform to expectation—even if our own experience is saying something different.

For Asch, it demonstrated our willingness to go along with the crowd, even when we know the crowd is wrong. This curious aspect of human psychology can partly explain everything from fashion fads, to street riots, to membership of the Nazi party in 1930s Germany.

It's a principle used in advertising when a brand of chocolate is described as 'the world's favourite chocolate', that 'two out of every three pet lovers choose this brand' or 'nine out of 10 dentists recommend Colgate'. If everyone else chooses that brand, why shouldn't you? It taps into our innate fear of exclusion and the power of conformity. Mark Earls is a leading thinker and practitioner of advertising. He refers to himself as 'The Herdmeister' because of his unflinching belief in the power of conformity. In his book, *Herd: How to Change Mass Behaviour by Harnessing our True Nature* (2007), he writes: 'We use other people's brains to navigate the world: to acquire skills and practices, and to access knowledge systems of long-dead strangers. We call this "culture".'

The third building block of collectivism is **action**. As outlined in Chapter 3, people are more likely to undertake the behaviour desired if they act towards your goal. This relates to cognitive dissonance—we like our thoughts, feelings and actions to be aligned. If we take a positive action towards a goal, we'll change our thoughts and feelings to be positive as well, as Leon Festinger's spool-turning studies showed. Further, actions are symbolic, acting as evidence of commitment to a cause. Collectivism will be even more powerful through action, rather than just asking people to go along with a thought or a feeling. However, there's still one missing ingredient—purpose—and that's where creativity comes into it.

Advertising has a way of 'spinning' ideas and of making action desirable. In these situations, advertising reaches for a higher purpose or aspiration and frames collective action around it. It's difficult to make people feel excited about collectively buying more products (as seen with the demise of group-buying platforms such as Groupon), so advertisers have to find a higher purpose to get people to rally behind a brand. People like to be involved in something with meaning. As the philosopher Nietzsche said: 'If we have our own why in life, we shall get along with almost any how' (1998). That is why it's important to make the 'why'as powerful as possible. This 'why' is third building block of collectivism: **purpose**.

When advertisers want to create collective action, they link it to a strong purpose—but the tricky bit is getting the purpose to be something the brand can actually deliver on. An example is Dove's 'Campaign for Real Beauty' that's been used since 2004. The campaign was based on a global white paper (Etcoff et al. 2004) that surveyed 3200 women aged 18–64 across 10 countries. It found that only 2 per cent of women saw themselves as beautiful. Rather than ask people to buy Dove's soap or other products because they were cheaper, or because they contained moisturising cream, Dove took a different route and asked women to join a higher purpose. That purpose was to fight against the powers that make women feel insecure about their looks. It encouraged women to stop buying into all the 'fakery' around women's beauty—fake products full of fake ingredients, sold by photoshopped models. It was a 'campaign for real beauty'. The reason Dove could claim this purpose is because of Dove's key point of difference—its higher levels of moisturiser compared with other soaps. The product could keep skin looking nice, without the artifice of other beauty products.

The campaign launched with a video, 'Evolution', showing how advertisers 'retouch' and transform a woman's appearance. This video, which you can see on YouTube (www.youtube.com/watch?v=iYhCnOjf46U) won the Grand Prix for film at the Cannes Lions in 2003 (the pinnacle of advertising creativity) and also won the IPA award for Effectiveness. The campaign is still going and in 2013, it created an online video called 'Sketches'. In this video an FBI trained 'forensic artist' draws a series of women without seeing them, instead relying on their description of themselves. These sketches are compared with a second series of sketches where other people describe the same women. The results are rather moving. You can see the video here: www.youtube.com/watch?v=XpaOjMXyJGk. At the time of writing, this video was the most watched online ad in history with 165 million views and growing. It also won the Titanium Grand Prix at The Cannes Lions in 2013. This campaign has encouraged women to join a common objective, a 'campaign for real beauty'. It's one of the most successful advertising campaigns of all time.

When we combine these four ingredients—obedience, conformity, action and purpose—we get collectivism (see Figure 7.2).

Figure 7.2 The building blocks of collectivism

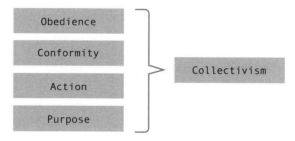

FBi COLLECTIVISM IN ACTION

An understanding of collectivism helped us formulate a strategy to save FBi. After organising a meeting with Meagan and Evan, I returned to FBi's offices to outline my approach.

'Right now, you see your audience as people you reach,' I began. 'I think you need to see them as the people who can "reach out" and communicate on your behalf. FBi needs to find a way to use the collective passion of its audience and turn that creative capital into cash. Your audience is the departure point, not the end point, for your campaign.' Meagan nodded, Evan looked perplexed.

'In the past,' I continued, 'you've asked many people to donate a small amount of money to keep the station running. As we all know, this approach hasn't worked well enough. So, instead of asking lots of people to donate a small amount of money, why don't you get them to all just ask one really wealthy person for the entire amount?' I paused, then shared what I knew was a radical and unorthodox idea. 'Let's get all of the FBi listeners to join in on a collective action, and get them all to ask Sir Richard Branson for $1 million.'

Shocked faces stared back at me. Meagan was the first to speak. 'Interesting idea. But why Richard Branson?' I thought Branson was a no-brainer. 'He's a music lover, he loves stunts and he's loaded. He also has business interests in Australia and regularly visits the country.' But, Meagan asked, 'Won't we alienate our audience by an association with Virgin?'

I pointed out that we were asking Branson personally, not Virgin.

'Do you think he'll give us the money?'

This was a great question. I had no idea if Richard Branson would come to the party. But for me, it wasn't the end goal. The purpose of this campaign was to get listeners to rally around the common action of asking Branson to donate a million dollars—quickly. We had to create the impression that 'everyone' was asking him for money so others would join in with this new norm—asking a rich guy for the money. Further, if enough people asked Branson for money, it would get his attention and once we had his attention, we would have publicity. If the station got enough publicity for something interesting rather than something desperate, people would want to be associated with the cause. It would make saving FBi cool.

In the meeting, someone finally piped up and said, 'Now that's a million dollar idea.' That brave comment started the positive momentum to give the idea a crack.

VISIT MY PLACE

If you want people to come over and see you (whether you be a suburb, town, city, state or country) then consider what the state of Queensland did with creative agency CumminsNitro. Their challenge was to make people understand that there were islands on the Great Barrier reef that had accommodation where tourists could stay, because tourists from the world over would take a day trip to see the reef—and then leave. Instead of using rational or emotional advertising to ask people to visit Queensland, CumminsNitro did something much more interesting. Sean Cummins (the founder of CumminsNitro, and now my business partner) explains how they conceived an idea that would become the most awarded campaign in the world:

> The strategy started with the idea that with the Queensland islands, people see the 'life below' the surface of the water. But there was also 'life above' in the form of luxury hotels, beautiful resorts and stunning islands. This idea of 'life above' spawned the notion that it would be great to live there. And, in fact, imagine if you worked there. That would be the 'Best Job in the World'.

The agency presented the idea—a chance to win the 'best job in the world', staying for six months on an island with a salary of $100,000 per annum—and it was instantly accepted by the client. Sean went on to describe the roll-out of the idea (Cummins pers. comm. 2013).

> We decided that the best way to communicate this notion would be to run job ads in the major newspapers in the key markets around the world. Creating the job as Island Caretaker with a hefty salary akin to US$100K captivated the world. All the winner had to do was 'feed the fish' and write a daily blog. The entries asked for a couple of minute video telling Tourism Queensland why they would be a great caretaker.

Overall, 34,684 people made videos and applied, while more than 450,000 people completed the form for a wild-card entry. More than 43,000 news stories on the campaign came up when searched on Google.

> Some of the entry videos were so elaborate—from stunning animation to an all-singing street musical that would put Ferris Bueller to shame. The appeal of applying for this 'job' became part reality show, part American Idol. CNN took interest in the competition, and would even announce the winner live from the Great Barrier Reef to over half a billion people.

But the idea spoke to human nature: 'I reckon I could do that.' It spoke to a collective spirit of optimism, of escapism and joy.

The secret ingredient was the timing. We waited till the next depths of winter came to our key markets of UK, US and Europe. And the response was phenomenal. Millions of views: 35,000 video entries and a phenomenon was born. It spun off to a one-season TV show on the Discovery Channel. It has been a much copied promotional idea, but was very much a one-off event.

From a budget of around one million dollars the state of Queensland received around $200 million in free PR, the competition attracted almost 35,000 applicants from 200 countries, and the campaign went on to win three Grand Prix titles at Cannes, a Gold Effie and two Black Pencils at D&AD. See the case study online (www.effies.com.au/attachments/7edab36f-4190-40b2-8f8a-59493f440440.pdf).

PURCHASING POWER TO THE PEOPLE

What if you could use the power of your purchases to influence businesses to become more environmentally friendly? Carrotmob (www.carrotmob.org) mobilises people to buy from a designated business if that business agrees to use the money for a green initiative. A café might agree to plant a herb garden, for example.

In early 2012, the City of Melbourne asked local businesses in Carlton to identify ways to reduce their environmental impact. Through online voting, one business would win the Carrotmob funding. With more than 50 per cent of the 1200 online votes, the winner was Cafe Lua. Over one week, 50 cents from every coffee sold would go towards the installation of solar panels. While the $1000 raised wasn't enough to cover the cost of the panels, the owner instead spent the money replacing the café's decrepit air-conditioner with a new, energy-efficient model. It shows that collectivism can be used to influence the behaviour you want.

This is just one example of a website that amalgamates data to allow users to compare their behaviour against others'. Other sites that do this include electricity and water suppliers where they show how much or how little power or water you use compared with others. Using social norms in this way can be an incredibly influential behaviour change driver.

BRANSON PERSUASION

The idea for 'Ask Richard' came to me when I was walking down the stairs at home. I was thinking to myself, 'What could we ask these creative individuals who are passionate about the station to do?', and thought, 'They could ask Bill Gates for the money'. That didn't feel quite right. I adjusted the thought to the left and came up with, 'Ask Richard Branson'. I mentioned the idea to one or two of the other guys in the agency. They didn't really like it, saying, 'It's good—but we can come up with something better.' I mention this not to embarrass that person but to make the point that it's rare for people to go: 'That's it. That's the best idea.' You need to believe in it yourself—and often have to convince others.

As mentioned earlier, the idea was signed off and it was time to begin the campaign to persuade Richard Branson to donate $1 million. Naked Communications created a logo with the outline of Branson's hair and beard that was available on a micro website. There was a downloadable toolkit with bumper stickers, cut out masks and badges. This gave the campaign visibility and made it appear as though many people were already involved—and signalled to others that they were a part of the movement. And there was a prize. The person who unlocked the cash from Sir Richard would be able to keep $50,000 of the bounty.

The campaign kicked off on the morning of 14 May 2009, outside Channel 7's *Sunrise* studios. When the cameras panned over the crowd, viewers saw hundreds of identical masks with the cartoon outline of Richard Branson. This flash mob was seen by *Sunrise*'s 1.2 million viewers and picked up by other media. Importantly, it gave the feeling that many people were involved in the 'Ask Richard' campaign from the start—a collective mob you could be a part of (note that this was before flash mobs had a bad smell about them).

People began to 'Ask Richard' for money in creative and ingenious ways. Some jumped out of planes wearing the logo and posting video footage online. Buskers in Newtown collected money. Five thousand cupcakes with the Ask Richard logo stuck on top were handed to morning train commuters. One supporter held a street to ransom, unfurling a huge banner that read, 'We play 'til U pay', saying the street wouldn't be released until Branson paid the million dollars. It was dubbed the 'Branson Ransom'.

'Ask Richard' games were created and 'Ask Richard' songs written and recorded. One not-so-ingenious chap put an 'Ask Richard' T-shirt up on eBay for sale—reserve price? $1 million. All of these stunts were covered on blogs, Facebook, Twitter and traditional media. Someone even managed to change Richard Branson's Wikipedia entry to mention FBi. The initiatives were quickly circulated through social and broadcast media, reinforcing the idea that many people were involved, which influenced people to act towards the cause of saving FBi. After a few weeks, it got the attention of Sir Richard Branson.

'I'm incredibly nervous,' revealed FBi morning presenter Alison Piotrowski as she started her show on 13 June 2009. The radio studio was filled with volunteers wearing T-shirts with the now famous silhouette of Branson on the front. 'He's a billionaire, an entrepreneur and an adventure-loving philanthropist. Over the last month we have basically been on first-name terms with him. Joining FBi live from his island, Necker, I do believe we have Sir Richard Branson.'

Over a crackly line, Branson revealed he'd trekked to the top of a mountain to make the call to Sydney. 'The first I heard about it I was having an early evening dinner on Necker Island and this rather soaking wet Australian girl stumbled into the dinner room and said she'd swum two-and-a-half miles from another island to get to our island to tell us all about your campaign. I contacted my Australian office to find out what was going on.' True or not, it was a great story from the king of PR stunts. But would he pay?

Sitting in front of a sagging FBi poster, Piotrowski asked, 'Would you be willing to help us out in any way, shape or form, Richard Branson?' With the audience hoping, and volunteers itching to find out if the radio station would get the cash it needed to survive, Branson broke the news. 'Well, I think the difficulty I have is that everybody every day asks for a million bucks or more or less. And we've got some big causes and campaigns on— some of which need entrepreneurial skills—like global warming or setting up a centre for disease control in Africa or creating measures to tackle global conflict. Other causes, like yours, we will sit down and come up with imaginative ways to help you get on your feet or raise money. So I'm afraid I won't be writing a cheque, but we will continue to support and help you to make sure you stay on air.' Branson paid $70 to become a member of FBi and donated a significant prize pool, including flights to London.

It wasn't the answer the supporters wanted to hear, but it was more than enough to make the campaign massively successful. Branson was a PR honey pot. Naked estimated that FBi received the equivalent of $7.5 million in publicity through traditional and social media coverage. It mobilised passionate support from listeners and flushed out cash from people who had a passive relationship with the station, which a traditional donor drive would not have generated. FBi raised $680,000—800 per cent more than any other fundraiser for the station (Ferrier & Cassidy 2010). Donations from current members increased from $14,000 to $206,000, with significant money from older, richer listeners. The campaign also brought in new sponsor dollars, with the extra money allowing FBi to open a not-for-profit, late-night venue called FBi Social to showcase new bands. Evan summed it up when he said, 'This campaign was a shot to the heart of any FBi listener. It was different to anything we had ever done before. FBi is saved, and that's a great result.' You can see the case study for the campaign on YouTube (www.youtube.com/watch?v=jK8a7zu3E1w).

The campaign won many advertising awards, including two Gold Effies (the awards for effectiveness), four Gold AIMIA awards (for digital marketing) and a Gold Clio in New York (for PR and Strategic Communications), and was considered by the Australian Marketing Institute (AMI) as the best Multimedia and Interactive campaign in Australia that year. Incidentally, the girl who apparently swam to Sir Richard's island was never identified.

This is how 'Ask Richard' used collectivism to influence others and change their behaviour:

1. Obedience—there was a clear and direct request from an authority (FBi) in the campaign to 'Ask Richard'.

2. Conformity—it was very easy for people to participate, and it quickly circulated through mainstream and social media. The campaign felt large from the start.

3. Action—a simple action was required, and easy to achieve; namely, find a way to get Richard Branson's attention and ask him for money. We used lots of devices to ensure it was easy for participants to signal to others they were getting involved.

4. Purpose—there was a clear purpose to 'Save FBi', but through creativity and fun rather than boring pleas for donations.

Maybe it's redundant to say, but these types of campaigns make an entire agency feel incredibly proud.

PUTTING THE PRINCIPLES TO WORK

The concept of collectivism can be applied to everyday situations, as well as advertising or public campaigns, as the following three cases attest.

MAKING MEETINGS PHONE-FREE

Almost compulsively, many people constantly check their smartphone for the latest email, status update or Twitter feed. It's become a big issue in meetings. There's generally no need to check your phone during a meeting—but because everyone else is doing it, the practice is copied and becomes a habit. It's rude. It's inefficient. And it's time to stop. Could you use collectivism to create a new social norm?

This is what I suggest you do. First, the majority of the office has to agree to the new behaviour before it's implemented. Once agreed, lobby the boss and argue that phone checking during meetings is both rude and reduces productivity (obedience). Then establish a 'naughty corner' in every meeting room for phones (action). If someone is caught checking their phone during a meeting, they have to put it in the naughty corner for the rest of the meeting. Name the campaign appealing to a higher purpose, such as 'The Busting Phoneys Project' (if you check your phone during meetings, you're not really paying attention to others—you're a phoney). At the beginning, have some high-profile busts. Take a photo of people's phones in the naughty corner. Circulate the imagery to establish conformity. To get your phone out of the naughty corner, you have to make a $20 donation to the office charity or cause. This fine might seem high, but studies show that fines only work if they're high enough to hurt (in fact, if fines are too low you may encourage the behaviour even more as people feel they can pay their way out of any moral conflict). Everyone must agree on the 'naughty corner' and everyone must have the right to police other people's phone behaviour. You'll soon create a new cultural standard.

DEALING WITH NOISY NEIGHBOURS

Another way to apply collectivism is if you live near a noisy neighbour who loves nothing more than to pump up the volume as you're trying to watch TV. Your first instinct might be to bang on their front door and tell them to turn it down, your anger barely concealed. But the reality is that changing behaviour in one-on-one conflict often requires 'social proof'—or consensus. This means showing the other party that a majority of people view their behaviour as contrary to social norms. You have to demonstrate that their actions are impacting on several people. I suggest gathering several neighbours affected by the noise and approaching the noisy neighbour as a group. This creates a 'diffusion of responsibility' and means the noisy neighbour can't get mad or have a war with just one person. Nominate two or even three people to speak, while the remainder stand in the corridor providing moral support. I know this approach works because I faced this very situation. The noisy neighbour stopped playing the loud music and moved out soon afterwards.

SEEKING MONEY

Whether you're raising money for your local school, seeking donations for a charity or need capital for a new business, asking for money is tough. People mostly use rational or emotional arguments when asking for money; the school library needs money to buy books, for example. If raising money for a new business venture, most people attempt to persuade you with facts, figures and balance sheets. The thing is that our ability to manage complexity is finite. We don't have time to research or take in all the information required. People generally say 'No' to your request because it's too hard to weigh up all the variables. Instead, I suggest using collectivism to unlock the cash. Make your cause look popular and part of popular culture, with a higher-order purpose that people want to be part of. In particular, ask people to act towards your cause in a way that creates a socially acceptable 'signal' to others. Good examples include buying a red nose For Red Nose Day, growing a moustache for Movember and wearing a pink ribbon for breast cancer. These signals work at two levels: a) the person receives social status for their involvement in for a cause for the greater good; and b) we look for cues on how to behave by watching others. We join a popular cause and avoid an unpopular one. According to Michael Lynn and Michael McCall (2009), we even give bigger tips if the tip jar is filled with high denomination notes rather than coins. (Lynn and McCall have loads of great tips on how to get bigger tips, if that's your thing.)

Think of creative ways people can get involved with your cause immediately. The more people who are involved in the collective action, the greater the likelihood that the money will come. Remember, with the 'Ask Richard' campaign we were not asking people for money, and nor did Sir Richard Branson end up donating the money himself—but because so many people got involved with the collective action the money found a way of arriving.

So how should the library raise money? Have a look at this brilliant case study from the library of Troy, Michigan (www.youtube.com/watch?v=AoT13m8-Kxo). They garnered support for a 0.7% tax increase to fund the library by embracing the collectivism action spur, albeit with a twist.

SUMMARY

Collectivism uses the psychological principles of obedience, conformity and action to influence behaviour. Offering the collective a higher purpose ensures collective action follows. Much of our behaviour is determined by watching how other people behave. Consciously or unconsciously we fear exclusion and go along with the crowd. Richard Branson wouldn't have responded if just one person asked him for money. It took a collective to get his attention. With collectivism, you need to create a perception that there's a social norm around the behaviour you want. You don't need to create the movement. You only need to create the *perception* of a movement.

The Insider: Mark Sherrington

It took me many years to figure out that, as regards your family and colleagues, you cannot reliably change the behaviour of others. You can only reliably change your own behaviour and your reaction to the behaviour of others.

When it comes to organisations we were long led to believe that in order to change behaviour you had to change attitudes, then the systems and processes, and finally a change of behaviour will follow. This is wrong—change the behaviour, and then the systems (or best of all, the two together) and then attitudes will follow. This is how change works in businesses and it has to be forced from the top.

Changing the behaviour of consumers is the hardest thing in marketing, because of course they are not consumers, they are people; and as people we rely on our inertia, patterns and reflexes to survive. Perhaps an incredible benefit or a massive incentive can force a change in behaviour, but the most effective method is a change in system or hardware. We can see this with the explosion of the internet and mobile phones—our behaviour (even the way we process information) has been changed by a fundamental change in system and hardware.

Our strongest survival technique as a species is the ability to copy. To create a widespread change in behaviour you have to create the momentum at a micro level. Every avalanche starts with the movement of one snowflake. You cannot change 'them' but you can change 'him or her' and allow others to copy. You can speed up this copying—Amazon do it really well by offering lots of ways for us to see what others have bought and making it easy to copy them.

Mark Sherrington is the founder of Added Value, a leading global brand consultancy, and was the global marketing director for SAB Miller, the largest brewing group in the world. I know Mark through my time at Added Value. Mark was a larger-than-life, charismatic, sports-loving leader of the company. He also wrote a very influential marketing book called *Added Value: The Alchemy of Brand-Led Growth*, which I strongly recommend you read if you want to know about how to create a strong brand. I always found both Mark and his writing inspiring.

REFERENCES

Asch, S.E. (1956). Studies of independence and conformity: I. A minority of one against a unanimous majority. *Psychological Monographs*, 70(9), 1–70.

Cialdini, R.B. (2005). Basic social influence is underestimated, *Psychological Inquiry*, 16(4), 158–61. Accessed at http://osil.psy.ua.edu/672readings/T3-Social%20Influence/Cialdini2005.pdf.

Cummins, S. (2013). Pers. comm.

Earls, M. (2007). *Herd: How to Change Mass Behaviour by Harnessing our True Nature.* Hoboken: John Wiley & Sons.

Etcoff, N., Orbach, S., Scott, J. & D'Agostino, H. (2004). *The Real Truth about Beauty: A Global Report: Findings of the Global Study on Women, Beauty and Well-Being.* Accessed at www.clubofamsterdam.com/contentarticles/52%20Beauty/dove_white_paper_final.pdf.

Ferrier, A. & Cassidy, G. (2010). *How to Save an Iconic Australian Radio Station: Ask Richard (Branson).* Australian Effie Awards. Accessed at www.effies.com.au/attachments/537e5466-5136-4f0e-9645-ad5e0f5b9835.pdf.

Festinger, L. (1962). Cognitive dissonance. *Scientific American*, 207(4), 93–107.

Lynn, M. & McCall, M. (2009). Techniques for increasing tips: How generalizable are they? *Cornell Hospitality Quarterly*, 50(2), 198–208.

Milgram, S. (1974). *Obedience to Authority: An Experimental View.* London: Tavistock Publications.

Nietzsche, F. (1998). *Twilight of the Idols.* London: Oxford University Press.

Sherrington, M. (2003). *Added Value: The Alchemy of Brand-Led Growth.* New York: Palgrave Macmillan.

OWNERSHIP: WHAT DO *YOU* THINK?

We've got four rules we follow. We let the community create the content. We let the community build itself—no advertising. We let the community help with the business; we add features based on user feedback. And we reward members of the community for participating.

Jacob Dehart, co-founder of T-shirt company Threadless

Too many people spend too much time trying to perfect something before they actually do it. Instead of waiting for perfection, run with what you got, and fix it along the way ...

Paul Arden, ad guy and author

HOW NOT TO DO THERAPY

Just after starting out as a psychologist, I had the demoralising experience of a patient leaving me midway through treatment. Meredith suffered anxiety and avoided interacting with people because she feared rejection. If she was with people she knew, such as work colleagues and friends, she felt okay. But any time she had to meet new people, she said she felt a sense of dread. It was starting to impact on her work and she was calling in sick on days when she had to meet new clients. Now, she worried about losing her job. I really wanted to help Meredith. She was a lovely person, intelligent and with good interpersonal skills. I was convinced we could quickly and effectively stamp out this social phobia (the diagnosis I had given her).

At each of the sessions we had together, I was always extremely well prepared and very enthusiastic about how effective therapy would be for her. I gave her advice and exercises to do between meetings, along with printed-out homework sheets. I thought things were going well and believed she would overcome her phobia. Then suddenly, after about three weeks, Meredith cancelled her appointments and I didn't see her again. Where did I go wrong?

As a psychologist-in-training, I had weekly meetings with my kindly supervisor, Anne, and asked for her advice. She said, and these words have stuck with me, 'Never get more excited about the possibility of change than your patient. They need to take ownership of their issues and lead the therapy. Not you.'

Not long after this, I began working with a new patient. When Allan walked into my consulting room, he kept his head down and didn't make eye contact. 'What brings you here today?' I asked after he sat down.

Allan kept his head lowered and didn't say a word. I waited for a minute or two and still nothing. I didn't say anything either—just waited. And then something painfully beautiful happened. Allan began to sob. After about 15 minutes, Allan said, 'Aren't you going to say something?'

In a gentle voice, I said, 'I already asked, "What brings you here today?"' He sobbed again before becoming silent. We stayed like this for some minutes more until he raised his head a little, caught my eye for a split second and asked, 'Do you know anything about sexual abuse?'

I worked with Allan over many months and he was an insightful and ultimately successful patient. During our sessions, I never took the lead and always waited until he was ready—I was by his side rather leading from the front. He was the one who had to do the work. In fact, I think the work I did with Allan was my proudest achievement as a therapist. He had control over the changes he wanted to make, and ownership of his progress in therapy, which was the key to his success.

CAN COKE GIVE OWNERSHIP?

What's your very first memory of Coke? What popped into your head? Was it an ad on a billboard? Perhaps you saw a bottle or can in the fridge at a milk bar or on a supermarket shelf. Or maybe you saw a TV advertisement with a see-through beach ball filled with jubilant teenagers tumbling over the ocean on a golden summer's day. Or was it a guy jumping from a plane 'skysurfing' with a Coke in hand? I'd suggest that your first memory of Coke was an advertisement that built an aspirational image of the brand with evocative imagery. Coke and its advertising have been inseparable—like healthy twins growing up side by side. Coke provides the classic example of a brand adopting the 'mass marketing' model: mass production, followed by mass distribution ('Always be within arm's reach of desire' was the unofficial Coke motto at one time), supported by mass advertising.

However, this strategy was slowly losing traction. No matter what Coke said, its beautiful and expensive ads weren't influencing consumer behaviour. The brand and the consumer were becoming disconnected. No amount of talking at the consumer was going to change their mind. What could Coke tell them that they didn't already know? It was time for a new strategy. In 2011 advertising agency Ogilvy (founded by advertising legend David Ogilvy) and Naked Communications collaborated on a campaign. We suggested that Coke needed to stop talking 'at' people and instead give them ownership of the brand.

WHAT IS OWNERSHIP?

Have you bought something from IKEA? Of course you have. I'm willing to bet it was cheap but did the job well enough. I'm also willing to bet that if you bought it a few years ago, or a few houses ago, you still have that cheap piece of IKEA furniture. For some reason you drag it from house to house, and find it hard to let go of it. I'm guessing you value it a little more than perhaps is reasonable. True?

There's a very good reason for this. When you co-create something—in the case of IKEA, assemble a piece of furniture—you value it more. It's called the 'IKEA effect', so named by dynamic young Harvard business professor Michel Norton.

The idea of assembling IKEA furniture fills me, and many others, with a sense of dread. This didn't deter Michael, who paid 52 people $5 each to participate in an experiment. Half were asked to construct a plain black IKEA 'Kasset' storage box. The other half didn't have to do any work—their IKEA storage box was already assembled. They just inspected the box to make sure it was in good condition.

Once the assembling was complete (assuming there were no missing screws), Michael asked the participants two questions: How much were they prepared to pay for their storage box? And how much did they like the box? As expected, the assemblers were prepared to pay significantly more for their box ($0.78 versus $0.48), and liked it significantly more (3.8 versus 2.5, on a 1–7 scale where 1 is 'Don't like it' and 7 is 'Like it very much') (Norton, Mochon & Ariely 2012). **People place a disproportionate value on something they build or help to create themselves.**

Let's break this down a bit more. IKEA saves on labour costs because it doesn't have to assemble the item, and they save on transport costs because the item can be flat packed. The outcome is lower prices. People are attracted by lower prices, but these findings also reveal that we value the item more *because* we have to finish the construction ourselves. This is perhaps the most striking example of ownership. In 2009 the founder of IKEA, Ingvar Kamprad (the IK of IKEA) was the fifth-richest man in the world (*Forbes* 2009) worth around $22 billion. No wonder: he found he could deliver unassembled products in flat packs more cheaply. However, the requirement to construct items created an unintended consequence—consumers valued the items more. This is because they felt ownership of them.

This was the first time the IKEA effect was researched and named (Norton also found a similar effect when folding origami and constructing Lego). However, it's an effect packet cake marketers took advantage of in the 1950s. When invented, instant cake mix was slow to catch on. Initially, all a baker had to do was add water. But sales were slow. Susan Marks outlines the situation in her book *Finding Betty Crocker: The Secret Life of America's First Lady of Food*:

> At this time, the company was still refining their approach to marketing. While they sought to promote a quick and easy product that still retained a 'fresh, "home-made" quality, the market was slow to mature'. ... The company called upon the market research of Dr. Burleigh Gardner and Dr. Ernest Dichter, both business psychologists.
>
> The problem, according to psychologists, was eggs. Dichter, in particular, believed that powdered eggs, often used in cake mixes, should be left out, so women could add a few fresh eggs into the batter, giving them a sense of creative contribution.
>
> As a result, General Mills (who own Betty Crocker) altered their product, abandoning the powdered egg in their mixes. The requirement to add eggs at home was marketed as a benefit, conferring the quality of 'home-made' authenticity upon the box cake mix.

Even though it was a small change, it made a big impact on sales. The reason is ownership. Ownership is about shifting power to the consumer and has three important components. The first is **autonomy**—the person determines what they will do (bake a cake). The second is **personal relevance**—there is a connection between the possession and the person (Dommer & Swaminathan 2013). They need to relate and have something invested in it (crack my own egg and mix well). And thirdly, it uses **cognitive dissonance**— when someone acts towards an outcome, thoughts and feelings follow (cracking the egg means more work, therefore I'm more invested in it). Through technological innovations ownership has become a popular tool in advertising and marketing. Now more than ever companies are giving ownership to consumers. The masters of it are IKEA.

Another example is T-shirt company Threadless (www.threadless.com). When you buy a T-shirt from this company, the shirts haven't been designed by an in-house design team. Instead, the T-shirts are selected from designs sent in by regular people. Each day, the company receives around 1000 design submissions from a community of consumers numbered at more than 2.5 million. This community then votes and decides which designs the company should make. The winning entry receives $2000 and the community can purchase the T-shirt for around $20. The company was founded in 2000 and is now a multi-million dollar business that has completely blurred the lines between consumer and producer. The quote from Threadless founder Jacob Dehart that opens this chapter demonstrates how much giving ownership to the consumer means to him and his company.

MEASURING THE POWER OF OWNERSHIP

The power of ownership can be seen in a study by Kahneman, Knetsch and Thaler (2009) from Cornell University. In their study, 238 people were recruited and divided into three groups. All groups were asked to complete a small task and, for their efforts, they were given a gift. The first group was given a coffee mug. The second received a chocolate bar. The third group could actually choose either the coffee mug or chocolate bar, with 56 per cent opting for the mug. Here's where the fun starts. The group that received the coffee mug was then asked if they would like to swap their mug for a chocolate bar. Eighty-nine per cent said no—and kept the mug. Notice the figure is much higher than the 56 per cent who, when given a choice, opted for the mug over the chocolate bar. The second group that received a chocolate bar was also asked if they wanted to swap gifts. Again, only around 10 per cent took up the offer. Even though the coffee cup and chocolate bar were roughly equally liked at the beginning of the experiement, by the end those who were given the coffee cup liked it more, and those who were given the chocolate bar liked it more. Just because they owned it, even if it was only for a brief period of time. The researchers dubbed this 'the **endowment effect'**—we place greater value on items because we own them.

It's why ownership is a powerful tool of persuasion and influence. As is evident when children fight over a toy, ownership has strong emotional and psychological pulling power. When you give someone ownership of your product, or even an idea, they become invested in it and find it difficult to let it go. This power is often out of proportion to the value of the item, as behavioural economists Ziv Carmon and Dan Ariely (2000) discovered in an experiment conducted at Duke University. Students who bought tickets to attend the National Collegiate Athletic Association basketball games were offered money to sell their tickets. But they would only sell the tickets if offered 14 times more money than the ticketed price. Why would someone knock back a considerable profit? Because, again, once you feel ownership of something, you value it more—sometimes much more. It's a tactic used by many companies today. One of the early adopters was McDonald's Australia.

WHAT SHALL WE CALL IT?

In 2007, McDonald's Australia had a problem. 'Sales growth of its largest category, beef burgers, was slowing,' explains Mark Pollard (2010), who worked for the company's advertiser, Leo Burnett. 'Despite the fact that McDonald's beef was just like the beef consumers bought from the supermarket, people thought that it wasn't great quality. In fact, only 34 per cent of people thought their beef was any good. Adjectives such as "plastic", "rubbery", "unhealthy" and "processed" were bandied about.'

Its problems went beyond poor perception of its beef. McDonald's also suffered from a disengaged customer base. 'People knew, hated or loved McDonald's, but didn't feel involved with it, viewing it as a big, distant multinational, easy to bash and a guilt-edged food choice,' adds Pollard.

The advertising agency asked the following questions:

- How do we get people to feel good about McDonald's by involving them in something?
- What if we could get people to feel good about eating beef at McDonald's by inviting them to name a new burger?

And so the Name-It Burger competition was born. Over four weeks, customers were encouraged to visit a website and enter their suggested name for a gourmet beef burger. The winner would become part of McDonald's celebrity 'Hall of Fame', be featured in a TV commercial and receive a $12,000 home entertainment prize.

Within the first 36 hours of the competition, a new burger name was submitted every six seconds. Over four weeks, the company received 143,332 burger name entries. Nearly a quarter of a million people visited the site, with 85 per cent submitting a name. The winning entry was the 'Backyard Burger' and McDonald's sold 4.2 million of them, representing a 12 per cent growth across the eight weeks of the campaign. Why did this work? Consumers were invited in, and given a sense of ownership of the brand. The company experienced the benefits of the Benjamin Franklin effect by asking for a favour. It also allowed consumers to co-create the brand. When you feel ownership, you're more likely to act positively towards the brand. You can see the case study on YouTube (www. youtube.com/watch?v=yhu4kI6TZzg).

This represents a huge shift in the production paradigm for marketers. In the past, a *producer* 'owned' the brand and would 'sell' it to the *consumer*. The producer came up with the recipes and names, and released new products into the market with little involvement from the consumer (except at the cash register). That's all changed. Now, producers ask consumers to help them 'crack' problems for them. Consumers help to name a product, create a flavour or design packaging. They give their ideas and creative energy to big brands. What they may not be aware of is this action also plays into ownership. If you help name the burger, you're more likely to buy the burger.

Curiously, people will contribute even without the incentive of a prize. In 2008, coffee giant Starbucks created a microsite called 'Mystarbucksidea', designed to canvass ideas and suggestions from consumers. Thousands of people shared their suggestions such as donating excess food to the homeless or giving nametags to baristas. Starbucks loudly and proudly implemented ideas generated by this community—giving them all a sense of ownership.

Let's think about how this could be applied. Could employees feel more engaged at work with a different office layout—one that gave them more ownership? When Macquarie Bank in Sydney built a new office, it moved away the traditional work station desk concept. As reported in *The Cool Hunter* (2010), it adopted:

> *... a new collaborative working style—Activity-Based Working (ABW), a flexible work platform developed by Dutch consultant Veldhoen & Co. Macquarie's 3000 employees now work in an open and highly flexible space where, for example, in the 10-storey atrium, 26 various kinds of 'meeting pods' create a feel of 'celebration of collaboration' and contribute to openness and transparency. The interior staircases have already reduced the use of elevators by 50 per cent, and more than half of the employees say that they change their workspaces each day, and 77 per cent love the freedom to do so. The result is part space station, part cathedral, and part vertical Greek village.*

Imagine arriving at work knowing you can sit somewhere different each day and next to different colleagues. It's a great incentive to arrive earlier in order to get the best spot. This is a small example of how ownership can be applied.

WANT A TISSUE?

If you are a marketer, or have commissioned an advertising agency to create a campaign or idea, you'll be familiar with the 'tissue session' (or sessions). It's when a creative agency shows the client a number of ideas, and the client says what they like or don't like about each one. It's called a tissue session because the ideas are thought of as disposable and can be thrown away. There's an interesting by-product of this process. Once the client contributes to the ideas process, they feel greater ownership of the outcome. This is normally not the primary role of a tissue session, but from an agencies perspective it's a useful by-product of such a meeting.

COKE CREATING OWNERSHIP

So can Coke give ownership to it's consumers? Yes, and it happened in September 2011. In the dead of night, Coca-Cola's distribution trucks placed brand-new stock on the shelves of supermarkets and convenience stores across the country. But instead of the usual branding, the cans and bottles had 150 of the most popular Australian names printed on them. The names 'Adam' and 'Ashley' sat next to 'Zac' and 'Zoe'. The next day, when people were shopping, they were surprised to see the new branding and went to social media sites, Twitter and Facebook, to ask, 'What's the deal with these Coke bottles and people's names???'

Coke didn't explain why it did this, but cleverly recruited these fans to become the face of the campaign. It then revealed its strategy and asked people to 'Share a Coke' using the best conversation starter of all—what's your name? For the first time, consumers weren't being asked to buy a Coke for themselves. They were asked to buy a Coke for a friend—to share a Coke.

In addition to printing the 150 most common names on cans, Coca-Cola placed 18 naming stations in Westfield shopping centres around Australia. Customers could step into a booth shaped like a giant can of Coke, buy a Coke and have a customised name printed on it and then share the Coke with their friend (and no, you couldn't write the word 'Pepsi' or something rude on the can). The response was incredible, with hundreds of people lining up to have their name or a friend's name added to a can.

There were other components to the campaign. Instead of the usual Coke billboards, people could SMS their friend's name and it would appear on the billboard. Stunts were organised such as getting 3000 men called Matt to sit together to watch football. You could even send someone a virtual Coke online with their name on the can. Consumers were then asked to nominate and vote on the next 50 names to be used; there were 65,000 entries. This was consumer ownership on steroids.

But what was the impact on sales? Let me give you some context. In recent years, the $4.5 billion dollar soft drink category in Australia has been declining by 0.7 per cent each year. During the Share a Coke campaign, sales increased 7 per cent against Coca-Cola's core target. In addition, 5 per cent of Australians drank Coke either for the first time or for the first time in more than a year. There were 121 million impressions on Facebook, 76,000 virtual Coke cans were shared and 378,000 custom Coke cans were printed at Westfield Shopping Centres (Cyron 2012)—all because the company gave ownership of the brand to consumers.

This was a big step for Coke. Its brand and logo was considered a sacred cow that was never to be tampered with. But this successful experiment in Australia was replicated across the globe. One of the reasons for its success was giving ultimate ownership of the brand to consumers. The name 'Coke' didn't appear on the bottle or can. It was your name or your friend's name. You can see the case study for the campaign online (http://vimeo.com/46072805).

A DASH OF OWNERSHIP

You might be thinking: 'Adam, that's great, but what if you can't offer to put someone's name on your product? Does a small amount of ownership work?' The answer is yes. By simply asking for an opinion, you'll elicit a degree of ownership in what I've dubbed 'the focus group effect'. When facilitating research groups, I've noticed that at the end of two hours, people leave the group feeling very positive about a brand even if they were negative about it at the beginning. At the end of a focus group I'd hear, 'I'm going to buy brand X from now on.' Why does this happen? Why does someone shift from disliking to liking a brand when asked for their opinion? To answer this, let's find out what happened at an electricity factory located outside Chicago called the Hawthorne Works.

In the 1920s, owners of the factory commissioned a study to see if worker productivity would change depending on the illumination level in their workplace. Would workers perform better under bright or dim lights? Some years later Henry Landsberger (1958) was examining the results from these earlier experiments and he discovered something rather interesting. Initially, it seemed dimmed lighting brought out the best in workers. But then something unexpected happened. As soon as the study finished, productivity slumped. Why did productivity improve and then collapse? Henry believed the improved work rate had nothing to do with lighting levels. Instead, he believed productivity increased because of the interest taken in the workers. When you know someone's interested in you, you want to make a good impression and so perform better.

This is now known as the Hawthorne effect[1] (or the observer effect) and it kicks in every time you respond to a survey or are involved in research. Even if you were disappointed in the service or a meal, your ability to vent that frustration reduces your dissatisfaction because you feel as though the company is trying to understand you better. It gives you a chance to express how you think something should be done, giving you a sense of ownership of the issue. You can see a video on the Hawthorne effect on YouTube (www.youtube.com/watch?v=IxZoxN5IjFE).

The easiest way to confer ownership is to seek opinions and share issues. It's about inquiring rather than telling. Rather than barking, 'Clean up your room!', instead ask, 'Why do you keep your room so dirty?' Instead of insisting, 'You must be home by 6pm', instead ask, 'What time do you think you'll be home tonight?' Instead of saying, 'I want a raise', instead ask, 'What do I need to do to get a raise?' It means every customer, or potential customer, can become a source of information. In asking for their opinion, you give them a feeling of ownership of your business.

LEVELS OF OWNERSHIP

So creating ownership is effective, but the level of ownership can vary considerably. As depicted in Figure 8.1 (over the page), this can range from giving someone full ownership (through independent creation of a product or content, as with the Threadless clothing company) down to a low-level, temporary sense of ownership (though the sharing of a general opinion). In between there's co-creation (as in the IKEA effect) and acquisition (as in the endowment effect). When using ownership to change someone's behaviour, the

---

1 The theory of the Hawthorne effect has many detractors, including Richard Nisbett (1998) of the University of Michigan. In an article, 'Scientific myths that are too good to die', he provides evidence that it's just a glorified anecdote, and 'once you have got the anecdote, you can throw away the data'. However, I've witnessed the Hawthorn effect repeatedly over many years—in focus groups. At the beginning of a focus group people will tell you how much they dislike the brand under investigation, but by the end of the group they'll tell you how much they like it. What's changed? They've had their opinion sought. Whenever doing research, people become more positively disposed to whoever is doing the research—because they believe their opinion is being valued.

greater the degree of ownership someone has, the more value is extracted and the more motivated they'll be to change.

Figure 8.1 Levels of ownership

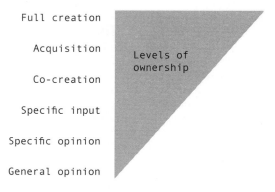

Full creation

Acquisition

Co-creation

Specific input

Specific opinion

General opinion

Levels of ownership

HOW OWNERSHIP WORKED ON ME

Along the river just north of Hobart is an eye-catching concrete building that houses the Museum of Old and New Art (MONA). When I visited the museum, stalls were set up outside the entrance to the museum with people selling food and drinks. As a person of rather low energy and self-motivation, I headed to a stall selling iced coffee. When I walked over, the man behind the counter said, 'Hey! You're on TV, aren't you?' This situation doesn't happen often. I replied, 'Yeah, I'm a panellist on *Gruen Planet* on ABC TV.' He said he thought I did a great job before adding, 'but not as good as Todd and Russel'—the regular panellists on the show. Despite the backhanded compliment, I appreciated the recognition.

The guy asked, 'Would you mind if I took a photo of you drinking a Rocket?' This was the name of his iced coffee. I agreed. Before I knew it, the guy took my photo and uploaded it to Twitter with the caption: '@adamferrier enjoying his first Rocket.' I retweeted his message, giving him exposure to another 5000-plus people. As I walked away I thought, 'How funny. My first product endorsement.' But then I realised I hadn't been paid—I didn't even get the iced coffee for nothing. He simply asked for a favour—a photo of me drinking his iced coffee that he tweeted and I did him another favour and re-tweeted his tweet. This was the Benjamin Franklin effect, plus ownership, at work.

Figure 8.2 The tweeted photo of me enjoying a Rocket

COKE AND OWNERSHIP II

In 2005, Coca-Cola had its biggest product launch in 22 years when sugar-free Coke Zero hit the market. Its launch in the USA earlier that year was a disaster, mainly because of the marketing campaign, in which a clean-cut twenty-something strums his guitar and raps, 'I'd like to give the world a break' as friends join him on a Philadelphia rooftop. Some partygoers are holding bottles of Coke as others set up speakers and amps. Assembled like a choir, the gathering sways in unison while singing, 'I'd like to teach the world to chill.'

Now, if you're a Coke aficionado, you'll recognise that the ad is a riff on the 1970s 'Hilltop' campaign that reworded the classic 'I'd like to teach the world to sing'. Not only was this reference lost on the male Gen Y market Coke was trying to reach (who were too young to remember the original), it also failed to explain that Coke Zero was a brand new, sugar-free version of the most popular brand on the planet. Result? In its first month, sales were a mere 0.9 per cent of the supermarket carbonated soft drink category (Robertson 2006). An Australian team was assembled to hatch a plan for Coke Zero's launch here that included staff from Coke, an agency called Kindred, a researcher from Pollinate, and the Naked team. The Australian campaign needed to start from scratch.

Pollinate (now Social Soup) was the research company who helped us with the launch. It was owned by Howard Perry-Husbands, an enigmatic, high-energy, mad-scientist type. With his help, we developed a plan to give ownership of the Coke Zero brand to influential opinion leaders before anyone else. In October 2005, two cases of Coke Zero landed on the doorsteps of one thousand 'early adopters' selected by Pollinate. Our target was men aged 16–35. We told them we'd like them to sample a new drink. They could consume the first case, but we'd like them to share the second case with friends. We then asked them to be researchers in the brand on our behalf. On average, each opinion leader gave a Coke Zero to 17 of their friends and compiled notes on their thoughts and opinions on the drink. That meant we had 17,000 opinions from a very influential group of consumers. A few enterprising influencers even tried to sell a single bottle of Coke Zero on eBay as an 'exclusive'. We received calls from Coke's head office in Atlanta asking why Coke Zero was all over (the then nascent) social media weeks before launch.

Howard and the team at Pollinte read the comments and feedback from our influencers. One discovery was the guys didn't like the colour of the can—in the US, Coke Zero came in a white can. They thought it looked feminine and similar to Diet Coke, and suggested a black can. After several impassioned phone calls with people at Coke's head office, the company approved the colour change. Our early adopters thereby became co-creators of the brand, had ownership of the brand and took 'action' towards Coke Zero. This decision had another effect—it gave staff in Australia's Coca-Cola office genuine ownership of the Coke Zero brand, which galvanised them.

The next step was to get as many guys as possible to try the product as quickly as possible. The Big Day Out is one of the most popular music festivals in Australia. As thousands of music lovers clicked through the turnstiles to hear the likes of Rhombus, Hilltop Hoods and Franz Ferdinand, many were handed a can of Coke Zero. Sampling took place across the country, with 20,000 Coke Zeros consumed on 26 January 2006. Called 'The Zero Movement', the campaign grew bigger and bigger, starting with a blog and some street stencils, and finishing with outdoor advertising and TV. This was only put in place once we felt our target market had discovered the brand on their own terms.

One month after the campaign launched, one million Australians had tried Coke Zero. Within three months, Coke Zero was outselling Pepsi Max. As Coca-Cola announced in 2006, 'The Coca-Cola Zero launch has been rated by AC Nielsen as the best new product launch in the past 10 years, matched against any other beverage, confectionery and personal care product.'

The Coke Zero campaign worked because we identified a group that had a greater propensity to change behaviour (men aged 15–36) and allowed them to sample and discover Coke Zero on their own terms by giving them ownership. The interaction between consumer and producer gave the consumer a sense of ownership of the brand and increased the positive association. We used the Benjamin Franklin effect by asking them to do us a favour in sharing the drink and giving us feedback about it. And, as the sales showed, they liked Coke Zero more as a result. It's worth noting that after its Australian launch, the strategy we created was embraced by Coca-Cola round the world. The colour of the can became black and the product is now embedded within the Coke portfolio.

AT WORK AND HOME

Can ownership be applied in your everyday life? Years ago, I lived in a share house and was lucky that one roommate was a 'clean freak'. She couldn't stand to have any mess in the house and cleaned up after everyone. But then she moved out. When the new roommate, Rachel, moved in, we had to negotiate a new approach to household domestics. Rachel organised a house meeting and asked for ideas on how the house should be cleaned. I suggested hiring a cleaner and everyone agreed. The other idea was a roster of duties in which you could pick the chore you hated the least. The roster was beautifully designed. In fact, our little chore board looked so good, it became something of a talking point with visitors. Both tactics worked and our house was clean and happy. When you ask questions, rather than tell someone what to do, it gives ownership and makes it more likely someone will undertake the desired behaviour.

I also like this suggestion from psychologist Jeremy Dean, who writes popular psychology blog, *PsyBlog*. In February 2012, he wrote a post titled 'The one (really easy) persuasion technique everyone should know', supported by 42 studies on 22,000 people. The technique is this. If you want to persuade someone to do something for you, first ask, 'But are you available to do this?' They can choose to accept or reject your proposal. Across all the studies it was found to *double* the chances that someone would say 'Yes' to the request. The exact wording of the request didn't matter. The phrase 'You're not obliged' worked just as well. However, the request had to be face-to-face rather than over email or other less personal forms of communication. When you allow people to feel they have agency—that they have ownership—you're more likely to get the result you want.

CANCELLING OUT THE ENDOWMENT EFFECT

Imagine you are in a shop that sells cosmetics. The shopkeeper, who understands the impact of ownership, encourages you to hold a particularly expensive brand of eye shadow to trigger the endowment effect. Because you have held onto the eye shadow for a while, you will feel a sense of ownership over it—and therefore value it more (you don't have to hold onto things for very long for the ownership spur to take effect). Now you are not sure about the eye shadow and want to make an objective decision about whether you should purchase it. What can you do?

The answer, remarkably, is to go and wash your hands.

In 2013, well-known Austrian researcher Arnd Florack and colleagues found that washing your hands after holding an item will mitigate the endowment effect. As they explain, 'the physical action of hand washing can reset the cognitive system to a more neutral state by reducing the asymmetrical perception of owned and not owned products' (Florack et al. 2013). Their findings support those from a field of study known as 'embodied cognition', which looks at the interrelationship between our cognitions, and how they are influenced by what happens to us physically. So if you're feeling uncomfortable about an impending sale, and don't want to overvalue something simply because you've held onto it, then go and wash your hands.

SUMMARY

When people feel ownership of a brand or an issue, they're more likely to exhibit the behaviour you want. From asking for an opinion, to giving people the opportunity to genuinely offer input, to allowing them to co-create or entirely create the entity, ownership creates desire and value. With social media and smartphones, brands can receive instant feedback and act on that feedback. This process can be genuinely scary because you expose yourself to criticism as well as praise. It often involves changing the company's behaviour first, before asking consumers to change theirs. Whether asking consumers to name a new burger or putting someone's name on a can of Coke, ownership empowers those you want to influence. They become co-creators of the brand. When you turn a directive into a question, people solve the problem with you. As a consumer, be aware that when you offer advice or feedback or suggestions for names or designs, you will value that item more highly—just because they asked you to do something for them.

The Insider: Michael Norton

Although those seeking to persuade often direct their full attention to their target (what can I say to this person to make her agree?), would-be persuaders would do well to divert at least some of their attention to another source: themselves. Research in leadership, negotiation and persuasion shows that self-aware indivudals—those who understand how their own thoughts and emotions are shaping their behaviour—are more effective at conveying the messages they intend and, as a result, changing people's minds. As an additional bonus, self-aware individuals are less likely to be persuaded by the weak arguments of others. Focusing attention inward increases the likelihood that we are the ones persuading rather than persuaded.

Michael Norton is an associate professor at Harvard Business School and co-author of *Happy Money: The Science of Smarter Spending*. I met Michael when speaking at a conference with him in recent years. Here's a prediction: Michael will become one of the most influential thinkers of our time.

REFERENCES

Carmon, Z. & Ariely, D. (2000). Focusing on the forgone: How value can appear so different to buyers and sellers. *Journal of Consumer Research*, 27(3), 360–70.

Coca-Cola (2006). *Zero to 100 Million in Thirty Days*. Media release accessed at http://ccamatil.com/InvestorRelations/md/2006/Coke%20Zero%20-%20Zero%20 to%20100%20million%20in%2030%20Days%20-%20090206.pdf.

Cryon, G. (2012). *Share a Coke*. Accessed at www.effies.com.au/attachments/1b9d8da6-2d7b-48d4-9b55-a9ded3b8ba8e.pdf.

Dean, J. (2012). The one (really easy) persuasion technique everyone should know. *PsyBlog*. Accessed at www.spring.org.uk/2013/02/the-one-really-easy-persuasion-technique-everyone-should-know.php.

Dommer, S.L. & Swaminathan, V. (2013). Explaining the endowment effect through ownership: The role of identity, gender, and self-threat. *Journal of Consumer Research*, 39(5), 1034–50.

Florack, A., Kleber, J., Busch, R. & Stöhr, D. (2013). Detaching the ties of ownership: The effects of hand washing on the exchange of endowed products. *Journal of Consumer Psychology*, 23, 127–37.

Forbes (2009). Forbes rich list: Ten years of top tens. Accessed at www.forbes.com/ lists/2009/10/billionaires-2009-richest-people_Ingvar-Kamprad-family_BWQ7.html.

Kahneman, D., Knetsch, J.L. & Thaler, R.H. (2009). Experimental tests of the endowment effect and the Coase theorem. In E.L. Khalil (ed.), *The New Behavioral Economics. Volume 3: Tastes for Endowment, Identity and the Emotions* (pp. 119–42). Cheltenham and Northampton: Elgar.

Lansberger, H.A. (1958). *Hawthorne Revisited: Management and the Worker, Its Critics, and Developments in Human Relations in Industry*. New York: Ithaca.

Marks, S. (2007). *Finding Betty Crocker: The Secret Life of America's First Lady of Food*. Minneapolis: University of Minnesota Press.

Nisbett, R. (1998). Scientific myths that are too good to die. *New York Times*, 6 December.

Norton, M., Mochon D. & Ariely, D. (2012). The IKEA effect: When labor leads to love. *Journal of Consumer Psychology*, 22, 453–60.

Pollard, M. (2009). *How to Sell 4.2 Million Burgers—A McDonald's Case Study*. Accessed at www.markpollard.net/how-to-sell-4-2-million-burgers-a-mcdonalds-case-study.

Robertson, D. (2006). Coke Australia takes Zero to hero. *Just Drinks*, March. Accessed at www.just-drinks.com/analysis/coke-australia-takes-zero-to-hero_id85967.aspx.

The Cool Hunter (2010). *The Macquarie Investment Bank—Sydney*. Accessed at www.thecoolhunter.com.au/article/detail/1701/macquarie-investment-bank--sydney.

PLAY: THE WORLD IS A GAME

We don't stop playing because we grow old; we grow old because we stop playing.

George Bernard Shaw, Irish author

It's only work if somebody makes you do it. [Calvin advising Hobbes]

Bill Watterson, US author of Calvin and Hobbes

THE PEEING GAME

If you visit Amsterdam during the Queen's Day holiday, you'll see a lot of orange. People wear orange shirts, hats, wigs, capes and body paint. Tiger suits are popular. Orange balloons and orange flags decorate the city. Even public water fountains spray orange-dyed water. The reason? Orange is the colour of the Dutch Royal Family. But there's another Queen's Day tradition—and that's peeing into one of the city's well-known canals. Even though numerous portable toilets are placed along the streets, many people—well, men mainly—relieve themselves directly into the canal. Thousands of people attend the celebrations so you can just imagine the effect on the canals, and the smell.

The city's water supplier hoped to change this behaviour. In 2012, it teamed with advertising agency Achtung!, which had the idea of turning outdoor toilets into gaming stations in a campaign called 'Piss Off'. It was described as 'a parlour game that makes peeing fun'.

Here's how it worked. Several brightly coloured urinals were installed along the Amsterdam canals. In each urinal, there were four stalls connected to a giant digital screen that was visible to the public. Revellers could step into the stall and use the power of their pee to float an image of a duck to the top of the screen. The first man—or woman—whose duck reached the top of the screen was awarded with the word 'Winner' flashing on the giant screen. There was also a prize for the person who generated the most pee during the day—they received a rebate on their water bill. It was a great success, with 850 people using the urinals and 920 litres of pee collected. The water company's cleaning bill was reduced and Queen's Day revellers avoided a nasty stench. You can watch the campaign on YouTube (www.youtube.com/watch?v=wvOh6fvIQPc).

The company influenced behaviour by turning a mundane activity into a game. Achtung! gamified peeing, which is not as hard as it sounds. Ask any guy if they've ever written their name using their pee stream—the answer will be yes. We enjoy playing games with our pee. In fact, we enjoy playing games full stop.

Using play to influence consumer behaviour isn't new. Do you remember buying a soft drink and checking under the lid to see if you'd won a prize? Often the prize was small—another soft drink. But there was also the chance to go into a lottery to win a significant prize. You bought the soft drink to play a game and, along the way, formed a positive association with the brand. **Play is great action spur to influence behaviour**.

PLAYING AT A HOTEL

The Art Series Hotels are three boutique-style hotels in Melbourne that are named after, and themed on, contemporary Australian artists. Step into The Blackman and you're met by Charles Blackman's paintings of melancholy faces and distinctive figures from his *Alice in Wonderland* series. The Cullen features the bold, lurid splashes of Archibald Prize winner Adam Cullen. The most upmarket of the three is The Olsen, graced by John Olsen's arresting abstract landscapes. The hotels have enjoyed pretty solid occupancy rates, with one exception—the summer break. From mid-December until the beginning of the Australian Open tennis in January, the hotels struggle to fill their rooms.

Marketing manager for the hotels, Liz Austin, asked if Naked Communications would be interested in pitching for their business. They wanted to fill 1000 beds over summer, double traffic to the website and generate publicity for the hotels. As part of the briefing process they informed us that there was scope for discounts, including a 10 per cent reduction for two-day stays and a 20 per cent reduction for three-day stays, along with other package deals. We had one week to come up with a winning strategy.

Over the past 10 years I've spent at least one night a week in a hotel room, so it's an experience I know well. And even though the industry is very competitive, there's surprisingly little differentiation between hotels. You book a room, check in at reception (a process that seems to still take much longer than it should) and get a swipe card. Unless you're Charlie Sheen, you sleep the night, wake up, shower and check out. Or in my case, just leave. I've never understood why you need to check out. The hotel will make sure you've paid.

In my experience, when a marketing category becomes well established, competitors start to copy each other. They behave in the same manner and develop category conventions. After a while these conventions become rules, and no one questions them. In the case of hotels, most promote themselves with discounts, or describe the quality of their beds or promise a restful stay. To generate greater interest, they offer free nights or a free breakfast. I decided it was time to approach vacancy rates differently.

In developing the pitch, we talked about how to turn the clinical and formulaic experience of staying at a hotel on its head. We also played with the idea that people like to get as much value for money as possible when they stay in a hotel room. Most people, especially travellers, take the little shampoos or accessories. It's not theft—you've paid for them—but it feels good when you pop them into your suitcase. And when you check out of the hotel, there's always the 'game' of being asked if you consumed anything from the mini-bar, with the temptation to say 'no' even if you have. We wanted to add value to the hotel experience by making it more fun to stay at the Art Series Hotels—rather than offer a promotion. We knew the idea should also be around art. That was the easy bit. But how could we turn art into a game? As we didn't have long, and the pitch was competitive, we bounced the question around the entire agency, hoping someone would come up with a great idea.

THE RULES OF PLAY

Dr Stuart Brown is a man who loves to play. In fact, he's the Director of the National Institute for Play in the USA. Stuart describes humans as the 'most neotenous animal on Earth'—which means we like to play. He says, 'We are, by physical anthropologists, by many, many studies, the most flexible, the most plastic of all creatures. And therefore, the most playful' (Brown & Vaughan 2009). He dives into this concept during a brilliant TED presentation evangelising for more play. (If you haven't heard about TED, it asks 'the world's most fascinating thinkers and doers ... to give the talk of their lives [in 18 minutes or less]'. See www.ted.com.) And while Stuart isn't the most playful-looking chap, make sure you watch the entire talk (see it on YouTube: www.youtube.com/watch?v=HHwXlcHcTHc). Brown believes play is important for intelligence and happiness throughout life, and has demonstrated a correlation between the success of people such as Steve Jobs and Sir Richard Branson and their willingness to engage in play (Brown & Vaughan 2009).

Play as a strategy to influence behaviour starts early. Just think of a parent encouraging their child to eat. As the child resists the food, the parent makes the behaviour of eating more fun. The food sitting on the fork magically becomes an aeroplane flying into a hangar—the child's mouth—tempting the child into eating.

There are four main types of play.

1. **Object play**—this is the equivalent of playing with an object, such as a toy. Turning a child's plate of mashed potatoes, meat and carrots into a cute dinosaur is a good example of object play in action. Object play teaches us about empowerment and self-efficacy. It helps us to explore how influential we are, and what we do and don't have control over. For example, have you ever tried to spin a pen in your fingers?

2. **Body play**—this is often used in health and sport where people explore the capabilities of their bodies. It could be a child fascinated by their hands or an adult testing how long they can keep their arms outstretched. Nike + and adidas miCoach are great examples of brands helping to gamify various aspects of body play. Body play teaches us about our body, health and physical possibilities.

3. **Transformational play**—this is where a person loses their sense of self and becomes another person either through imagination or technology. It could be a child imagining they are a sporting legend kicking a goal, or an adult pretending to be a powerful businessperson in a role-play situation. Imaginative play teaches us creativity and open-mindedness. It can also be an extremely useful tool for problem solving.

4. **Social play**—this involves interacting, competing or collaborating with others in a safe, semi-structured environment to reach a goal or achieve an outcome. It includes kids playing in a sandpit or a group of friends catching up for a game of tennis. Social play teaches us the value of collaboration and competition, along with social skills and social problem-solving skills. Advertisers often use social play.

If Stuart Brown is the modern father of play, Jane McGonigal is the mother of **'gamification'**. Gamification uses game mechanics and game structures to make situations playful. Most situations can be gamified, and this leads to higher engagement. For example, a child walking along a footpath could be pretty bored unless she decides to gamify the walk and make stepping on a crack an opportunity to rhyme—'Step on a crack, break your mother's back.' What about buying a chocolate bar? What if the wrapper contains details of a competition to find a special golden chocolate bar with clues on its location? You've gamified the purchase of a chocolate bar. Gamification makes an activity more engaging and enjoyable and therefore more appealing. As a consequence, people are more likely to agree to do that behaviour.

WHY ADVERTISERS LIKE GAMIFICATION

The reason humans like games rests with our brain's reward mechanism: dopamine (Koepp et al. 1998). When we engage in an activity that has a reward, our brain gets excited as it anticipates the reward. Like playing a poker machine,[1] we don't know how much the reward will be—it could be large or nothing. Nor do we know when the reward will come—if it comes at all. But our brain's response to this unpredictable pattern is deeply ingrained. It's what motivated us to keep hunting for food when we were hunter-gatherers. Psychologists refer to it as 'variable positive reinforcement'. Today, this drive has been transferred to checking emails and Twitter feeds. (When is the next good one coming? How good will it be? Better keep checking that phone.)

There's another reason 'gamification' has become big in advertising—technology. The advent of smartphones and social media has created massive multiplayer games across the planet. Advertisers use gamification to entertain people with daily quizzes and questions on Facebook. Technology, especially social media platforms, allows brands to interact with people in real time, making them more immersive.

Advertisers have also embraced gamification because they can create a win–win with the consumer. In the traditional model, advertising interrupted people during their entertainment, such as during their favourite TV show. But now, gamification makes the 'advertising' entertaining. As indicated in Figure 9.1 (over the page), gamified advertising allows people to interact with the brand (what the advertiser wants to happen) and the consumer gets the chance to play a game (what the consumer wants to happen). Gamification allows a consumer to play a game while being marketed to.

---

1 I once had a poker machine client and they wanted to create a more effective poker machine. Manufacturers know general principles about poker machines that work (many of which are listed in later chapters); however, they still have little idea what type of machine will be successful and what will not. I found it extraordinary that with all the information and money they had available, whenever they made a new game they never knew if it was going to be successful. It's a constant and beautiful reminder that while there are some things we are starting to understand about human behaviour, there is a lot more we don't have a clue about. Gamification is a difficult business—be wary of anyone over-promising anything in this area.

Figure 9.1 Gamification allows consumers to enjoy the process of being advertised to!

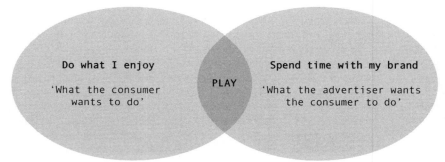

In short, **play is an effective way to influence behaviour, but only when you can control and manipulate the wider environment**. When a mother turns food into a plane when feeding her child, she controls the entire environment. However, getting all of the variables right when creating gamified environments can be very difficult (hence the need for control). It's also effective when the behaviour you want to change is complex or requires multiple or ongoing interventions. **Play is ideal for behaviour that gets better by degrees** such as losing weight, being less violent or doing exercise, rather than one-off behaviours such as buying a certain brand of ice cream.

MAKING CRIME PLAY

It was a week later and we had created something playful that we thought met the brief for the Art Series Hotels. The three ideas we developed were written up simply, one idea per A4 piece of paper. It was just me and Aliya, one of our strategists at Naked, who journeyed over to the client to 'pitch' the ideas.

What game would influence you to book a room at a hotel? With stark white floors and walnut panelled walls, the foyer of The Olsen Art Series Hotel showcases a giant mural by John Olsen, with vibrant yellow brush strokes and flecks of red and blue. The Olsen is the most conservative and upmarket of the hotels and the venue for our pitch to the Art Series Hotel team. After walking through the stylish foyer, we were ushered into Liz's small, windowless office. After tea and coffee arrived, we got down to business. Liz thanked us for our time and for participating in the pitch, before politely asking what our ideas were.

I said we needed an idea that would stir people to take action to book a room at the Art Series Hotels. So why not tap into Melbourne's history of art theft—such as the theft of Picasso's *Weeping Woman* from the National Gallery of Victoria in 1986? (Incidentally, rather than a straightforward theft, this was a politically motivated act by the 'Australian Cultural Terrorists', who threatened to destroy the painting if arts funding was not increased. The painting was eventually returned anonymously, and the case remains unsolved.) Why not exploit the darker side of human motivations? I talked about creating controversy around art, luxury and intrigue. When people stay at hotels, they take a break from their regular life and behave in unexpected ways. They swipe the little soaps and shampoos, and sometimes steal towels and bathrobes. All of which taps into our innate desire to break conventions, bend the rules and explore our own dark side. There is a saying in forensic psychology, '**Bad men do what good men dream**' (Simon 2008). Have you ever wondered why true crime is so popular? I believe it's because a little bit of all of us wants to commit the crime. Further, crime and art are often linked in a glamorous, decadent way. Think art heists, forgery and *The Pink Panther*.

So what about this concept? We invite people to stay the night and steal the art.

Since each hotel room contains expensive art, Liz was understandably surprised. I explained the 'game' would focus on one piece of art purchased especially for the campaign. The one we had in mind was by Banksy, the satirical street artist whose stencil-style art can be seen on random walls across the world. In 2003, Banksy visited Melbourne and secretly spray-painted images of parachuting rats and *Little Diver*, a figure in a vintage deep-sea diving helmet. The work we wanted to purchase, called *No Ball Games*, was already associated with theft, after the original was cut from the side of a shop in Tottenham Green, London, with the help of an angle grinder.

In our proposed campaign, people had to book a room at any of the Art Series Hotels between 15 December and 15 January. During their stay, they could search the hotel for the Banksy art. *No Ball Games* would be moved between the three hotels to encourage bookings at all Art Series hotels and increase the cat-and-mouse intrigue. If a guest found the art and could steal it from the hotel without being caught, it was theirs to keep. If they were caught, it went back on the wall for someone else to potentially steal.

They loved it. We pitched two other ideas—I can't remember what they were. At the end of the meeting, I said our favourite concept was 'Steal Banksy'. In fact, I went a bit further and admitted that the other two ideas were just there to make up the numbers, and the only good idea that was presented, the only idea that would meet their ambitious targets, was 'Steal Banksy'.

Liz phoned the next day and said, 'We love it and so does the CEO. We're up for it. Now what?'

PLAYING FOR SAFER ROADS AND MONEY

One of the most creative uses of 'play' in an advertising campaign happened in 2009, when German car company Volkswagen launched its BlueMotion technologies, part of its new environmentally friendly cars. In deciding how to market these cars, Volkswagen's advertising agency, DDB in Stockholm, believed the cars needed to be associated with fun. I mentioned part of the campaign in Chapter 1 in which stairs exiting a train station were transformed into a giant piano. The piano stairs example kicked off a global competition to come up with a fun solution to common problems. It was called 'The Fun Theory'.

The winner was Kevin Richardson from San Francisco, USA, who also happens to be a producer for Nickelodeon's games division. His idea was the Speed Camera Lottery. As he explained in DDB's video of the campaign, 'The Speed Camera Lottery does two things. One, it would photograph speeders and give them a citation and that money goes into a pot. But if you're obeying the law, your picture will also get snapped, you'll be entered into a lottery and win some of that money from those speeders.' You can see the case study on YouTube (www.youtube.com/watch?v=iynzHWwJXaA). He posed this question: could we get people to obey the speed limit for fun? 'I really think fun can change human behaviour and I was really thrilled to see that my idea that really started as a scribble submitted into this competition might even become reality.'

Less than a year later, his idea was trialled in Stockholm, Sweden. A speed camera was placed outside a school zone that had a speed limit of 30 km/h. Drivers who obeyed the limit were sent a lottery ticket with the prize being the money generated from fines levied on drivers speeding. Over three days, 24,857 cars passed the speed camera. The average speed before the experiment was 32 km/h. During the experiment, it was 25 km/h, reducing the incidence of speeding by 22 per cent. The chance to be financially rewarded for obeying the speed limit influenced driver behaviour.

Could play encourage people to save money? Dressed in a white skivvy and red jacket, 87-year-old Billie June Smith smiles as she holds an oversized cardboard cheque in front of her. The cheque has her name and $100,000 written on it. People standing around her are clapping and smiling. How did she get this cheque? The retired daycare supervisor won the money from her credit union, just because she opened a savings account.

Billie June Smith is part of an experiment in the USA to encourage people to save money as part of Prize-Linked Savings (PLS). Rather than buying lottery tickets, people are asked to put money into a savings account that has a lower interest rate than its competitors, but offers the chance of winning a cash prize. It's been called the 'no lose lottery'. Every $25 put into a share certificate provides a chance to win in a monthly draw, or the annual mega-draw. Over three years in Michigan and Nebraska, 25,000 people opened savings accounts, totalling $41 million in savings. Rather than feeling like a sacrifice, saving money was turned into an exciting game.

LET THE GAMES BEGIN

With the Art Series Hotels signing off on our ambitious game exploring the dark side of human nature, we set about acquiring some art. First, we tracked down Banksy's art dealer, a man by the name of Pest Control, and parted with two cheques: one for $16,000 for a reproduction of *No Ball Games* and one for $4000 for another Banksy print called *Pulp Fiction*, which was purchased in case the first was successfully stolen early in the game. Liz was clear that the idea needed a direct call to action. Simply generating PR was no use—it had to generate sales by getting people to actively participate in the game. To this end, the advertising to attract potential thieves offered the invitation: 'Stay the night. Steal the art.' *No Ball Games* was initially hung in The Blackman and would be shifted to different locations at the three hotels. As soon as it was on the wall, people started to play.

On the first night, there were several attempts to steal *No Ball Games*. Many people impersonated hotel staff. Others tried to distract staff by pretending the TV or other equipment in their room was broken, while an accomplice waited in the foyer. The attempts were creative and generated a playful and fun atmosphere, with guests and staff chatting about it and the various attempted robberies. Then, four days into the campaign, someone told hotel staff they worked at Naked Communications and had to move the art to another hotel. The only problem was she didn't work at Naked and *No Ball Games* was stolen! The thieves were two young women, Megan and Maura. As Megan reveals (*Mumbrella* 2011):

> We dug into LinkedIn, Twitter, Facebook and Google to source the names we would need to drop to impersonate an insider. In the wee hours of the night we role-played different scenarios to practise keeping cool to pull the wool over the eyes of the helpful, unknowing staff. Early the next morning Maura headed down to reception posing as a PR lead from Naked Communications, the agency behind the activation, and Megan was on call to corroborate nearly any story. The next 20 minutes were a blur. The concierge, Rob, fired question after question, but Maura replayed the answers from the previous night's rehearsal and he eventually took the bait.

We didn't think the painting would be stolen so quickly (in fact, we were confident it wouldn't be stolen at all), however, we were prepared. Luckily, we had bought the second (much cheaper) Banksy, just in case this very scenario happened. The newly hung Banksy, *Pulp Fiction*, featuring Vincent Vega and Jules Winnfield (John Travolta and Samuel L Jackson) holding bananas instead of guns, then started doing the rounds of the hotels. There were again many attempts to steal it—even champion tennis player Serena Williams had a crack (she was staying at the hotel and tweeted that she was going to try to steal it). At the end of the campaign, *Pulp Fiction* was still hanging and we donated it to Crime Stoppers.

During the campaign, 1500 hotel rooms were booked, which was 50 per cent above target. Visits to the website increased by 112 per cent. The campaign was reported in news media and blogs in 61 countries, generating an estimated $2.1 million in PR value (Ferrier, Houltham & Hasan 2012). The idea was successful because it was easy to play, it was easy to share and it allowed people to undertake an activity not normally permitted—theft. Reflecting on the success of the idea, Liz recently told me, '"Steal Banksy" really set us apart from our competitors and put us on the world stage as a cool hotel group, one that was willing to take risks. But importantly the idea also talked back to our brand essence. It was all about the art experience, so it helped reaffirm who we are.'

In 2012, only nine advertising campaigns across the globe were awarded the much-coveted advertising double—a Gold Lion at Cannes for creativity and a Gold Effie for effectiveness. This campaign was one of those nine. You can see the campaign on YouTube (www.youtube.com/watch?v=wO8TVILY2LM).

AND YOU THOUGHT HOUSEWORK COULDN'T BE FUN

Could you influence your family to do housework by turning it into a game? Why not create a points system for different cleaning tasks? Say, emptying the dishwasher earns 10 points. vacuuming the house is worth 50 points and folding a load of washing gets you 30 points—and you can watch TV while you complete the job. Points are deducted if someone doesn't complete their chores and there are bonus points if you complete someone else's chores. If you fail to complete tasks, you have to do something embarrassing, such as uploading an awful photo to Facebook. A chart tracking everyone's achievements can be placed on the fridge, with each person in the house given a designated colour so they can watch their progress. In fact, this has all been done for you: you can join an online community and play 'chore wars' (www.chorewars.com).

GAMIFYING RETAIL?

Could gamification increase the number of customers at a café? When buying coffee, the choice of where to buy involves a bit of habit and taste. Incentives, such as receiving a tenth cup free, are widespread and no longer a point of difference. One option is to offer a twelfth cup free, but stamp three cups after the first purchase. This starts customers on the loyalty journey and increases the likelihood they'll return to your café in order to complete the card. Also, purchases increase in frequency when people are about to receive the free coffee (Kivetz, Urminsky & Zheng 2006).

Melbourne's KereKere café has an even more playful approach and gives people a playing card every time they order a coffee. When it's time to pay they place the playing card into one of four jars, each representing a different charity. A percentage of the profits from your coffee purchase is given to that charity. The owner of the café is a lovely bloke called James Murphy (who is both an entrepreneur and qualified social worker). James is a tall, good-looking character with a continual flow of ideas on how to make consumerism more fun—and more fair. I ran into him once as he was loading pineapples and whole legs of ham into his car. 'These are the prizes for the basketball competition we've been running down at the café,' he partially explained. James spends his time creating gamified business models where everyone can win. As he says, 'Why does the owner always have to be the winner? Why can't many people win?' This simple example of gamification creates loyalty and potentially increases the number of coffees purchased. Incidentally, as I was leaving, James casually mentioned that his next venture was going to be a 'reverse soup kitchen' where the staff would be the homeless people, handing out soup to regular citizens.

One of the best ideas I've ever presented (in my less than humble opinion) that wasn't bought was to a retail client I had for many years. This client had a very traditional advertising model and often ran promotions such as 'buy one, get one free' (known as a BOGOF in advertising—pronounced 'bog off'—which I've always found pretty funny). I suggested the client introduce 'The Game of Giving' for their next BOGOF promotion. The idea was simple: when a customer made a purchase, they could either choose and keep another item of the same value, or they could choose not to take the extra item and give the money equivalent to a charity instead. We believed it would be engaging for customers and generate media attention as well. I also thought the game would encourage people to return to the stores more frequently. The idea wasn't used. The marketing director liked it, but the CEO wasn't so sure. Sometimes it's difficult to get people to do something new—it's human nature to avoid change, which can be frustrating.

Rory Sutherland (one of the 'Insiders' in this book) once said that advertising's job 'is to make the new familiar and the familiar new'. Currently, gamified retail models are still on the fringe. However, as corporations get better at manipulating data, and technology companies create better retail infrastructure, I believe it will be a new frontier of retail. We'll see variable pricing models that will make retail fun become commonplace.

PLAYING OUR WAY TO A BETTER WORLD?

Advertisers, me included, are largely interested in gamification techniques that can increase consumer purchases. However, some believe it has the potential to solve some of the world's most challenging problems. Jane McGonigal (2011) has been an advocate of using the powers of gamified environments to solve many of the world's significant issues and asks us to imagine what could happen if the collective energy and intelligence that completes meaningless missions in games such as *World of Warcraft* were to be applied to solving real-world problems.

As an example, in collaboration with the World Bank Institute, McGonigal created a game called EVOKE. It asked online players to come up with solutions for several hypothetical problems identified in Africa in 2020. Players accomplished each mission by uploading blogs, videos and photos. If players encouraged other players' efforts, they received credits and more time in the game. The game ran over 10 weeks in 2010 with 20,000 players from 150 countries registering. During the game, players submitted 23,500 blog posts, 4700 photos and 1500 videos. There were 178,000 unique visitors during the game. Interestingly, many ideas generated during the game were applied later on:

- Ten ideas received seed funding.
- Twenty-two projects received a post-game mentor for further development.
- Fifteen projects were invited to the EVOKE Summit in September 2010.

You can see a trailer for the game online (http://vimeo.com/9094186).

In 2004, a bunch of socially minded 'game creators' in the USA started the non-profit company Games for Change, which 'facilitates the creation and distribution of social impact games that serve as critical tools in humanitarian and educational efforts' (see www.gamesforchange.com). Some of the ideas generated in this community include:

- Want to lose weight? You can participate in *Zombies, Run!* Outrun the zombies and lose weight as you exercise.
- Want to donate bikes to developing countries? Play *SideKick Cycle*.
- Want to learn how your body works? Help Fred survive a terrifying night in the woods with *Code Fred: Survival Mode*.
- Or how about playing *The Best Amendment*? You'll need to distinguish between the 'good guys with guns' from 'bad guys with guns' in this game about gun control.

Another project is using the potential of gamification to help in the detection of malaria. It takes a specialist around 30 minutes to look for malaria through a microscope in a blood sample. First, you need to detect the parasite in the sample. Then you have to count the number of parasites that appear in the sample. The greater the number of parasites, the worse the infection. Dr Miguel Luengo-Oroz (Luengo-Oroz, Arranz & Frean 2012), from the Universidad Politécnica de Madrid in Spain, had the idea of using online gamers to do the detection, devising a game called *MalariaSpot*. In his study, volunteer online gamers were invited to play a web-based game in which they had to identify and count parasites in blood smears that appeared on their computer screens. When you start the game, music plays and you're shown a screen that reveals what the parasite looks like. Then you're invited to 'Click on the parasites'. The screen goes pink and you can see various blotches. When you correctly click on the parasite, a nasty grey cartoon face appears. When you click on other material, a red cross appears. An hourglass in the top left hand corner of the screen counts down, as you race to identify all the parasites. Your score can be seen in the top right-hand corner of the screen. It's quite addictive, and you can compare your score against the efforts of other gamers (see www.malariaspot.com/game).

In this study, which took place over one month, anonymous players from 95 countries played more than 12,000 games, generating a database of more than 270,000 clicks on the test images. When 22 games from non-expert players were combined, there was a parasite counting accuracy higher than 99 per cent. When malaria detection became a game, people were influenced to play.

SUMMARY

Humans have an innate need to play. Play is ideal for influencing behaviour that gets better by degrees (rather than one-off behaviours), but is only effective in influencing behaviour when you can control and manipulate the wider environment. Gamification is the art of putting rules and structures around play, and of turning play into a game. Technology makes this easy to do, thanks to smartphones and social media. When you turn something into a game, you make it enjoyable and fun. Instead of signs saying, 'Do not urinate here', the Amsterdam water supply company turned urinals into gaming stations. It used an understanding of human behaviour to achieve its desired outcome. The credit union that wanted more customers turned the mundane experience of opening a savings account into an exciting possibility to win money. It understood that a chance to win, rather than an opportunity to save, was far more motivating. If you asked people to volunteer to identify malaria in a blood sample, I doubt many would be interested. But turning malaria detection into a game that allows you to earn points and compete against others makes it an entirely different proposition. The chance to steal art from a hotel encouraged an increase in bookings. Gamification turns a stick into a carrot to influence behaviour.

The Insider: Faris Yakob

Why do we do what we do?

It's one of the biggest questions we grapple with, what drives human behaviour. As marketers we try to both understand and influence it.

Behaviour does not correlate strongly to beliefs. This we know, but it's a hard thing to know because it contravenes our own experience of reality. It seems like we make decisions and then act, but emerging research suggests that consciousness itself may be an epi-phenomenon, a manifestation of decisions made below the threshold of awareness.

It's not as simple as one thing or the other, of course. Your body and mind and stimulus and context interact in the most complex multivariate system in the known universe to create behaviour. Emotions are the lubricants of reason. In systems, it is the interactions of elements that are important.

What do we know?

That behaviour is like water, following the pathways of least resistance, obeying system defaults more often than not. That we are predisposed to mimicry and reciprocity. That heuristics lead us to make non-optimal economic decisions, but in a predictable way. That behaviour is mysterious, but knowable. That asking someone why they do what they do is useful only as therapy, not as research, predictive or explanatory. That behaviour does not aggregate in a linear way, as interactions create emergent behaviours. Crowds do not act like people, and markets do not respond like focus groups.

Clay Shirky says, 'Behavior is motivation filtered through opportunity', making us detectives of human behaviour. The great revolution to come is in decoding influence and working with people to create positive behavioural loops. People fear and resist being influenced overtly, unaware that everything influences behaviour. If we can expose the fact that everything influences, we can help people help themselves.

Faris Yakob is a good friend who I met working at Naked Communications. Faris left to become a global thinker and provocateur as chief innovation and technology officer at Advertising Holding Group MDC. Faris now travels the world speaking at conferences and coming up with very clever ideas for his clients.

REFERENCES

Brown, S. & Vaughan, C. (2009). *Play: How it Shapes the Brain, Opens the Imagination, and Invigorates the Soul.* New York: Avery.

Ferrier, A., Houltham, M. & Hasan, A. (2012). *Steal Banksy.* Australian Effie Awards. Accessed at www.effies.com.au/attachments/3267db17-3567-40fb-b4ba-34881f0d3705.pdf.

Kivetz, R., Urminsky, O. & Zheng, Y. (2006). The goal-gradient hypothesis resurrected: Purchase acceleration, illusionary goal progress, and customer retention. *Journal of Marketing Research*, 43, 39–58.

Koepp, M.J., Gunn, R.N., Lawrence, A.D., Cunningham, V.J., Dagher, A., Jones, T. et al. (1998). Evidence for striatal dopamine release during a video game. *Nature*, 393(6682), 266–26.

Luengo-Oroz, M.A., Arranz A. & Frean, J. (2012). Crowdsourcing malaria parasite quantification: An online game for analyzing images of infected thick blood smears. *Journal of Medical Internet Research*, 14(6), e167.

McGonigal, J. (2011). *Reality Is Broken: Why Games Make Us Better and How They Can Change the World.* New York: Penguin Books.

Mumbrella (2011). How we pulled off the Banksy heist. Accessed at http://mumbrella.com.au/how-we-pulled-off-the-banksy-heist-68934.

Simon, R. (2008). *Bad Men Do What Good Men Dream: A Forensic Psychiatrist Illuminates the Darker Side of Human Behavior.* Washington DC: American Psychiatric Publishing. The advertising to attract potential thieves offered this invitation: 'Stay the night. Steal the art.' *No Ball Games* was initially hung in The Blackman and shifted to different locations at the three hotels. As soon as it was on the wall, people started to play.

UTILITY: NO MORE EMPTY PROMISES

Advertising is the wonder in Wonder Bread.

Jef I Richards, US advertising lecturer

The best ad is a good product.

Alan H Meyer, US ad guy

SPORTS FAN

In 1985 the West Coast Eagles were admitted into an expanded AFL (Australian Football League) competition. This may not mean much to most of you, but for a boy growing up in Perth, Western Australia, who was fanatical about Australian Rules football, this was very exciting. The Eagles were Perth's team, and I can still remember waking up and reading about the news in the *West Australian* newspaper. I yelled out to mum and dad to get out of bed so I could share the news with them. Tragic, I know.

It was seven years later when the Eagles won their first AFL premiership, another day seared into my memory. After the triumphant game, I remember walking down Perth's Stirling Highway with a mate wondering which pub we should visit to celebrate the win. However, we couldn't find a crowd anywhere. Instead, we wandered around the streets, a bit lost, having our own little party. It was an odd experience: I felt euphoria that our team had won, but disappointment that we weren't in the right place at the right time to share the win with other Eagles fans. We knew they were celebrating—we just couldn't find where they all were.

Fast-forward to Melbourne in 2013, when sporting giant adidas was the official guernsey sponsor of the AFL's Hawthorn Football Club. Adidas wanted us to come up with an idea that demonstrated its support for Hawthorn. Further, the Hawks (as they are known) wanted the idea to be digital in nature. The Hawks were the number-one team in the competition, and they wanted an idea that was progressive and innovative—that no other club had done.

Upon receiving a brief from a client, all agencies will start an 'insights' process; that is, they will look for interesting 'insights' or 'findings' that will help point them in the right direction for an idea that will solve the brief. When we instigated this process, one of the first things we found out was that the state of Tasmania was one of the team's major sponsors. This had a significant impact on their fans as it meant Hawthorn played several games in the island state. We wondered how many Hawthorn fans made the trip south, and how they got in touch with each other. Where did they stay? What did they do before the game? Where did they sit during the game? And what did they do after the game? Further, we discovered that many Hawks fans live in Tasmania. How did they know where to go or what to do when they visited Melbourne to watch their team?

We discovered a core group of Victorian fans made arrangements to meet during Tasmanian games, but there were many other fans who weren't connected. They travelled to Tasmania at the last minute and hoped to bump into other fans. I was reminded of my lonely experience on Stirling Highway looking for a pub to celebrate the Eagles win in 1991 and realised one way to reward fans was to help them connect during away games.

HOW UTILITY WORKS

According to Barden (2013), 'the more relevant a brand is to a particular goal the consumer has, then the greater the reward the consumer expects. The greater the reward they expect—the more value they perceive. The more value they perceive, the more they are willing to pay, or the more effort they are willing to make to attain that brand.' Therefore, a marketer needs to truly understand a customer's goals in order to deliver value. Imagine you're really thirsty, yet dressed in a very nice suit as you are about to go for a job interview. You stop in the café at the bottom of the building where your interview is about to take place to purchase a flavoured milk. There are only two options. Option A has a wide spout (so you can drink it quickly), while option B has the added utility of a straw attached on the side and a punch hole on the top. In this situation your goal is to drink the flavoured milk without spilling it over yourself. Which of the two flavoured milks do you think you'd choose? Of course, it's option B—and I'm sure you'd pay more for it too, as it more clearly meets your goals. The added utility of the straw means you can consume the drink without spilling it on your suit. Therefore it becomes more valuable to you. This can be expressed in the following equation:

$$\text{Value = Ability to meet my goal/Price}$$

If utility can help make the brand or product better meet the consumer's goals, they'll value it more and their motivation to get it will be increased, leading to a greater likelihood of behaviour change. One of the best examples of utility is Nike's FuelBand. This very cool-looking bracelet tracks and calculates how much energy the wearer expends—which is part of the newly dubbed 'quantified self' movement.[1] However, if we take a step back, the goal that the Nike brand may fulfil for many of its consumers is: 'I want to feel a sense of victory by participating in sport.' The Nike FuelBand helps the consumer meet this goal. This added utility creates more value for the consumer as they get to track how much energy they are expending, and measure their level of participation in sport. It's not just

---

1 The 'quantified self' is a recent fascination of advertisers and something that is appealing to consumers. With the proliferation of data, people are beginning to track their own behaviour via the data that they can collect about themselves. This is also a massive opportunity for marketers. Marketers are beginning to offer data about people, the energy they use, the cooking habits they have, the kilojoules they consume and so on. People can compare this data to other people and judge how 'normal' they are (or not). The quantified self proves we are all a little narcissistic and find ourselves endlessly fascinating (which is probably a nice thing).

another product for Nike but a way of adding value to the Nike brand. **The more value that can be injected into the brand (making the brand increasingly valuable to the consumer), the stronger the brand becomes.** Advertisers are beginning to take the dollars previously spent on 'advertising' and putting it towards building utility for consumers that meets their goals.

FROM WONDER TO BREAD TO UTILITY?

Utility is an emerging part of advertising. Let me explain with the help of Wonder Bread, a brand of bread created in North America in 1921. It was the first brand of bread to be pre-sliced, generating the expression 'the best thing since sliced bread'. This bread has enjoyed an eventful history, including a government-sponsored program of enrichment in the 1940s, when vitamins and minerals were added to it. However, the key to the bread's success historically has been its advertising. As Michigan State University advertising lecturer Jef I Richards says, 'Advertising is the wonder in Wonder Bread.'

Let me outline three notable pieces of advertising. The first is from the 1950s, and shows a little boy amazed at the wonderful nutritional properties contained in Wonder Bread. It's a minute-long television commercial (TVC) (ads from this era were often a minute long, or even longer, as media was relatively cheap to purchase then), which you can see in the commercial on YouTube (www.youtube.com/watch?v=GEfWShkO4Ac). The next piece of film comes from 2006. Here Wonder Bread's promotion has moved from straight commercials to creating 'branded content' through its sponsorship of the hit movie *Talladega Nights: The Ballad of Ricky Bobby*, starring Will Ferrell. In the footage, Ricky Bobby's driving suit and car are completely dominated by Wonder Bread's name and colours (www.youtube.com/watch?v=vIxSSbjz1k8) as they become toast. In the final clip, from 2013, we see the car of real-life Nascar driver Kurt Busch rebranded as 'Wonder Bread'. After its previous owners went bankrupt, Wonder Bread's new owners, Flowers Foods, decided to pay homage to *Talladega Nights* and sponsor a real Nascar team, echoing the film—a classic example of life imitating art, http://www.youtube.com/watch?v=9TCuJ2hQcRo.

Now although these three clips show a steady progression of innovative communications from Wonder Bread—from a TVC, to branded content, to postmodern sponsorship—all three forms of advertising are about image creation. All three clips are trying to build the 'wonder' of Wonder Bread through cool, aspirational imagery. Advertising is the aspiration wrapped around the bread. It's what transforms a standard loaf of white bread into 'wonder' bread. Advertising excels at creating a desirable image to wrap around a product. In this case, it's the 'wonder' or perceived value. It's intangible.

But advertising and image creation only get you so far. The product has to deliver and meet consumer demand. If consumers say, 'Hang on. Maybe Wonder Bread isn't so wonderful. I want a healthier alternative', what can an advertiser do at this point? It can't continue to build value through aspirational imagery. The product needs to change. In fact, it's what the manufacturers of Wonder Bread did—creating wholegrain and whole-wheat versions of the brand.

Let's imagine a further restraint for an advertiser. The brand isn't selling and the owners can't alter or change the product, which is a common scenario. How can you persuade consumers to purchase the product? The solution is to make the product appear more valuable to the consumer. At this point, you give it 'utility'.

Writing in advertising magazine *Adage*, marketing consultants Fred Pfaff and Art Cannon (2013) argue that advertising has to move from image creation to utility:

> Advertising giants built the brand business on sentiment, which falls short in an age where I want to do something. Marketing can't just communicate your ethos anymore; it has to deliver access to your brand through mechanisms that let people experience the value in everyday life. That means the brand job only starts at aspiration and has to incorporate a range of technologies for realization.

Sometimes it's not enough to tell someone how great a product is. Sometimes you have to add value—or utility.

In the case of Wonder Bread, you might include a free lunch box with every loaf. You're not changing the image or the product, but providing utility. Alternatively, you could add a wooden butter knife into the packaging (popular in Scandinavia) so people could butter their bread without it tearing. You could create a mobile app that gives consumers information on the nutritional value of its bread compared with other foods. Or it could create an app that offers 'wonderful' inspiration for sandwich fillings. With smartphones, advertisers can create utility like never before.

EXTRA VALUE WITH EXISTING ASSETS

If we accept the equation that Value = Ability to meet my goal ÷ Price, nirvana for a marketer is an ability to deliver on that equation without increasing their costs. The more value the brand can give the consumer without increasing costs to themselves (or increasing the price to the consumer), the more desired that brand will become. In 2013 we created extra value with the existing assets we had at our disposal for the Art Series Hotels. After our successful 'Steal Banksy' campaign (see Chapter 9), we needed to come up with another way to encourage people to book a room at the hotels, particularly during the quiet summer season. We wanted to offer something of value, but didn't have a big budget. Instead, we looked at what the hotels already had—their assets. In the case of a hotel, it was its empty rooms. What value could we offer that didn't cheapen the brand and could make money?

Our solution was the 'Overstay Checkout'. With this utility, guests at the hotels didn't have to check out of their room unless the room they were staying in actually was booked. Each morning, after staying the night, guests could ring the front desk and ask for an overstay checkout. If no one had booked the room, they could stay on for free. The next morning they could ask again if they could stay on. Some guests stayed on free for over a week. Although these free nights were desired by the consumer, the hotels were not actually incurring any costs as the rooms would have just remained empty anyway.

The utility for the guest is obvious. But the hotels benefited as well. Bookings increased because guests wanted the chance to stay for longer for nothing. There were more people staying at the hotels and spending money at their bars and restaurants. The idea also generated positive PR (estimated at $1.5 million) and social media mentions. Room bookings were

55 per cent above the forecast. The hotels now have a mechanism they can turn on and turn off to increase patronage—based on utility. The campaign won a Silver Lion at Cannes (Creative) and a Gold Effie (Effectiveness). Further, this campaign won the Warc (World Advertising Research Centre) $10,000 prize for the world's most innovative campaign in 2013. The main reason the campaign was seen as so effective was because we managed to create extra value for the consumer out of the hotels' existing assets (unused hotel rooms). You can see the case study on YouTube (www.youtube.com/watch?v=nkLY3GOU0tc).

UTILITY INCREASES MOTIVATION

Let's see how you go with the following brief received by Ogilvy France from their client IBM. IBM had informed Ogilvy France that their next idea had to do a number of things. First, they wanted to express their 'Smarter Cities' proposition by using the advertising to give consumers utility; that is, they had decided before the campaign that the best way to express the proposition of smarter cities (IBM 2013) was to do something smart (and useful)—not just talk about it. Second, it was decided that the key medium to be used would be outdoor advertising, so it would appeal to everyday city dwellers and business leaders alike. What would you do? How could you use utility to provide value?

Now to appreciate the cleverness of Ogilvy France's solution, imagine walking past a billboard that advertises IBM. Would you notice it? If you did notice it, what would it make you think about IBM? Not sure? I guess it depends what the ad says.

Now imagine you're walking to work and the skies suddenly open and it begins to pour with rain. You look for shelter and the only shelter you see is an outdoor advertisement, except the top quarter of the outdoor ad has been deliberately curved away from the wall to provide enough shelter for you to rest under. The billboard is coloured bright blue and says, 'Smart ideas for smarter cities. Join the conversation at www.people4smartercities. com.' And in big letters at the bottom of the billboard: 'IBM'. What would you think of the ad now? You may even visit the website. It certainly makes IBM seem smart!

Now imagine you continue walking to work and your shoelace comes undone. You need a place to sit to retie your shoelaces. Then up ahead you see another billboard. This time the bottom of the billboard is curved up to provide a platform for people to sit on; the billboard is also painted to resemble a park bench. This time written at the top of the billboard is, 'Sitting on a smart idea for your city? Share it at www.people4smartercities. com.' And again, 'IBM' appears at the bottom.

These two billboards were part of a series of outdoor ads IBM and Ogilvy France created. As Susan Westre, Worldwide Creative Director at Ogilvy and Mather, said after winning the Grand Prix for Outdoor at the Cannes: 'We were looking for an idea that reached regular citizens as well as city leaders. That's how outdoor became the medium. IBM is a strong believer in providing "utility" in its communications—from offering useful information and facts to educational experiences' (Ogilvydo.com 2013).

The utility both expresses the brand's proposition (smarter cities) and gives consumers a genuine benefit. This is the goal of utility. You can see a case study online (http://vimeo. com/68144832). The campaign had only recently launched at the time of writing, so there were no statistics about its degree of success. However, it clearly demonstrates how providing people with extra utility can help influence them to do what you want them to do.

EXPERIENCING RENTAL RAGE?

Here's how the utility action spur was applied when real estate website, realestate.com.au, expanded from selling property to also offering rental properties in Sydney. The rental market was very competitive, with people finding it difficult to find a place to rent. Those looking for a property found the process stressful as they rushed from place to place, joining long queues with other rental hopefuls. Research revealed those looking for rental properties weren't treated well by agents, who saw them as second-class citizens compared with those buying homes. The experience was horrible and degrading. Renters were so stressed they experienced 'rental rage'—a term our company, Naked, helped to create and disseminate in the media.

We also created a utility-based solution for renters. It was called the 'Real Estate Renters Retreat'. An entire floor of a luxury hotel was converted into a haven for stressed renters, with hundreds of two-day stays up for grabs for those who registered on a website and could prove they were looking for a rental property. We held a cocktail party to get people talking and invited key journalists and celebrities to stay at the hotel.

As a result of this utility, there was a 7.8 per cent increase in unique site visitors in October 2007. In addition, 42 per cent of people who registered on the site opted to receive regular information about realestate.com.au. It offered empathy and value to renters and was more engaging than a traditional advertising campaign.

UTILITY MAKING THINGS EASIER

This is another example of utility adding value for consumers. In 1999, UK supermarket giant Tesco opened stores in South Korea under the name 'Home Plus'. But after several years in the market, Home Plus was still the country's second largest supermarket after E-Mart. It faced the challenge of how to increase sales despite the fact it had fewer stores than its competitor. Advertising agency Cheil Worldwide came up with an idea that used utility to encourage more sales. How? Subway stations became virtual supermarkets. As commuters waited for their train, they could stand in front of a glass wall that had pictures grocery items laid out just like a supermarket. It was as though you were standing in an actual supermarket aisle. Commuters could choose items from virtual shelves stocked with drinks, cereals and bread. Even the meat looked as it would at a real supermarket. The commuter scanned the QR code on their smartphone and checked out when finished. If their train arrived mid-shop, they could continue shopping online on the train, thanks to connectivity. The goods were delivered soon after they arrived home. It combined the familiar habit of shopping with modern technology. In three months, sales increased by 130 per cent, with the number of registered users increasing by 76 per cent. See the case study on YouTube (www.youtube.com/watch?v=MGJifBHm8_s).

This is a great example of communications as 'utility' and of advertisers influencing behaviour by offering additional benefits and services. The money that would traditionally be spent on advertising was spent on utility—on adding value.

HELPING HAWKS FANS STAY CONNECTED

This understanding of utility informed our strategy when advising adidas and the Hawthorn Football Club. The value we decided to create was an app that would help fans to connect during games in Tasmania. We called it 'Hawkspotter', and the inspiration for the idea came from Grindr, a website that allows gay men to locate each other and, if they so desire, 'hook up'. Hawkspotter would allow fans to see where all other registered Hawks fans were three hours before, during and three hours after each game, so that they could share the excitement of each game with other Hawks fans nearby. Each week, fans can click on the app and discover where other Hawthorn fans are hanging out. Here's how Hawthorn announced the new app to their members.

⊛ New adidas 'Hawkspotter' app launched

adidas Australia, in partnership with Hawthorn Football Club today unveiled a revolutionary smartphone application allowing Hawks fans to go all in with each other by pinpointing the exact location of fellow supporters on match days.

The 'Hawkspotter' app is a world first for football fans of any code and is designed to enhance the game day experience by allowing fans to login via Facebook or create a profile and search for other fans before, during and after each game.

The free app, which is available on IOS, will give Hawks fans a unique opportunity to link up with fellow fans around Australia, while the updates feed notifies fans of special offers and pop-up events.

With a significant number of the Hawthorn faithful now also based in Tasmania, this app offers new security for supporters who regularly make the pilgrimage across Bass Strait.

Fans will be able to quickly and conveniently flock to a Melbourne or Launceston pub filled with other Hawks supporters.

The app facilitates the coming together of Hawthorn diehards everywhere, so wherever you are on game day you can be sure you're not watching the match alone.

The new 'Hawkspotter' smartphone application is available for download from iTunes this week.

Exclusive to hawthornfc.com.au.

Source: Hawthorn Football Club (2013).

There have been mixed results for Hawkspotter. It's been downloaded thousands of times, but repeat usage has been low because of functionality issues. As an advertiser, this feedback is useful. It's harder to create value for consumers, as we have a lot more work to do than just build nice imagery. When the Hawkspotter app is improved, it will mean fans will willingly spending several hours each week with the adidas brand through their phones. It means adidas can offer special promotions with retailers. Instead of just talking about how adidas supports the Hawks though advertising, it can show it by creating utility for Hawks fans.

UTILITY AT HOME

How can you use the principles of utility to influence others? When I was growing up, the only way my mum could get me to clean my room was to wait until the weekend when I needed her to drive me somewhere. When I asked her for a lift she would invariably say, 'Only if you clean up your room'. The utility (getting a lift) became positive reinforcement for my behaviour. Another thing: people put effort into a task if they know there's a reward, and it works much better than punishment. My mum agreeing to drive me somewhere if I cleaned by room was far more motivating for me than if she grounded me for *not* cleaning my room. Positive reinforcement works best if used at an appropriate time (happens soon) with an appropriate reward (as small and desirable as possible) and with consistency (so people are able to predict the reward).

Utility as an action spur can also make a task easier. Let's say your friend always arrives late to your expensive personal training sessions. What can you do to make her turn up on time? You've already begged and pleaded for her to arrive on time. She tells you the reason she's late is because she can't get out of bed in the morning. Using utility, you could:

- Give her a watch with an alarm.
- Give her a pre-programmed alarm clock.
- Ring her on the day of training.
- Pick her up on the way to training.

Utility identifies barriers to behaviour and makes it easier to perform. It creates extra value for the behaviour you want to happen.

SUMMARY

Utility allows the consumer and the advertiser to win. If utility can help make the brand or product better meet the consumer's goals, they'll value it more and their motivation to get it will be increased, leading to a greater likelihood of behaviour change. So if an advertiser diverts budget into creating utility for the consumer, the consumer gets something beyond image. In our examples, Hawks fans have a way of connecting with each other and guests at the Art Series Hotels can stay additional nights for free. This value can increase motivation such as the 'Real Estate Renters Retreat' that gave stressed renters the chance to win a weekend at a luxury hotel. From shopping at the subway, to finding shelter in the rain courtesy of IBM, utility offers more than advertising.

The Insider: Rohit Bhargava

Sometimes we change behaviour because it's in our own self-interest. That's certainly the best case, but it doesn't always happen that way. Instead, many times we change our behaviour because of someone, not something. When we do, it usually comes down to one thing—inspiration. The leaders who inspire us are the ones who can lead us to change.

We follow the people first and the ideas second.

That's why so called 'leaderless revolutions' don't work. So what's the lesson in this? If you really want to motivate people to change, it's not enough to have a great message. You'll need an inspired messenger to deliver it as well.

Rohit Bhargava is the best-selling author of *Likeonomics* and Founder of Influential Marketing Group. I met Rohit in 2013 at a conference, although our paths nearly crossed when he worked at Leo Burnett advertising agency in Sydney. It's funny he's written a book called *Likeonomics*, as he's one of the most likeable guys I've met.

REFERENCES

Barden, P. (2013). *Decoded: The Science Behind Why We Buy*. Chichester: John Wiley & Sons.

Hawthorn Football Club (2013). *New adidas 'Hawkspotter' App Launched*. Accessed at www.hawthornfc.com.au/news/2013-06-27/new-adidas-hawkspotter-app-launched.

IBM (2013). *Smarter Cities*. Accessed at www.ibm.com/smarterplanet/us/en/smarter_cities/overview.

Ogilvydo.com (2013). *IBM Smarter Cities: Grand Prix and Gold Lion Winner*. Accessed at http://cannes.ogilvydo.com/ogilvy-scoops-more-grand-prix-awards/#.Un7bXKUss1g.

Pfaff, F. & Cannon, A. (2013). Why marketers need to reorganize around the most powerful behavior principle of all: Utility. *Adage*, 15 April. Accessed at http://adage.com/article/guest-columnists/utility-powerful-behavior-principle/240860.

MODELLING: MONKEY SEE, MONKEY DO

In modelling: He with better looks is more in demand than he who has read better books.

Mokokoma Mokhonoana, South African author, philosopher and non-conformist

The advertising world had space men in it before spacemen existed.

Fred Allen, US comedian

FANCY A JARRAH?

'Let's have a coffee,' a woman announces to two friends seated in her living room. She enthusiastically springs up from the sofa asking, 'Would you like Swiss, French or Vienna-style?' 'Swiss,' responds one. 'French,' says the second. 'Then I'll have Vienna.' As she scurries into the kitchen, one of the friends asks, 'If it's not too much trouble?' The host makes fake coffee machine noises. She has no need for an espresso machine—she's got all-in-one coffee by Jarrah Coffee. The advertisement is from 1987 when Jarrah Coffee was commonly found in the pantries of suburban kitchens across Australia.

Invented by an Australian chemist in the 1970s, Jarrah Coffee was seen as a convenient coffee choice in offices and homes. Fast-forward forty years and the brand was struggling for relevance. The market had, as they say, moved on. Not only was all-in-one coffee viewed as a bit suburban, but consumers were also concerned about drinking a product that had so many unknowns. What are the ingredients that create the flavour? What's the milk powder made of? Does it contain real coffee? In addition, Jarrah had been ridiculed by popular TV comedy *Kath & Kim*, which parodied Australian suburbia. 'Fancy a Jarrah?' the new-age sex therapist, Marion, would ask at the end of her unorthodox sessions. In 2012, the company wanted to rejuvenate the brand.

The first task was to work out which behaviour to influence. We arranged for a series of strangers, half of them regular Jarrah drinkers, to meet with the Naked Communications team. Seated in a shopping centre, the group discussed their thoughts and feelings about the brand. As they chatted, I watched the faces of the Jarrah drinkers and noticed that when the drink was discussed, each had a reserved smile. It was as though they held a terrible secret. The reaction of the non-drinkers explained why. When they spoke, they openly scoffed at the brand and described its drinkers somewhat disparagingly. The people who loved Jarrah kept quiet during the onslaught. I realised there was a massive perception issue with the brand. Those who loved it stayed quiet and those who thought it was 'uncool' voiced their displeasure loudly.

MODELLING BEHAVIOUR CHANGE

We thought the best action spur to promote Jarrah would be modelling—a concept based on social learning theory developed by one of the most influential psychologists of all time, Albert Bandura (mentioned in Chapter 2). Born in 1925, Bandura spent most of his working life at Stanford University. A kindly looking man with a warm smile and gentle eyes, Bandura pioneered an approach to psychology that was based on observing how we behave in groups. He believed that how we interact with others was a much better indicator of human behaviour than how we behave on our own. Social learning theory asserts that **we learn new ways of behaving by watching 'models'**. We copy them.

It reminds me of my mum, who nagged me about keeping my room tidy as a kid. The problem was the rest of the house wasn't tidy (sorry mum, but it's true). Even she admits the place was (and still is) frightfully untidy, full of mess and dust. In the early 1980s, mum cleaned out the kitchen cupboard and threw away everything priced in shillings and pence—decimalisation happened in 1966! So when she berated me about keeping my room tidy, I'd say, 'Why should I keep my room tidy when the rest of the house is a complete mess?' That may sound a little obnoxious, but it seemed a reasonable assertion to me. She'd respond with her favourite saying: 'Do as I say, not as I do.' I found this incredibly frustrating and it didn't motivate me to clean up my room. We argued about it for years.

Eventually, after studying psychology at university, I took great pleasure in telling mum the principles of modelling. I told her that, according to Bandura and social learning theory, her words are not as powerful as her actions. If she wanted me to keep my room tidy, she would need to keep the rest of the house tidy. Only now can I fully appreciate just how annoying my comments must have sounded to her. My smugness aside, my mother's 'Do as I say, not as I do' approach was always going to be futile because we learn by mimicking others. As Bandura (1977) said:

> Learning would be exceedingly laborious, not to mention hazardous, if people had to rely solely on the effects of their own actions to inform them what to do. Fortunately, most human behavior is learned observationally through modeling: from observing others one forms an idea of how new behaviors are performed, and on later occasions this coded information serves as a guide for action.

The classic psychological experiment that demonstrates modelling was conducted by Bandura (Bandura, Ross & Ross 1961) and was one of the first experiments I learned when studying psychology at university. In the experiment, a child and an adult are brought into a room. The child is placed in front of toys and the adult is seated in front of a play set, mallet and blow-up doll with sand in its base that's shaped a bit like an egg—a Bobo doll. It stays upright if pushed or punched. In the first group, after about a minute of playing with the toys, the adult directs their attention to the Bobo doll and acts aggressively towards it, punching the poor doll, and hitting it over and over again with the mallet.

In the second group, the adult plays normally with the toys and then goes over to the Bobo doll. However, instead of a concerted attack, the adult plays nicely with the doll. After 10 minutes, the child is taken into another playroom filled with toys and is allowed to play for two minutes before the toys are taken away, building frustration in the child. The child is then taken back into the room that has the Bobo doll. Any guesses as to what happens next? That's right, the children who watched the adult hitting the Bobo doll were much more likely to copy that behaviour and hit it in the same way. Have a look at the rather stark results on YouTube (www.youtube.com/watch?v=hHHdovKHDNU).

THE MODEL BECOMES THE NORM

Modelling has flow-on effects. If the child in the Bobo doll experiment went into the playground and acted violently they may become a model for others—creating a cascading effect. As my old boss Mark Sherrington from marketing consultancy, Added Value, writes, 'Every avalanche starts with the movement of one snowflake. You cannot change "them" but you can change "him or her" and allow others to copy' (see 'The Insider' box, p. 101).

We can see Mark's words in action in a video (www.youtube.com/watch?v=GA8z7f7a2Pk) taken at a dance festival held on a hillside. If you can, stop reading for a few minutes and take a look. I promise you'll enjoy it. The video shows one lone guy dancing with free abandon. After a while, another person joins in, followed by two more and suddenly, there's an avalanche of people having a wild and crazy time together. A 'new normal' has developed on the hillside.

Modelling is very powerful when it tips over to create a new 'social norm'. And there's generally a tipping point when *not* participating in the action becomes the odd behaviour. In the case of our hillside revellers, the social norm shifted from 'watching the crazy guy dancing' to 'dancing like the crazy guy'. When most people danced, it was acceptable for others to join in. How would you encourage an entire hillside of people to start dancing?

1. Would you do as the guy did, and just start dancing yourself?

2. Would you use advertising that asks people to dance?

Clearly the answer is 1. The expression is 'Monkey see. Monkey do', not 'Monkey told. Monkey do'.

Social psychologist Robert Cialdini has undertaken extensive studies on social norms and their impact. He and his colleagues distinguish between two types of social norms: 'descriptive norms' and 'injunctive norms' (Cialdini, Kallgren & Reno 1991):

- *Descriptive norms* are existing norms around a particular behaviour ('Are other people actually doing this behaviour?').

- *Injunctive norms* are norms around assumptions of normal behaviour based on signs, rules and regulations; that is, whether significant people in your life would approve or disapprove of the behaviour ('What would people think if I undertook this behaviour?').

Schultz and colleagues (2007) demonstrate how these two norms can get confused by examining campaigns that ask young adults not to binge drink. They found that most of these campaigns used descriptive norms that effectively said 'underage drinking is a problem'. This approach was problematic because it gave the impression that *many* underage people drank too much—that it was the norm to drink to excess (even though the campaign was about reducing the incidence of underage drinking). A better strategy in this case is to use 'injunctive norms' that imply a majority of young people *don't* drink too much.

For an example closer to home, I recently received this email from Faye in our office seeking donations for an office initiative to send canned food to the Philippines, which had just suffered a devastating earthquake.

```
-------------------------------------------------
Hi all,

As you know Jax has been collecting all manner
of items from clothing to cans of food to send
across to the Philippines to help those who've
lost everything.

I have to say the box down on level 3 is REALLY
bare and she's due to send the box tomorrow.

So, can we all rally tonight, search your
pantries for a can you can spare. Look in your
wardrobe for that old tshirt, shirt, jeans etc
you haven't worn in years and PLEASE help us
fill the box tomorrow.

We'd really appreciate it and I promise you'll
feel great doing it.

Maraming salamat sa 'yo!

:-)
-------------------------------------------------
```

According to Cialdini's principles, this email (as well intentioned as it is) suggests that people not donating is the norm. Perhaps the email could have used more injunctive norms and been written like this.

```
-------------------------------------------------
Hi all,

As you know Jax has been collecting all manner
of items from clothing to cans of food to send
across to the Philippines to help those who've
lost everything.

So many of you kind-hearted folk have already
donated, and even more have said you will donate
but have forgotten thus far. Well, Jax is due
to send the box tomorrow.

So, can we all rally tonight, search your
pantries for a can you can spare. Look in your
wardrobe for that old tshirt, shirt, jeans etc
```

>>

```
you haven't worn in years and PLEASE help us
fill the box tomorrow.

We'd really appreciate it and I promise you'll
feel great doing it.

Maraming salamat sa 'yo!

:-)
```

This email implies many people have already donated, and that you will be looked upon favourably (by the other 'kind-hearted' folk) if you do the same.

In short, if people are not behaving as you'd like, do not emphasise this. Rather, use injunctive norms to reframe the desired behaviour as something that's already happening and that's likely to get the approval of significant people in their lives.

COOL MODELS

When I worked at Added Value (great company, but not such a great name), I was employed as a global cool hunter. In my late twenties, I got to fly around the world and stay in cool, luxurious hotels. The job involved going out on the streets to spot trends for my clients Pepsi and Levi's. I got the gig because I completed a clinical psychology thesis titled 'Identifying the Underlying Constructs of Cool People' (Ferrier 2014). One of the most interesting findings was that cool things, brands, products and hotels all had one thing in common—as soon as cool people stopped using them, they were no longer cool. Brands are only cool if cool people use them. This spurred my supervisor, Adele Hills, and me to uncover the attributes of cool people. To do this, we asked people to list the coolest and uncoolest people they could think of. Once we constructed a list, we presented it to our participants asking, 'How are these people similar to and different from each other?' This process allowed us to generate a very, very long list of factors. Through statistical analysis, we boiled down the five factors that make someone cool. They are:

1. **Self-belief and confidence:** They have a strong and unwavering sense of self and belief in themselves.

2. **Defying convention:** They follow their own path, especially if it means doing something different.

3. **Understated achievement:** They are successful in whatever they do, but are understated about it. This coincides with a generally strong ability to regulate their mood and put on a 'cool affect'.

4. **Caring for others:** They are often humanitarian, with a caring attitude of others. This is probably related to being an outsider themselves.

5. **Energy and connectedness:** They spend time with other people, the media and the world.

I liked the acronym SeDUCE, or 'The Seduction of Cool' to remember these factors. 'Cool' people tend to be men,[1] adults (i.e. over 18) and with careers related to their true passions: human rights, politics (generally left-of-centre), music and the arts. My time as a cool hunter involved identifying these cool people and understanding their hopes, dreams and lifestyles. I'd feed this information to my clients and they would (theoretically) use this information to develop products and communications that cool people would want.

Cool is an intriguing topic. When I finished my thesis, media outlets from around the world published articles about it, claiming I'd cracked the codes of cool. It even made the front page of the *New Zealand Herald* (perhaps cool is very important to New Zealanders). This was some time ago (2002) and I've since noticed that every two or three years, a Master's student writes a thesis on cool and it's picked up by the media. According to journalist and historian Thomas Frank, author of *The Conquest of Cool* (1997), we all aspire to be cool, at least on some level. Long before my work, advertisers had been taking the codes of cool (outsider, aloof, follows own path—that kind of thing) and feeding it back to consumers. Being cool is still the dominant aspiration aesthetic of our time, and it's the reason cool people are often used for modelling.

MAKING CLICKING COOL

Lynx (or Axe as it is known in most countries) is one of the world's great brands. I say that because it has a clearly defined brand proposition; namely, Lynx 'gives guys the edge in the dating game'. Or more simply—use Lynx and women will find you more attractive. Can you imagine how much fun advertisers have had bringing that promise to life? No wonder it's one of the most desired accounts for an agency. I worked on Lynx for five years and what follows is the first and most audacious piece of work we ever did for it.

Our contact point at Unilever, which produces Lynx, was marketing director Sharon Parker, a no-nonsense Irish woman. She needed assistance launching a new product, Lynx Click, into the Australian market. The launch was global and the brand had secured none other than Hollywood actor Ben Affleck to be part of the campaign.

---

1 Here's something you might find funny. I once gave a talk to a client on how to make brands cool (as you can imagine, a lot of marketers are interested in this subject). The talk was to the entire marketing team of this particular large corporation—and like many marketing teams, it was largely female. As mentioned briefly, one of the things that makes someone cool (according to our research) was being male. One hundred per cent of the cool people nominated by males were male. Well over 50 per cent of the cool people nominated by females were male, too. So males see only other males as cool, while females see both males and females as cool. This is the reason many brands divorce themselves from overt femininity. If you want a car to appeal to both sexes, you model the car with a male driver. I explained this to the marketing team and it didn't go down well. Later that evening, when we were all having a drink, someone (who I'm guessing had a little too much to drink) threw a glass of wine over me, called me a 'sexist pig' and walked off.

Seated in her office, Sharon showed me and my colleague, Paul Swann, a story board for the proposed ad, with line drawings depicting each frame of the ad. It starts with Ben walking down a street with a 'clicker' in his hand. Every time a girl looks at him, he 'clicks' the device. During the day, he racks up a large number of clicks. Then he gets into a lift and stands next to a scrawny looking man who is also holding a clicker. Ben glances down at the guy's clicker and sees it has hundreds more clicks than his. Scrawny man has a secret weapon: he uses Lynx. Turning to Ben, he shrugs as if to say, 'What can you do? Wear Lynx.' Sharon asked for our opinion. We thought it was okay but lacked relevance and context. Paul then asked, 'Why are Ben and the Lynx guy using clickers to keep score of how many girls check them out?' Sharon replied, 'Ha! That's your job. We want you to make clicking popular before this ad is released.'

It was an amazing brief. Unilever has a reputation as a formidable marketer that's not afraid to take risks. Our task was to 'make clicking when girls check you out cool'. If we could achieve this before the ad was shown in Australia, it would look as though Lynx was ahead of the curve with this new trend—giving it cool status.

The first step was to find a person to model clicking and context in which it was suitable to click when girls checked you out. The context was important because 'clicking girls' could seem artificial, sexist (okay, *very* sexist), narcissistic or just plain silly. We thought hip-hop music would be the perfect context because it already involves guys strutting around, expecting to be checked out by girls. In this genre, it's acceptable to demonstrate your sexuality. Further, music is always a popular way to connect with the youth market. We decided to use a hip-hop musician to make clicking cool. This was decided in the taxi ride back to the office.

We enlisted the help of Kim Carter, a talent agent with links to the hip-hop world. She found the up-and-coming Australian duo Ken Hell and Weapon X. They were our ground zero in the quest to make clicking cool. We returned to Sharon's office at Unilever and presented our concept, playing Ken Hell and Weapon X's music and announcing the group would launch the 'International Click Tour' (international was Australia and New Zealand). The group would tour Australia and New Zealand and, at each concert, the band would hold clickers in their hands and click constantly. The crowd would be given free clickers, so they could click when they were checked out, too. 'Clicking' would be the band's signature thing. A website would feature chat-up tips and a running tally of 'clicks', along with footage captured on pinhole cameras worn by the band. Sharon agreed with the strategy and we set out to make clicking cool. Sharon ended up buying the idea, and we set about making it happen, pretty much as we pitched it.

And so Ken Hell and Weapon X did the tour, promoted clicking and, within this subgroup, clicking became a social norm. Later when the ad with Ben Affleck was released, many young guys were now accustomed to (or at least exposed to) the idea of using a clicker. Ken Hell and Weapon X were the equivalent of the lone hillside dancer starting an avalanche. I know it sounds manipulative, but I tell this story to show you how modelling can influence behaviour. It's about making behaviour a social norm.

And the results? Lynx Click was the most successful launch of a brand variant in Australia. The action spur of modelling made a new type of behaviour socially acceptable. You can see the campaign case study on YouTube (www.youtube.com/watch?v=b47J3kytnvg).

...SING USES MODELLING

...odelling principle has broader applications. When we watch certain ...opy it and others copy us. It's how fashion works. You observe the clothes ...wear (or that models in magazines wear) and are influenced to buy similar ...ese are other modelling techniques marketers use:

Testimonials—ask people to write positive comments on 'independent' websites such as *Expedia*. By writing the endorsement, you're modelling the brand to others.

- **Celebrity endorsements**—pay well-known celebrities or credible people to spruik a message.

- **Selective targeting**—identify an aspirational group and ask them to endorse the brand; for example, personal trainers at a gym.

- **Influence targeting**—use models that are experts in a particular niche and have a high degree of social influence. Perhaps the easiest way to measure someone's social influence is to look at their 'Klout' score (www.klout.com), which measures your degree of social influence with a score between 1 (not influential) and 100 (very influential).

- **Social media proofing**—encourage 'Liking' a brand on Facebook or other social media, so people act as models to their friends.

- **Public relations hype**—use PR to make it appear as though many people are involved or excited about a certain brand.

Advertisers spend a lot of time working out who will be the best model for their advertising campaigns. The biggest considerations are accessibility and aspiration. You want someone who is accessible to your audience ('I'm like them', or 'I could be friends with them') yet also aspirational enough to make the brand feel attractive ('I wish I could be more like them'). It's like a tennis 'bumper board' where you can challenge people who are above you in order to move your way up the ladder. Most people will only ever challenge people who are one, two, or three places above them. Challenging the top person doesn't make sense because you're likely to lose.

Broadly speaking, models are category- and task-specific. A well-known cool celebrity might be the perfect choice to model a new brand of gin, but the same celebrity won't be effective in modelling power tools. Effective models have the following characteristics:

1. **Expertise**—the greater their expertise or perceived knowledge of a task, the more successful the model will be.

2. **Attraction/liking**—modelling is more effective when someone likes or can relate to the model. Advertisers work out how much a 'model' is liked using 'Q Scores' or other similar measures. Q Scores, developed in 1963, rank actors, athletes, stars and personalities according to their levels of likeability and awareness (Finkle 1992).

3. **Attention getting**—models who are interesting or unexpected, as well as relatable, will be more effective.

4. **Fit for the job**—this is a 'brand' question. Are they the best person to represent the brand?

CELEBRITY INFLUENCE

One of the most effective models at the moment is Britain's Princess Kate. When Kate wears a particular outfit, women rush to buy it; this has been dubbed the 'Kate Effect'. It's the same with her baby. When Kate bought Prince George a cotton muslin wrap made by aden + anais, demand spiked. Australian aden + anais owner Raegan Moya-Jones told the *New York Daily News*, 'Not in a million years did I ever anticipate the future King of England was going to come out in an aden + anais swaddle. I was dismissive, because I really thought it was a joke. It's been great for business.' Importantly, Princess Kate isn't paid to endorse items, which increases her appeal.

In advertising, we spend a lot of time matching the model and the brand. Beyond Q Scores, in truth there is often little science to the task. It's more a case of:

'Is Ricky Ponting still liked by school kids?'

'Yeah, I think so.'

A client that manufactures yoghurt wanted to use model Miranda Kerr to promote its product. Very little 'science' went into the decision. Kerr was available and interested. In the end, the yoghurt company decided not to use Kerr because she'd endorsed too many other brands at the time.

One of the riskier, yet effective, strategies is when a celebrity is able to demonstrate the effectiveness of a product by putting the theory behind that product into action. In November 2008, comedian Magda Szubanski became an ambassador for weight-loss company Jenny Craig. She already had a popular profile thanks to her role as Sharon on *Kath & Kim*, and the investment by the company initially paid off, with a 50 per cent jump in inquiries after Szubanski signed on. We watched as she shed the kilos and thanked Jenny Craig in magazine articles and interviews.

However, the relationship (and the weight loss) didn't last, and Szubanski broke ties with the company in June 2011. But while Szubanski modelled the behaviour prescribed by Jenny Craig, she influenced others to copy her and sign up to (and perhaps later dump) the weight-loss program.

Another example of an effective celebrity endorsement is Nespresso, in which handsome George Clooney beguiles and amuses women in advertisements filmed across the globe. The company reported a 30 per cent increase in worldwide sales following his endorsement. Why? Clooney is suave and debonair—which is exactly the feel of the product. It's for wealthy, handsome people, like George, who are so busy travelling the globe they don't have time to deal with coffee bean mess. They need pods. Does George keep a Nespresso machine in one of his many homes? We can wonder. Also, George is likeable. In fact, many celebrities are. We like them because they are familiar to us—a perception that is reinforced in magazines, movies and TV. Obviously, we can't all afford to pay George Clooney to model the behaviour we want. But it's okay—other models work just as well.

According to Brown and Fiorella (2013), celebrity endorsements, or celebrities as models, were originally used by emerging brands to reach more people. Today, it's more a case of ensuring the model has the right degree of influence (measured by Klout scores, Q scores and general popularity with the target market) and they have the right brand fit.

JARRAH MODELLING

So how did we use modelling to reinvigorate the all-in-one coffee, Jarrah? We knew Jarrah drinkers liked the taste because sales were steady. The issue was the users' embarrassment about liking the brand. We needed to 'out' Jarrah drinkers so they could see they were not alone. We knew if we modelled an aspirational person consuming it, and enjoying it, others would follow suit. The challenge was finding the appropriate model.

Jarrah's brand proposition was 'a break from the usual'. We wanted people to drink Jarrah instead of their current beverage—normally coffee. Various names were suggested until someone said 'Dame Edna Everage.'

Every Australian knows the purple haired, gladioli-toting character created by performer Barry Humphries. And thanks to appearances in American TV show *Ally McBeal* and several British shows, she has international appeal. Created in the 1950s, Dame Edna satirises narrow-minded Australian suburbia. As a character she felt like an ideal choice because she embraced the slightly dowdy side of the brand, while simultaneously being well known and memorable for the target audience. While not aspirational, focus group participants liked her attitude and irreverent take on life. So how did she perform against our list of characteristics displayed by effective models?

1. *Expertise*—Dame Edna's expertise was 'suburban housewife' and her character would know what to bring for an afternoon hot drink.

2. *Attraction/liking*—Dame Edna is well known and liked. She doesn't have a Q score but focus groups loved the idea. She had the right level of aspiration and accessibility.

3. *Attention getting*—Satirical suburban housewife with purple hair? Tick!

4. *Fit for the job*—The brand proposition was 'a break from the usual'. We thought Dame Edna demonstrated that in spades.

COFFEE TIME

Instead of traditional advertising, we ran a competition inviting people to have coffee with an Australian icon—without letting them know who it was. After interviewing a number of entrants, we selected Helen from Melbourne suburb Moonee Ponds, the 'home' of Dame Edna. During July 2012, we told Helen that an Australian icon was coming for afternoon tea. The plan was that this footage of Dame Edna knocking on their door and surprising them would then become television commercials, as well as a series of online content.

Wearing canary yellow and black, Dame Edna walks along the footpath telling the viewer, 'I'm going to give someone a break from the usual.' After knocking on the front door, it opens and Helen screams, 'Oh my goodness!' Inside Helen's home, Dame Edna prepares some Jarrah coffee, claiming she's always found Jarrah 'rather stimulating'. 'Do I have a

'French Liaison' or a 'White Delight'?' she asks, thumb and forefinger placed along her chin. 'To see Helen and me reveal more, check out the Jarrah Facebook page' intones Edna before clumsily knocking over the promotional pile of Jarrah products. It's irreverent and fun. See the ad on YouTube (www.youtube.com/watch?v=-mZ3aT4LtQo).

When filming the TVC, we filmed other footage of Dame Edna expressing her desire to have a Jarrah with other celebrities and people of influence. It was hoped that in singling out other people of influence, they would become models for other subgroups in the population. The desired effect can be seen in Figure 11.1. This additional content was to be available online, and sent to the various models directly in the hope they would share it on their own social media channels. The content was tweeted to Shane Warne in the hope he would re-tweet it to his million-plus Twitter followers (he didn't).

Figure 11.1 Using multiple models taps into multiple influenced populations

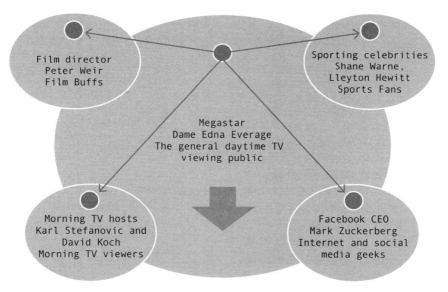

We hoped Dame Edna celebrating the suburbs, and Jarrah, would make people feel better about buying the product. Not only that, because we could use Dame Edna's image on packaging, supermarkets prominently stocked the product. The campaign had mixed success. There was a strong uplift in sales and the retail partners (the supermarkets) were very supportive of this ambitious advertising plan. This is important because retailers like brands to advertise and drive demand because they make money on every sale. In fact, retailers often pressure brands to spend more on advertising in order to maintain a good position on the supermarket shelf. The campaign with Dame Edna was expensive; and even though there was an uplift in sales, it wasn't as high as we had hoped. Our client loved the campaign (as did we), but it wasn't used the following year.

USING MODELLING TO INFLUENCE ACTION

You don't need a high-profile model to elicit the behaviour you want. Think about health professionals who want to influence your behaviour. Are you likely to follow guidance about weight loss from a doctor who is overweight? Other health providers, such as physiotherapists, often have difficulty getting patients to do their exercises. You might know the routine. You visit a physiotherapist in their consulting room and they work out what's wrong with you. You are then given a sheet of paper with a series of exercises written on it to practise at home. Patients that are highly motivated will do the exercises, but many others don't. How could you help patients undertake the behaviour needed for their rehabilitation?

Physiotherapist Anna-Louise Bouvier answered this question with a classic example of modelling. In 1995, she devised a program called Physiocise (www.physiocise.com.au), a series of one-hour classes in which patients learn functional movement and posture from a physiotherapist who leads the class. In a room with full-length mirrors along one wall, up to eight patients watch, and then mimic, the movements demonstrated by the teacher—the model. They do the exercises—undertake the behaviour—with modelling as the spur. People are more likely to practise the behaviour because the teacher is modelling the behaviour.

If you're running a meeting or workshop, model the behaviour you want by speaking first. If you want people to stand when they speak, then stand during your presentation. If you want presenters to sit, then you should sit. If you don't have the skills, choose a suitable model to exhibit the behaviour you want. I have a word of warning, though. Most of us like to believe we are unique individuals who don't conform to the group. If a model is too overt, or the behaviour modelled restricts individual expression, it won't necessarily be copied. Further, the model needs to be the right model according to the criteria discussed previously.

If raising money for the local high school, find out who is influential in the cohort before targeting them. Recruit those who are more influential and have them support your cause. Check their Klout scores. I know it sounds icky, but these scores are now used by brands in their marketing strategies. In May 2013, American Airlines gave people with a Klout score above 55 free entry to their Admirals Club lounges. In 2010, those with high Klout scores were targeted by hotels and offered discounts to stay with them. The hope is they would tweet their network and promote the hotel. The Klout score is a proxy for popularity, and popularity is an important attribute in a model. Why? Because they will reach and influence more people.

MODELLING EVACUATION

Here's further evidence of the copying instinct. One night in 2012, authorities closed the Sydney Harbour Tunnel that connects the northern suburbs and city centre. As yellow flashing arrows directed traffic along a detour on the Cahill Expressway, authorities from the fire brigade drove trucks into the northbound tunnel; 240 metres from the northern exit of the tunnel, the fire fighters stopped their vehicles and placed an old wrecked car in the left hand lane. Then they set it on fire.

As flames and smoke spread through the tunnel, 32 volunteers aged between 16 and 81 were instructed to drive into the tunnel behind a lead car. When they were 100 metres from the burning car, a sign instructed them to stop. And for almost a minute, there was nothing. The volunteers didn't know a group of safety experts were observing their behaviour. Would they follow instructions?

During that first minute, before an announcement was heard through their car radios and public announcement system, the volunteers showed a large amount of indecision, with some people getting out of their cars and then getting back in. Others wound down their window and stuck their head out to see what was happening. One driver even took a photo of the smoke. Then, the safety instructions played, telling people to leave their cars and meet at a marked door that would take them into the southbound carriageway of the tunnel.

The researchers (Burns et al. 2013) observed that drivers appeared reluctant to be the first to leave their car. When interviewed after the evacuation, one said, 'I opened the door when I saw the sign above, then saw others still in cars, so got back in and shut the door.' Another said, 'When other people hesitated to leave their vehicles, it made us unsure.' Another wound down his window to see what others were doing and said, 'As soon as one person opened the car door, so did we.' The first to leave their car was a group of young men. The volunteers were then guided north to the Sydney Harbour Tunnel offices while the burnt wreck was extinguished and removed.

Ninety-four per cent of participants in this study said their decision-making was influenced by the action of others. Even in a potentially life-threatening situation, we work out how we should behave and act according to how other people behave and act. If you find yourself in an emergency situation—try and be aware of the behaviours you are modelling to others. Seriously, Philip Zimbardo (of Stanford Prison Experiment fame) has started up a program called 'Everyday hero'. It teaches people how to act in emergency situations so that lives can be saved.

SUMMARY

In marketing, many of the models used are cool. This is because being cool, the values of cool and the aesthetic of cool are all highly desired by many people in our society. So whether it's a brand of coffee or a 'clicking' trend, we often copy other people—particularly cool people. It's why modelling is a powerful fool of influence. Modelling is most effective when the behaviour is easy to do but there's low motivation. To use modelling to influence behaviour, select the most appropriate model, get people's attention, model the behaviour and watch others play along. At the same time, you have to practise what you preach. There's no point advocating recycling if you don't exhibit the behaviour as well, because people copy your actions rather than your words. Finally, ensure you are modelling the desired behaviour and not the 'descriptive' norm.

The (sort of) Insider: Anna Bongiorno

I think modelling is really important—you've got to do what you say. Say, 'This is the way it should be done', do it and show them, and then get them to do it after you. You have to do this consistently and don't get slack. If I take clients out for a coffee then I'm more conscious of what I'm doing and how I do everything, as I want to provide the best modelling I possibly can. And if I'm dealing with my son, it's the same thing. Children learn by what they see around them, and by who they are living with. So if they see a good caring person, then hopefully they'll become a good caring person. But Adam, I don't want to be quoted in the book.

Anna Bongiorno is my wife, and loving mother to our son Asterix. She's also a social worker working with homeless women, providing them with emergency housing.

REFERENCES

Bandura, A. (1977). *Social Learning Theory.* Englewood Cliffs: Prentice Hall.

Bandura, A., Ross, D. & Ross, S. A. (1961). Transmission of aggression through the imitation of aggressive models. *Journal of Abnormal and Social Psychology*, 63(3), 575–82.

Brown, D. & Fiorella, S. (2013). *Influence Marketing: How to Create, Manage, and Measure Brand Influencers in Social Media Marketing.* New York: Que Publishing.

Burns, P., Stevens, G., Sandy, K., Dix, A., Raphael, B. & Allen, B. (2013). Human behaviour during an evacuation scenario in the Sydney Harbour Tunnel. *Australian Journal of Emergency Management*, 28(1), 20.

Cialdini, R., Kallgren, C. & Reno, R. (1991). A focus theory of normative conduct: A theoretical refinement and re-evaluation of the role of norms in human behaviour. *Advances in Experimental Social Psychology*, 24(20), 201–34.

Ferrier, A. (2013). Identifying the constructs that underlie the concept of a cool person. Figshare.

Finkle, D. (1992). Television; Q-ratings: The popularity contest of the stars. *New York Times*, 7 June. Accessed at http://www.nytimes.com/1992/06/07/arts/television-q-ratings-the-popularity-contest-of-the-stars.html.

Frank, T. (1997). *The Conquest of Cool.* Chicago: University of Chicago Press.

Schultz, P.W., Nolan, J.M., Cialdini, R.B., Goldstein, N.J. & Griskevicius, V. (2007). The constructive, destructive, and reconstructive power of social norms. *Psychological Science*, 18(5), 429–34.

PART

3

EASE ACTION SPURS

EASE ACTION SPURS	The following three ease action spurs increase ability to perform a behaviour: skill up, eliminate complexity and create commitment. In this Part, a chapter is devoted to each
>>	of these spurs.

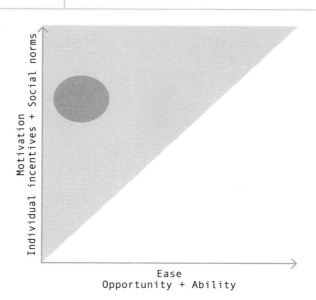

SKILL UP: STOP THE 'I DON'T KNOW HOW'

People ask me what my hobbies are in interviews, and I always say biking. But all I bike for is to get to rehearsal more quickly.

> *Jesse Eisenberg, US actor*

Chess is as elaborate a waste of human intelligence as you can find outside an advertising agency.

> *Raymond Chandler, US author*

PLAYING CHESS

This chapter is about skill. To explain why it's a powerful tool of influence, I'd like to share this achievement. In my youth, I was Western Australian Under 12 Chess Champion. The reason I was so good at chess is because of my grandfather, Rudi. My grandparents, Rudi and Ruth, were Jewish immigrants from Germany. Rudi was lucky to funnel some of the family's money into a plan that allowed for both he and Ruth to escape the Nazis (with the exception of his two brothers, Rex and Gunta, his family was killed in the Holocaust). Rudi and Ruth made their way to London before boarding a ship bound for Sydney. During the voyage, Ruth was so seasick that when they docked in Perth, she decided they were far enough from the war and she was not getting back on that ship. That's why the family settled in Perth.

I was a difficult child. My sister Becky, on the other hand, was wonderful. She was super-smart, extremely diligent and very creative. (As an aside, Becky also works in advertising and scored her first job at Saatchi & Saatchi in Singapore while we were on holiday, after showing them her portfolio from Advertising AWARD School.)[1] Becky was born on Rudi's birthday and was always his favourite—all the grandkids knew and accepted this.

I remember Rudi as an elegant, charming, intelligent and much-loved man. He was also a talented bridge and chess player. It was Ruth who decided Rudi should teach me to play chess—as a way to forge a bond between us. I still remember our early games. We'd pull out a large chess board with green and white squares and place it on a glass coffee table. Rudi would sit in his blue velvet chair and I'd kneel on the floor. In the early games, Rudi would sacrifice all his pieces except for his king, queen and a few pawns. He still beat me, but it didn't matter. I still remember feeling excitement when we started playing. I loved it. I loved the intense concentration, thinking up strategies and trying to keep multiple moves in my head. We'd often play several games in a row—so he must have enjoyed it, too.

---

1 If you live in Australia and want to become a 'creative' within an advertising agency, one of the traditional and effective ways to do this is to attend AWARD school.

Eventually, after a year or two of consistent playing, I started to occasionally beat Rudi. At this point, he took me to play chess with his friends at their houses. There I was, a rambunctious little kid, playing chess well into the evenings with six or seven elderly Jewish immigrants. My Mum encouraged my interest in chess and entered me into several chess competitions. Before the tournaments, she prepared meals containing fish (brain food).

In time, I became relatively good for my age, this was due more to practice than innate talent. In his 2008 book *Outliers*, Malcolm Gladwell makes the case that a skill becomes proficient after 10,000 hours of practice. I don't know if I made it to 10,000 hours, but at the peak of my powers, I was a pretty good chess player.

Having played so much chess so early in life, I was able to recognise patterns on the chessboard instantly and could review potential strategies in my head before deciding on my move. Kahneman (2011) believes chess uses both System 1 thinking (where tentative plans come together) before the brain employs a deliberate process that works through rationales and System 2 thinking (see Chapter 5 for more on system thinking). The more proficient you are at a task, the more complexity you can handle. Chess Grand Masters can beat ordinary players, often several at once, operating entirely in the System 1 mode. I didn't find chess tiring or stressful; to me it was a pleasurable experience—and whenever anyone asked me for a game I'd eagerly accept. When people find it something easy to do, they'll be more likely to do it.

THIS CLIENT IS CRAP

Simon Griffiths used to lecture in economics at the University of Melbourne and now works as a social entrepreneur. This means his businesses are attached to, and help support, social causes, working to a socio-capitalistic business model (basically doing good whilst making money). He needed help with a new venture and arranged to come to our offices. Before the meeting, I did a Google search and discovered Simon had these achievements:

- First class honours degree
- Short-listed for the Rhodes Scholarship in 2006
- Exhibition (highest mark) for Finance for New Ventures, University of Melbourne, 2005
- Golden Key Honorary Member, 2013
- SOCAP Conference (USA) Scholarship Winner, 2010 and 2012
- Summit Series (USA) Fellow, 2011
- TEDxMelbourne Speaker, 2011
- Fellow of the Unreasonable Institute (USA), 2010
- Fellow of the School for Social Entrepreneurs (Australia), 2010
- Shortlisted for Echoing Green (USA) Fellowship, 2010.

Okay, so we had one very smart cookie coming to meet us. When he arrived at our offices, he didn't match our expectations of a serious academic type at all: he was young, hip and extremely confident. Simon shared his venture with us. He wanted to produce and sell toilet paper. Now, at first glance, that's not very exciting until you discover that the production process for this toilet paper would use fewer toxins than regular toilet paper, and 50 per cent of the profits from its sales would support clean water and sanitation projects in the developing world. Simon started the company when he and his business partners learned that 2.5 billion people across the world don't have access to a clean toilet. That's roughly 40 per cent of the global population and means diarrhoea-related diseases fill over half of sub-Saharan hospital beds. It kills 2000 children aged under 5 years every day. Sobering statistics.

Simon told us he needed to raise $50,000 to have the first shipment of toilet paper manufactured. The name of the toilet paper was Who Gives A Crap. As an aside, Simon and I discovered we attended the same primary school in Perth—Swanbourne Primary. 'Swanny' was a fantastic school and has a dear place in my heart. We told Simon we'd love to be involved and calculated our fee at 20 per cent of every dollar raised over the $50,000 target. He agreed.

'SKILLING UP' AND ADVERTISING

If you're reading this book in order (or even if you're not), you'll notice that this is the first chapter dealing with ease action spurs. As explained in Chapters 3 and 4, many advertisers have traditionally tried to change behaviour by increasing people's motivation to do something. However, what if the motivation is already there—but people just don't have the skills to do what it is that you want them to do? In an increasingly complex world, the biggest barriers to people not buying your brand, or not doing what you want them to do, may simply be that they don't know how to do it.

So, though it might not seem obvious, teaching skills is important in advertising. Just as I didn't buy a chessboard until I knew how to play chess, I didn't order a glass of whisky at a bar until I knew the language of whisky. This is the reason whisky brands spend money hosting whisky tasting events. It's not only so people can taste the product but also to educate attendees on whisky language and the nuances of styles and flavours. People leave with a better understanding of the culture surrounding the drink, but more importantly they've been skilled up in how to talk about (and describe the taste of) whisky. This makes it far more likely that they will buy the product in the future, particularly in bars or pubs as they won't be so worried about being seen as ignorant.

Some people like to remain blissfully ignorant about how to perform certain tasks so they can avoid doing them, such as a child claiming they can't wash the dishes—'I don't know how'. Others will quietly avoid doing something if they don't know how. Not having the skills to do something is a real and everyday barrier to people adopting a behaviour you want them to. To remedy this situation, the first thing you do is to give them the skills they claim they're missing. It's the same with advertising. People aren't going to buy your product if they don't have the skills to use it. **It's no longer good enough to make people 'aware' of a brand. They need to know how to use products, too.**

EXPLAINER VIDEOS

Ever wondered how to place a baby in a car seat capsule? It was only while making preparations for the birth of our son, that my wife said, 'You know you're going to have to drive us home from hospital. You know it means we need a car-seat capsule for the baby.' In that moment I realised I had no idea what was involved—I'd never paid attention to baby seats and had never placed a child in one. I was obviously motivated to find out how to strap my son into the baby seat to be safe and sound, but I lacked the skills to do so. So I went to a store, bought a capsule and had a guy install it for me. When he'd almost finished putting the seat in the car, I asked, 'Mate. How do you actually put a baby in that thing?'

Instead of ridiculing me, the guy pulled out a plastic doll and said, 'Meet Dorothy.'

Then the guy asked if I had a smartphone: 'You can film me demonstrating what to do and watch it when you need to.'

And so, on a chilly Saturday morning, I filmed a guy placing a doll called Dorothy into a car seat capsule. I've got say, that video helped me, and my wife, several times. It was a great training tool. We also watched explainer videos to find out how to use our Bugaboo pram, and I now use both the capsule and pram proficiently.

Writing in the *Huffington Post* (2012), Jim Kukral claimed, 'Explainer videos are the new infographic.' Normally quite short (1–3 minutes), these videos are easy to share across online platforms and can be added to newsletters, social media and websites. They have become popular because: a) people need to quickly learn new skills or adapt to a new piece of technology; and b) smartphones and ISP internet bandwidth improvements allow video messages to be played anywhere.

Sunny Arora (2013) at *Bloggers Passion* believes explainer videos can be used to:

1. **launch a product**—help people internally understand the new product or service

2. **elaborate on complex information**—such as using a pram

3. **connect with your customer**—often it's much easier to demonstrate something visually than describe it in writing, such as unfolding a Bugaboo pram

4. **reach out to more people**—video content is sharable, so there's no reason why an explainer video can't be compelling and sharable, too

5. **differentiate**—if you're the only company using explainer videos, you can potentially be a more effective communicator than the competition.

In my experience, explainer videos are a fantastic way to influence behaviour because they give people the skills to make a purchase and, if entertaining, increase the time spent with the brand. Obviously, video content is increasingly important as more and more people buy products online, but consumers won't buy what they don't know how to use. Providing them with the ability or skills is crucial.

A FEEL-GOOD TOILET EXPERIENCE

How could we use the 'Skill Up' Action Spur to help Simon raise $50,000? I enlisted the help of psychologist Simon Thatcher, who specialises in the relationship between the mind and body. He also happens to live in an isolated bush cabin and is one of the most interesting and lovely people I know. Simon told us that going to the toilet was 'the most mindful experience most of us have in our day'. He explained that being mindful is about being in the present moment—of not worrying about the past or the future. He said that sitting on a toilet was about 'going into an isolated small room and thinking about nothing else but your body. In the moment of doing a poo, all other worries fade away. When someone goes to the toilet, they want a "feel-good experience".'

We took these insights and created a frame (see Chapter 5) around the idea of 'feel-good toilet paper'. With 50 per cent of profits going to sanitation projects in developing countries, people should feel good that their money is helping those in need. Our challenge was to explain this rather complicated story to people who had never heard of the brand. We needed to tell them about the brand proposition, explain the cause, and make it easy for them to donate. We decided the best way to educate people about the brand was through an explainer video—one that people would want to watch.

This is how Simon raised the cash. When you click 'play' on the video, you hear 1950s-style music and see the words, 'What if every crap you took made a difference?' Blue-eyed, ginger-bearded Simon introduces himself, and then the camera pans out— his pants are around his ankles and he's seated on a toilet. Using a roll of toilet paper as a prop, he explains his cause, with plenty of puns thrown into the pitch. At the end of the video, Simon announces he won't shift from the toilet until $50,000 is raised—and to prove it, you can watch him on live streaming video. The donation was framed as a challenge. Because **people respond to scarcity**, donations could only be given within a specified time frame; and we **built authenticity** by using Simon, the CEO of the company.

The explainer video (at www.youtube.com/watch?v=WdWZ8WVv6qk) was shared across the globe and the donations came in. Simon raised the first $50,000 in 50 hours and got off the toilet with glee. He decided to 'have a second push', raising a total of $65,000. More than 77,000 people visited the site and more than 1300 people donated money or bought toilet paper.

The stunt struck a chord with media around the world. One headline exclaimed, 'Holy crap: Why's this guy stuck on the toilet?' (Paine 2012), with the video embedded in the news story. It was mentioned in publications as diverse as *Fast Company*, *Huffington Post* and *MTV*. It trended on Twitter, reaching 2.5 million people, aided by influencers such as Guy Kawasaki, TEDx, Missy Higgins, Unicef, Innocent Drinks, Triple Pundit, Unmarketing, GOOD, Paul Pollack and Andrew Bloc. And www.indigogo.com, the crowdsourcing site that housed the video, now uses it as an example of how to create these types of videos. Further, they listed it as one of their top 12 campaigns of 2012 (Nunnelly 2012). The business Who Gives a Crap is now up and running. You can read more about them at http://whogivesacrap.org. As they say, thanks for giving a crap. See the case study on YouTube (www.youtube.com/watch?v=rz1T-qXmx_I).

DON'T EVER ASSUME

Advertisers often assume that to change behaviour, they need to increase people's motivation. Sometimes, however, they just need to make the behaviour easier to do. When I stayed at the W Hotel on Sentosa Island, Starwood's 'hip' hotel brand, everything was designed to look super-cool. Some of the features were so cool I didn't know how to use them. When I used the shower on my first morning, I tried to turn on the tap. After a few befuddled attempts I read the sign above the shower handle that instructed:

1. Please lift

2. Turn to your desired temperature

While this little sign helped me to work out how to use the shower handle, what did it say about its functionality? Although it was designed to be cool, the shower handle wasn't designed for ease of use.

A more serious example comes from North Dakota in the USA, where it gets very, very cold, with an average maximum of around −5°C for five months of the year. As a consequence, many people are susceptible to the flu, especially those over the age of 65 (90 per cent of those who die from flu-related causes are aged over 65). A flu shot in a place like North Dakota is a big deal because it can mean the difference between life and death. However, it's difficult for those living in the rural parts of the state to get one. Even though the flu shot is fully subsidised (that is, free), knowing where, when and how to get the shot was proving a significant barrier.

Psychologists from North Dakota State University tested if different messages increased flu immunisations (McCaul, Johnson & Rothman 2012). They mailed 16,000 letters to North Dakota rural residents aged over 65. Some received a 'reminder letter' and others received an 'action letter'. Both letters included general information about the flu and its health risks (McCaul, Johnson & Rothman 2012):

> The flu season will soon be upon us, and it's time for you to make arrangements to get your flu shot. Flu, or influenza, is an easily spread virus, and flu shots are for anyone who wants to reduce the risk of catching the disease and avoid illness and hospitalization.

The action letter also included information on the exact times and places when health units would be conducting flu shot clinics, and informed people about exactly how they could get their flu shots (what they had to bring and so on). The letter concluded by stating:

> Medicare B pays for flu shots. Please bring your Medicare card with you to the flu clinic.

The results are telling. The letter with the action message (informing them exactly what they needed to do to get the shot) increased flu shot redemption by almost a third, from 19.6 per cent to 28.2 per cent. The simple act of including practical information about how to receive the flu shot increased compliance. The information gave the people the skills to get their flu shot—it made the behaviour easier to do.

HOW SKILLING UP HELPS

Skilling up is about making a task easier through capacity building and providing resources to confidently engage in the behaviour. Influencing behaviour is often as simple as showing someone how to do a task—of giving them the skills. There are several ways to impart skills, including:

- Provide **training** through instruction manuals, guides, videos and programs. (Take a look at the instruction guide for an iPhone these days. It's very short, very simple and very easy to read and apply.)

- Allow people to **practise**, try out, sample or get experience before committing to a purchase (or any other type of behavioural change).

- Provide tools that give useful **information**, such as bus/train/ferry routes and schedules, and guides on the most efficient way to do things. (When done well, this assists behaviour, but it can go horribly wrong as the doomed Microsoft Paperclip showed.)

- Give people **extra resources**, such as offering interest-free periods to buy items, helping them to fill out forms or providing assistance to get from home to a store.

These strategies increase someone's ability to undertake behaviour and assists with influence. Teaching skills improves your chances of behaviour change.

Skilling up also relates to a concept known as '**self-efficacy**', which refers to a person's belief in their ability to succeed in a given situation. The higher our self-efficacy, the greater the likelihood we'll see challenges and obstacles as simply tasks to be mastered. I read about this concept in Dr Bob Montgomery's book *The Truth about Success and Motivation* (1988). I like Bob Montgomery not just because he was President of the Australian Psychological Society for several years or because he is one of Australia's most respected psychologists or because he taught me during my postgraduate year at university. I like him because I've applied many of his ideas to my life and they've made a positive difference.

Bob believes we have two fundamental life drivers: a drive for **pleasure** and a drive for **mastery**. We feel pleasure during a holiday, an indulgent meal at a restaurant or a massage. But we won't feel completely satisfied unless we also aim for mastery, such as overcoming obstacles, making our mark, or setting challenges and achieving them. Mastery includes both internal drivers, such as pride and satisfaction, and external drivers, such as money and status. One of the main things that prevents people from achieving mastery is ability—they don't have the skills. Therefore giving people the skills to do something increases their sense of self-efficacy, and therefore their ability to master their environment.

Australian psychologist Mary Luszcz (1993) looked at the interrelationship between ageing and memory function. In her experiment, she asked 40 young people (with an average age of 23), and 40 older people (with an average age of 73) to indicate how good they thought their memory was. She then gave them a series of memory tests. Interestingly, she found that age wasn't a predictor of memory ability; rather, those who believed that getting older meant their memory would deteriorate had poorer memories. Sometimes 'skilling up' can look like 'revving up'—helping someone to realise they already have the skills to do something.

SKILLS CHECKLIST

When creating a strategy to upskill a targeted group of people, use the following approach:

1. **Audit** the current understanding and capabilities of behaviour. Do people understand what's required of them? Do they have the ability to do it? Do they believe they have the ability to do it? What are the gaps?

2. Develop a **program** to upskill the group. Create tools to help people become skilled, such as an explainer video.

3. Remember that **mastery beats reward**. Where possible, tap into internal motivators to build a sense of mastery. People are not only motivated by external rewards such as money but also by a sense of satisfaction and mastery.

ANGER MANAGEMENT

Ability and skill isn't restricted to physical tasks; you can teach psychological skills as well (Schacter, Gilbert & Wegner 2010). In fact, strategies to manage anger were an important part of my work at a minimum-security prison in Oberon, NSW. Many inmates had difficulty controlling their anger, and even though most were motivated to change, they didn't know how to stop themselves from erupting when they became angry. Many grew up in homes that solved problems using violence, and they continued this practice in their own lives.

When working at the jail, I implemented an 'anger management' program where, on a Wednesday afternoon, six to 10 inmates would gather in a small room. With tables and desks pushed to the side, we'd sit on flimsy chairs placed in a circle. The inmates were dressed in green tracksuits and smelt of 'White Ox', a brand of roll-your-own tobacco many were addicted to. The energy of the room was pretty chaotic. To give you an idea, think back to your school days and the most badly behaved kid. Now, double the disruptiveness and apply it to everyone in the classroom. That's the kind of energy we had in the workshop.

The course taught them different options they could pursue rather than swinging a punch. I told them about meditation, deep breathing and calming techniques. I also talked about irrational thinking patterns and how to replace unhelpful thoughts with more helpful ones. We discussed the fight-or-flight response and why your heart beats faster as the body deals with stress or anger. Later in the course, the inmates practised real-life skills and role-play. I'd often play the role of their loved one or a person they'd met at the pub who aroused anger in them. Although straightforward, I believe this injection of 'skill' helped the inmates reduce their violent behaviour.

Skills can also help with the treatment of phobias (Choy, Fyer & Lipsitz 2007). People learn that when they are exposed to a particular stimulus, they feel fearful and their anxiety rises. If they allow themselves to accept this feeling, despite exposure to the fearful stimulus their anxiety will eventually subside and they will feel better. It involves incremental exposure. In the case of a fear of spiders, you start with a photo of a spider, then introduce a dead spider and, eventually, a live spider. It's unrealistic to expect to change someone's fear without giving them skills. Without these skills, it doesn't matter how motivated they are to change, they won't be able to achieve it.

One of the easiest ways to remove the barrier of 'I don't know how' is to show or demonstrate the skills needed to undertake the behaviour. If your child complains that they don't know how to stack and unstack the dishwasher, create a video using your smartphone. At the office, if someone is nervous about how to run workshop, create a video tutorial. If someone doesn't know how the office recycling works, pair them with a 'buddy' or appoint a recycling coach to give them the skills.

DON'T JUST SAY NO

Changing behaviour without teaching appropriate skills can be ineffective and even futile. One example is the 'Just Say No' anti-drugs campaign championed in the 1980s in the USA by former First Lady, Nancy Reagan. The campaign encouraged young people to resist peer pressure by saying 'No' if offered drugs. While Reagan certainly increased awareness of drugs, and no one can deny the destruction caused by drug abuse, a direct relationship between reduced drug use and the Just Say No campaign was never established.

Nancy Reagan had a simplistic solution to a complex problem. The campaign failed to give people the tools to deal with drug-taking situations. It also failed to acknowledge that many people experiment with drugs and don't become hard-core addicts.

Fisher and Birch (1999) at Penn State University examined the Just Say No effect on children who liked to eat 'cookies'. Families were divided into two groups and each mother was given a full jar of cookies to take home. In the first group, the mums were told to say 'No' when their child asked for a cookie. In the other group, the mums sometimes gave a cookie when asked, and sometimes refused. The results are fascinating. The group that was told 'No' became more obsessed with the cookie jar. They talked about it more often and asked more often than the other group. When you tell children they can't have something, it can increase their motivation to ask for it.

Successful behaviour change is rarely about just telling people to do something. Enduring and self-directed behaviour change is achieved by giving people the skills to work things out for themselves. As Confucius said, 'Tell me, I forget. Show me, I remember. Involve me, I understand.'

SUMMARY

It's often claimed that advertisers brainwash consumers to buy, buy, buy. There's a perception the advertiser creeps into your mind and motivates you to make a purchase. But if you don't know how to make the purchase, no amount of motivation will work. My sister has never bought a chess set, yet I've bought several—but only after I learned the skills of the game. The more people learn about your business or mission, and how to engage with it, the easier it is for them. It sounds like an obvious consideration, but it is so obvious that people forget to do it. If someone lacks the skills to undertake behaviour you seek, your attempts will be futile. Your task is to give them the necessary skills, as in the case of prison inmates who needed to learn skills to reduce their violent behaviour. Similarly, the Who Gives a Crap case revealed that people are willing to support a worthy cause: they just needed to know why and, most importantly, how to do so.

The Insider: Jon Casimir

My first response is that maybe you should consider not doing it at all. Maybe you should leave other humans alone for a change, particularly if you're a brand marketer. There are already way too many people trying to change our behaviours, most of them taking aim at behaviours that don't need to be changed. And let's be frank: it's hard enough keeping up with our lives, trying to bring meaning to them, without the constant, nagging incursions of boundary-ignoring marketers. So if you want to change behaviour to sell us something we don't need, why not try something else for a living? Landscape gardening looks like fun ...

All right, that's a narrow view (of behavioural change, not gardening). Many behaviours *do* need to be changed, and almost all of us are, in some way, in the persuasion business: Watch this! Buy this! Learn this! Eat this! Think about this! Vote for this! Believe in this! So my small piece of advice is to give more than you take. Be as altruistic as you can be. At the core of the *Gruen* programs, there's an acknowledged desire for behavioural change. We'd like people to think more about the messages they consume; about the ways in which we are all bought and sold. As television producers, we try to respect viewers by making a program that is entertaining and full of ideas, that more than repays the investment in time and attention. We have never made the show to become wealthy or to boost someone's bottom line (though it does provide a happy work life for us). We make the show because we think it's part of the solution rather than the problem, in the hope that it will stimulate a conversation we reckon Australians ought to have. And, if we're really honest, because we'd be crap at gardening.

Jon Casimir is the co-creator and executive producer of the *Gruen* series on ABC TV. But he is also a published author (four times over), and before that a journalist. I met Jon when he was doing the rounds interviewing advertising people to be on his show. I have gotten to know Jon bit by bit over the years: he's fascinated by people, and seems determined to create TV that helps people as it entertains. Jon is also a funny guy, and great company.

REFERENCES

Arora, S. (2013). Ten compelling reasons to go for explainer videos. *Bloggers Passion*. Accessed at http://bloggerspassion.com/ten-compelling-reasons-to-go-for-explainer-videos.

Choy, Y., Fyer, A.J. & Lipsitz, D.J. (2007). Treatment of specific phobia in adults. *Clinical Psychology Review*, 27(3), 266–86.

Fisher, J.O. & Birch, L.B. (1999). Restricting access to palatable foods affects children's behavioral response, food selection and intake. *American Journal of Clinical Nutrition*. 69(6), 1264–72.

Gladwell, M. (2008). *Outliers*. New York: Little, Brown & Co.

Kahneman, D. (2011). *Thinking, Fast and Slow*. New York: Macmillan.

Kukral, J. (2012). Explainer videos are the new infographics. *Huffington Post*, 19 September. Accessed at www.huffingtonpost.com/jim-kukral/social-media-marketing-videos-_b_1895514.html.

Luszcz, M.A. (1993). When knowing is not enough: The role of memory beliefs in prose recall of older and younger adults. *Australian Psychologist*, 28(1), 16–20.

McCaul, K.D., Johnson, R.J. & Rothman, R.J. (2002). The effects of framing and action instructions on whether older adults obtain flu shots. *Health Psychology*, 21(6), 624–8.

Montgomery, B. (1988). *The Truth about Success and Motivation*. London: Thorsons.

Nunnelly, A. (2012). Indigogo's top 12 campaigns of 2012. *Indigogo*. Accessed at http://blog.indiegogo.com/2012/12/top12.html.

Paine, C. (2012). Holy crap: Why's this guy stuck on the toilet? News.com.au, 12 July. Accessed at www.news.com.au/national/holy-crap-we-interviewed-a-guy-on-a-toilet/story-fndo4eg9-1226424152625.

Schacter, D.L., Gilbert, D.T. & Wegner, D.M. (2010). *Psychology* (2nd edn). New York: Worth Publishing.

ELIMINATE COMPLEXITY: KNOCK DOWN THE HURDLES

To me, error analysis is the sweet spot for improvement.

Donald Norman, *US cognitive scientist*

It's possibly the most disgusting ad I've ever seen in my life. It might be the most disgusting anything I've ever seen in my life.

Will Burns, Forbes *(2012)*

PIMPLES AND 14-YEAR-OLD BOYS

The body plays a cruel trick on the average 14-year-old boy. It's called puberty and when it hits, it releases hormones that not only make a boy sex-obsessed, but can also play havoc with his skin (a rather unfortunate combination). The result? Pus-filled pimples—and lots of them. Enter Mentholatum, creator of pimple cream Oxy, a product especially designed for teenage boys. The issue was how the company could connect with zit-afflicted boys and convince them to use the cream.

From the outset, there were a couple of stumbling blocks. For starters, Oxy was only stocked by pharmacies. Can you tell me the last time you saw a 14-year-old boy at a pharmacy? These stores are packed with embarrassing, foreign products for a start. Another problem is that many teenage boys are too embarrassed to ask their mum or dad to buy them pimple cream. If the cream is already in the bathroom, they might use it—but most would never ask for it directly. Those who do ask often don't know brand names, which is an issue for supplier and advertiser alike. Our task was to make it easy for young boys with pimples to request an Oxy sample. The company had assembled 10,000 samples to give away in the belief that once boys tried Oxy pimple cream, they'd ask for it by name. A complicating factor was that the company had a very limited budget.

In working out the strategy, we went to Google and typed the word 'pimple' into the search bar. After Wikipedia, the second most popular result was a YouTube video titled 'Best Pimple Pop Ever', with an image of two fingers placed ominously around what appears to be a massive pimple. The video is really gross. But of interest to us was the number of views for this video: 12 million and counting. It wasn't the only one either—there were many pimple popping videos available and most had loads of views. Who would go to YouTube to watch pimples being popped? It was our target audience: teenage boys. From this insight, our strategy took shape.

ZOMBIES AND ELIMINATING COMPLEXITY

By and large, people are relatively lazy (or at least their brains are). We use the least amount of effort and thinking possible. There's a view in psychology (popularised by celebrity psychologist Dr Phil) that 'the biggest predictor of future behaviour is past behaviour'. This is particularly the case with criminals (Mossman 1994). Humans learn patterns of behaviour, they repeat the behaviour and these behaviours become habits. As we learnt in Chapter 5, we like to use System 1 thinking—that is, to operate on autopilot (Kahneman 2011).

This chapter is about **'eliminating complexity'** and making it easier for people to undertake behaviour. It differs from skilling up (Chapter 12), which is about teaching skills or increasing people's ability to do a behaviour. The boys targeted by Oxy never went into pharmacies, rarely went into supermarkets and seemed reluctant to ask their mothers to buy a pimple cream. They had the ability to ask for it, but their life circumstances meant they didn't have a suitable opportunity. **Eliminating complexity is about modifying the environment or context of the behaviour to make it easier.**

Modifying the environment to make a behaviour happen may at first might seem like wasted effort. If people are motivated to do something, and have the skills to do it, then surely they'll do it? This might be true if someone has high motivation to complete a task, but what if their motivation is relatively low, or almost non-existent, and we still want them to do something? This is where the zombies come into it.

While we are on auto-pilot we operate like zombies and stick to routines. Think of the archetypal zombie, who walks slowly, arms outstretched, searching for victims. If something is placed in their path, they stop and repeatedly walk into it. So think of the zombie when eliminating complexity: you have to remove any barriers that get in their path.

When we go shopping, for example, we generally use System 1 thinking—autopilot. We select the same items and ritualise the shop as much as possible to minimise the cognitive effort required. It's the reason supermarkets charge more if a brand is stocked at eye level.[1] The zombie doesn't like to bend over or reach to retrieve the product. Barden (2013) argues that products have to be easy to identify and read because the consumer doesn't want to think. In other words, eliminate complexity by using large, clear graphics and strong colours, and ensuring every part of the packaging communicates the same story about that brand. Eliminating complexity means thinking about the large and

---

1 Many brands will pay supermarkets extra to have their brands stocked at eye level, rather than higher (making the zombie reach up) or lower (making the zombie bend down). This extra payment is called a 'slotting fee'. If you go to your local supermarket and look at the shelves, you may notice that the brands at eye level are the supermarket's home brands (if no one pays the slotting fee, they'll put their own brands there). The other thing you may notice is that the supermarket's home brands are often designed to resemble the market-leading brand of that category. The supermarkets have realised that if they stock their own brand at eye level and design the packaging to look similar to the market leader, people (in their zombie-like, System 1 state) tend to absent-mindedly choose the brand that's in front of them (even if it's just a poor imposter).

small barriers that prevent people from undertaking a task. The fewer steps needed for a purchase, the less people have to think, the more likely it will happen (whether shopping offline or online).

WHY ELIMINATING COMPLEXITY WORKS

Further recapping Kahneman's system thinking, System 1 thinking is fast, intuitive and emotional, and connected to the world through the senses. It makes snap judgments and uses generalisations, stereotypes and rules of thumb. By contrast, System 2 is the slower, reasoned and rational part of the brain. It's the part that actually stops and thinks. To illustrate this point, have a go at answering this equation:

$7 \times 13 = ?$

What's your answer? Please have a go now—it's not that hard. Here's a clue: the answer is less than 100. Are you still resisting? If so, was it too hard to solve? Why didn't you work it out?

What if I'd asked you to work out 2×4? Would you do that?

$2 \times 4 = ?$

It's much easier, right? What I hope you experienced was the difference between System 1 and System 2 thinking, and the laziness of your brain. Rather than shifting to System 2 thinking, your brain likes to stay with System 1. So even if you did answer the first equation, you probably experienced a brief pause while your brain mentally shifted gears to deal with a problem that couldn't be answered automatically. If you didn't bother to work out the answer (which is 91, by the way), your brain was likely finding it too taxing to make the switch to System 2 to work it out. But rather than admit to laziness, the brain comes up with rationalisations for this behaviour. In the case of this maths problem, you might have said, 'I can't be bothered', or 'I'll pretend I tried', or 'It's not important', or 'I could work it out if I wanted to but I don't see the value in it.' In *The Simpsons* (1992), Homer, the ultimate anti-hero slob tells his son Bart, 'If something's too hard to do, then it's not worth doing.' It's an amusing inversion of the usual advice. If a task is difficult, we often procrastinate or invent a reason for not completing it. If we can't easily achieve an outcome, especially in cognitive tasks, we'll park it and rationalise our avoidance of it, just as Homer does.

RED MEANS GO AND GREEN MEANS STOP?

Have you ever checked in for a flight online? Or have you used one of those little computers in the airport terminal (where the people used to be)? At the page that asks if are you carrying any dangerous goods like knives, poisons or guns, you'll notice something odd. There are two response buttons to the question. One says 'No' and the other says 'Yes'. The interesting thing about these buttons is that the 'No' button is green and the 'Yes' button is red. Which one would you press?

Figure 13.1 Are you carrying dangerous goods on a flight?

YES (Red background)	**NO** (Green background)

This is a deliberate ploy by the interface designers to make you stop and carefully consider your options. Normally, we expect green to indicate permission: 'I am not carrying any dangerous goods, so I can continue'. Red means stop: 'I am carrying dangerous goods, so I have a problem!'. Normally, when trying to eliminate complexity we want things to be as smooth as possible, and to operate seamlessly. However, in changing the colour from one that's expected to one that's unexpected, you can halt the zombied self making people stop and actually think.

This is a clever adaptation of the Stroop effect (Stroop 1935). Named after American psychologist John Ridley Stroop, it is one of the most commonly cited and repeated effects in psychology. It's been replicated more than 700 times (MacLeod 1991) and has found its way into brain-training games that assume the brain has a high degree of neuroplasticity (Pinaud, Tremere & De Weerd et al. 2006). The Stroop effect is illustrated through a list of colour nouns that are written in colours different from the noun itself; so the word 'orange' is written in blue, 'yellow' is written in green, and so on. It's easily found on Google. Bring up the image and read the names of the colours out loud as quickly as possible. The incongruity of the word being printed in a different colour from what you are being asked to read aloud creates confusion.

This is a cognitively complex task because we have two bits of competing stimuli to process. Therefore, it takes cognitive effort to say the correct colour (and not the name of the contradictory colour). We may be okay at it at first, but we quickly tire and it becomes increasingly difficult. To do this task, you need to operate in System 2, and this soon becomes hard work and tiresome.

Again, we like to process the environment around us assumptively—and believe it's going to be intuitive. If we see green buttons, we'll assume they mean 'Go'. If we see doors with flat metal plates on them, we'll assume they are for pushing, not pulling, and so on. To encourage a particular behaviour, we need to eliminate any possible complexity that could get in the way of that behaviour—no matter how trivial it seems.

LESSONS FROM A POKER MACHINE

Imagine creating a device that people repeatedly and voluntarily put money into without any certainty of a return. Of course, you don't need to imagine it—it already exists. In fact, the poker machine is a perfect example of a device that eliminates complexity.

I encountered my first poker machine on a cruise ship during a family holiday in the Greek Islands when I was 12 years old. Despite the sun and scenery, a great on-deck pool and other activities, I became glued to the three poker machines on the ship. I begged, borrowed and probably stole money to play them. I'd plead with my parents, 'Can I please have 20 drachma?' (the Greek currency at the time). I remember placing a coin in the slot and pulling a long handle with a small black ball on the top. A solid 'click' would sound as I waited for the three rotating discs to stop. The first wheel would then stop, closely followed by the second. If there were two gold bars in a row, I'd get excited. Where would the third wheel stop? Damn. On the cherries. Every attempt at winning was great fun and full of suspense. The wait seemed to go on forever.

Since then, I've loved gambling, but today I realise that the more I gamble, the more I lose. It's the business model. Poker machines pay around 85 cents for every dollar down the slot, which means if you play for long enough, you'll lose. It's a fact. The machines take significantly more than they give. Even though many people know this, they keep on playing—using System 1 thinking. System 2 thinking tells people they shouldn't play, and the makers of poker machines know this. Therefore they make it as easy as possible for someone to use the machine, and try to make it more compelling for them to keep playing. It's why poker machines have changed so much since I was a kid on that cruise ship:

- The handle has disappeared and been replaced with a big bright button. Pulling a handle is more difficult and time-consuming. A big red button is quicker and easier, and the red communicates urgency.
- The newer machines are much faster. The fruits line up—or more often, don't line up—much more quickly.
- There are flashing lights and noises of bells and whistles with every win, but silence when you lose.

Poker machines have eliminated complexity so people like me can play, and keep on playing. There's no long wait for the wheels to drop, as I might become distracted or ask, 'What am I doing? This is silly.' In *Wired* magazine (Venkataramanan 2013), gambling expert Natasha Shüll describes how poker machine manufacturers have eliminated complexity by:

1. tilting the screen at 38 degrees to maintain the player's posture so they don't feel tired
2. creating a sound cone around the player to avoid the distraction of the outside world
3. providing comfy seats to encourage longer play
4. using credit play—machines now accept large bank notes or casino reward cards, which are one step removed from 'real' money, encouraging more spending
5. developing player tracking; that is, using behavioural data to monitor individual player behaviour
6. offering multiple play lines, which implies that if you play lots of lines, you're bound to win on most of them
7. supplying big and comfy buttons that can be played with one finger (and often are).

Now, I'm not opposed to the manufacture of poker machines. Companies have a right to run a profitable business and make their machines as easy to use as possible. But if I were a politician, I'd heavily regulate the use of poker machines because their design is a gold-class case study in 'eliminating complexity'. None of these adjustments to poker machines gives a player additional skills, or increases their motivation to play. They simply remove barriers to playing, and make it easier to keep on playing (whilst in autopilot).

When influencing behaviour, the take-home message is to focus on autopilot thinking. People will undertake the behaviour without even thinking about it.

A PSYCHOLOGICAL BY-PRODUCT OF ELIMINATING COMPLEXITY

It's not rocket science to conclude that we like doing things when they are easier. But this is a particularly important concept for advertising because consumers tend to purchase brands they already like (Haefner, Deli-Gray & Rosenbloom 2011). In a recent study, Brasel and Gips (2013) found that people who use touchscreens to view ads are more likely to feel psychological ownership of a brand than those who use a screen with a mouse or wireless touchpad. The touchscreen minimised psychological distance. In making the design easy to use, it feels almost intuitive and means people can develop closer attachments to the brand and feel that it's part of their extended self. People desired the brand more and were prepared to pay more for it—all because they enjoyed the interface more.[2]

WE KNEW IT WOULD BE A VIRAL SUCCESS

How could we eliminate complexity for teenage boys with zits so they could buy Oxy? We knew that videos of guys popping pimples tend to go viral, judging by the long list of previous 'big zit' viral successes. As mentioned earlier, the biggest predictor of future behaviour is past behaviour, so we decided to create a video of all the zit-popping videos spliced together—a zit-popping extravaganza comprising the best zit-popping content from YouTube. Incidentally, we contacted the creators of the video content and asked if we could use it, giving them $100 as thanks. If you want to feel the emotion of disgust, just watch it (www.youtube.com/watch?v=l0cAaYW5Ri4). You have been warned!

At the end of the video we added a sampling mechanic that read, 'Click here for your free sample home-delivered'. If they clicked 'request sample' and gave us their address, we then sent them samples of Oxy in the post, delivered within 24 hours in brown paper bags. It was perhaps the most elegant example of 'eliminating complexity' I've worked on (disgusting, sure, but elegant). We created content teenage boys wanted to watch and would want to pass on. As they watched, we eliminated the complexity of sourcing the pimple cream through the direct 'request a sample' mechanic. Around 700,000 people watched the

---

2 In his book *Emotional Design* (2004), Donald Norman looks at how the design of objects can make us like them more (or less). As you'd expect, Apple features heavily in the book as the ultimate example of design that eliminates complexity. Take a look at the instruction manual for an iPad—it's miniscule. It doesn't need to be large because the design of the iPad is so intuitive. The book also looks at how simple design of everyday things can evoke powerful emotions.

video and the 10,000 samples were gone within 24 hours. When you eliminate complexity, you identify the hurdles to behaviour and knock them over.

As Will Burns (2012) wrote in *Forbes* magazine in an article titled 'When Disgusting is Good Strategy':

> In the video, the payoff to the zit-popping scenes is the line, 'Man Sized Problems'. It appeals to the manly aspirations of the teen boy, and, better yet, positions the giant zit itself as a manly thing. Which is just the opposite of how teens currently think of zits—as a lowly teenager problem. And, of course, the Oxy Face Wash brand is squarely positioned as the ultimate hero of the film as the 'Man Sized Solution'. So smart on so many levels. Very bold. Very gross. And, my guess, very effective.

Burns concludes his article: 'I'll never look at a mirror the same way again.'

WAYS TO ELIMINATE COMPLEXITY

Behavioural economist Richard Thaler uses the term 'choice architects' to describe the people who design systems that incorporate choices (Thaler & Sunstein 2008). These are the people who design supermarket layouts and websites, as well as menus that are not only pleasing to the customer but also maximise profit for the restaurant.[3]

Thaler and Sunstein's book *Nudge: Improving Decisions about Health, Wealth, and Happiness* (2008) lists seven principles that nudge people in a particular direction. (And with a bit of creative licence, the first letters of each of the words even form the acrostic 'NUDGES'.)

- **IN**centives—offer clear incentives and make them immediate.
- **U**nderstand mappings—translate data to minimise the gap between the representation of the data and its meaning.
- **D**efaults—set the default at the option you want the person to choose.
- **G**ive feedback—we repeat what works, and don't repeat what doesn't—so give feedback when it works.
- **E**xpect error—assume people will make mistakes, and design for those mistakes.
- **S**tructure complex choices—minimise choices and differentiate them as much as possible.

Let's look at three of these principles in more detail.

---

3 Menus are one of the most frequently researched items in behavioural economics because it's easy to see the impact of various tweaks to a menu in terms of how much people spend, or what they order. If you're designing a menu, or when you next eat at a restaurant, be aware of the tactics that encourage you to spend more money (Poundstone 2010). These include no dollar signs on the menu, the use of florid and warm descriptions of the food, prices not neatly aligned in a column and the most profitable meals listed in a box. There also may be one or two really expensive items on the menu to anchor your price expectations—so everything else looks relatively more affordable. Finally, it's unlikely that prices will end in the number '9' as this equates to value but not to quality.

SET THE DEFAULT AT THE OPTION YOU WANT THE PERSON TO CHOOSE

When given a choice, more people go with a default option than make the decision to either opt out or opt in. This can be seen with the emotionally charged issue of organ donation. If you look at the rates of organ donation in Europe, you'll notice some countries have very high rates, such as Sweden, with 85.9 per cent of citizens giving permission for their organs to be used after their death. Close neighbour the Netherlands, however, has a 27.5 per cent rate of organ donation. As psychologist and behavioural economist Dan Ariely points out, these countries have similar values and you would expect them to have the same attitude towards organ donation. Something else must be at play. It turns out the decision about organ donation depends on the question asked by the authorities. The Netherlands has an opt-in system: 'Tick this box if you would want to participate in the organ donation system.' Sweden, by contrast, has an opt-out system: 'Tick this box if you would not like to participate in the organ donation system.' In both cases, people are failing to tick the box and opting for the default. Ariely (2008) writes:

> You might think that people do this because they don't care. That the decision about donating their organs is so trivial that they can't be bothered to lift up the pencil and check the box. But in fact the opposite is true. This is a hard emotional decision about what will happen to our bodies after we die and what effect it will have on those close to us. It is because of the difficulty and the emotionality of these decisions that they just don't know what to do, so they adopt the default option (by the way this also happens to physicians making medical decisions, and also to people making investment and retirement decisions).

If a decision feels too difficult, we opt for the default. Keep this in mind if you want to influence the location to meet friends. Instead of asking, 'Where should we meet?' you could say, 'Should we meet at Newmarket Hotel?' The first question has no default and no compliance. With the second question, you've set the default. If you're ordering a bottle of wine, you'll be more influential if you ask, 'Should we choose Shiraz?' Shiraz becomes the default. Just remember to set defaults responsibly.

EXPECT ERROR AND DESIGN FOR *IT*

Most people become annoyed when something is too complicated. When you design around errors, you anticipate mistakes and design around them. It's easier to take one multivitamin than several single vitamins, for example. Or what about resealable cheese? Many people were finding it difficult to store cheese once it was opened and were tossing it out when it became hard and dry. This dissuaded repeat buying as people didn't like the waste of money when they threw out the cheese. Now the resealable design keeps air out and makes cheese easy to store, and eliminates costly waste.

Kahneman (2011) uses the example of the Paris Metro system, where the metro cards have readers on both sides, as well as up and down, so no matter how you swipe the card the machine reader will accept it. The card has been designed around errors. (In my view, a product crying out for new design is the TV remote control.)

Could you eliminate the complexity of getting up each morning? Thaler and Sunstein (2008) cite the example of Clocky, an alarm clock developed in 2005 by Gauri Nanda, a graduate student at MIT's Media Lab. Clocky looks like other alarm clocks but has one significant difference. Clocky has two rubber wheels sitting on either side of its centre. When the alarm goes off, Clocky's wheels start turning, making it roll from the bedside table onto the floor and away from the bed. The only way to stop Clocky's beeping is to get out of bed, walk to it and turn it off. And now you're out of bed—the goal of Clocky. When it was created, Clocky received media attention in the USA with *Good Morning America's* Diane Sawyer declaring, 'I would kill Clocky in about two days.' Clocky even became a case study at Harvard Business School's Marketing and Innovation course. Why did Clocky capture the imagination? Because it solved a problem: getting up in the morning. It didn't increase someone's motivation to get out of bed—it redesigned the environment to encourage that behaviour.

STRUCTURE COMPLEX CHOICES

A marketer's job is to minimise choices. The fewer the choices, the better the products. In his influential book *The Paradox of Choice: Why More is Less* (2004), Barry Schwartz says when items are similar, it's harder to choose between them, but (paradoxically) the decision is less important—as any of these similar products will more or less do the job. Therefore, marketers should try to make a product stand out as much as possible, and ideally make it become its own category. If your product becomes a category, you have a 100 per cent share of that category. Here are some examples:

- fashionable cheap watches—Swatch (very 1980s, I know)
- micro-blogging services—Twitter
- MP3 players that connect to buyable music—iPod
- free and legal streaming of music—Spotify
- Just-in-time affordable fashion—Zara.

As Schwartz says, when it comes to choice, 'more is less'.

CAN YOU MAKE RECYCLING EASIER AT HOME?

Eliminating complexity also can be applied to recycling. Even though people say they believe in recycling, some become lazy and place all their rubbish in the one bin. To encourage recycling behaviour, think about how you could eliminate complexity. One suggestion is to use recycling bins that are larger in size than regular bins and placed in more prominent locations. Or you might place two bins side by side—one for regular waste and the other for recycling, with the recycling bin easier to access. My brother-in-law's house has two floors, with the kitchen on the top floor. He's designed a pulley system in which recycled garbage can be literally thrown off the top balcony and into the recycling bin, and this means his family recycles almost everything they can. Think about other kitchen chores. Is it easy to return clean dishes from the dishwasher to the cupboard? If not, could you store your dishes nearer to the dishwasher? It's what we've done at our house. It makes the task easier and I'm more likely to unpack the dishes as a result.

If you have a problem with colleagues checking their smartphones during meetings, you could eliminate complexity by creating a storage spot for the phones. When people enter the meeting room, they pop their phones in the spot and collect them once the meeting is over (just make sure the phones are in silent mode). Alternatively, you could purchase a phone-jamming device for use in meeting rooms in your workplace. If you disable the phones with such a device, it's easy for people *not* to check their phones because they don't receive any new messages. Design your environment to eliminate the barriers that get in the way of people behaving the way you'd like them to.

If you want your partner to stop leaving her keys and bag on the dining room table, buy a table that sits by the front door. As she walks in the front door, she can put her keys and bag on it instead. Make the behaviour as easy as possible.

STOPPING HARMFUL BEHAVIOURS FROM HAPPENING

When I was working as a psychologist, some of my clients had alcohol dependency issues. They would work hard to stay sober and resist the temptation to drink, until one day they'd find themselves standing outside a pub with time on their hands, so they'd walk in and order a beer, and begin drinking again.

I would explain to my patients that they didn't just suddenly appear in front of a pub. Rather, what led up to being outside the pub was a series of what I'd call SUDs—'seemingly unimportant decisions'. To explain this, I would ask people to imagine a chap at home on his own. He believes he needs some exercise, so he decides he will go for a walk. He then decides he needs some food for dinner, so he walks to the shop. He needs money to buy food, so he decides to take his wallet. He leaves home to walk to the shop and on the way to the shop is his favourite pub. Lo and behold, he finds himself outside the pub with money in his pocket.

So what happened? The chap in question made a number of 'seemingly unimportant' decisions to wind up where he was. He decided to go for a walk, he decided to take his wallet and so on. Each of these decisions took him one step closer to being outside the pub on that particular afternoon.

Sometimes the best way to stop a harmful behaviour happening is to put up barriers or increase complexity. Having to exert mental effort to overcome a barrier can momentarily stop the behaviour from happening long enough to make the person reconsider their actions. This is why smokers put elastic bands around their cigarette packets and dieters place the yummiest (and most fattening) food right at the bottom of the fridge. Just as eliminating complexity can help to make a behaviour happen, increasing complexity can work to stop a behaviour we don't want to happen.

BUILDING BEHAVIOURAL CHANGE SYSTEMS TO SAVE MONEY

Most people I know are motivated to try to save money, such as for a deposit for a home or an international holiday. There is some motivation to save, but things get in the way. We need to transfer the money over to our savings account (hassle), we see a nice pair of shoes we want to buy (distraction) or we end up having a big night out with friends (unplanned expense).

This is a classic example of where we should not worry about building someone's motivation to change or save more. Instead we should work with them to design systems that make it impossible *not* to save. Here's what can be done:

1. Set up a recurring direct transfer between your accounts.

2. Download the automatic 'Impulse Saver Button' (www.westpac.co.nz/branch-mobile-online/while-you-re-mobile/impulse-saver-for-iphone-app), an app that allows you to impulsively save money whenever you like. (Launched in 2012, it currently only works if you bank with Westpac and live in New Zealand—but you get the idea.)

3. Ask your place of employment to pay some of your salary directly into the savings account.

4. Set the account up so withdrawals have to be counter-signed.

As you can see, all of these techniques 'design around errors' (our inability to save) and do not require increased motivation. You can see more suggestions for how designing the environment can help people save money by reading Thaler and Benartzi (2004). The same approaches can be used for losing weight, becoming more organised and so on. If the motivation is there, think of the ways you can eliminate complexity to make the desired behaviour happen.

SUMMARY

Eliminating complexity is about removing barriers to behaviour. Because we like to use the least amount of effort and energy to do tasks, successful advertisers and influencers need to make those tasks as straightforward as possible. Keep these three elements in mind. First, the biggest predictor of future behaviour is past behaviour and you shouldn't expect too much change. Second, people behave like zombies (System 1 thinking) and when something blocks their path, they're likely to stop, so you need to anticipate possible obstacles and design for these mistakes. Third, the easier the desired behaviour is to do, the more likely people are to do it (remember the poker machine that's designed to maximise playing time). Combine these insights when working out how to eliminate complexity. The easier it is for a behaviour to happen, the less the motivation is needed to make it happen. So consider working with the environment to create systems of behavioural change.

The Insider: Joseph Jaffe

Missouri is known as the 'Show Me' state and this idea becomes the backdrop for how behaviour change is shifting and evolving from a 'tell and sell' to a 'participate and play' approach. Ultimately, talk is cheap and it is talk that has characterised advertising pre-digital. With interactivity that has become ubiquitous, communal, social and mobile, our mandate is anywhere on the continuum of a healthy balance between 'talk' and 'walk' to an extreme pendulum swing from 'talk' to 'walking our talk'—in other words, a behaviour change that is less suggestive, persuasive and inferential to one that is based on referrals, credible recommendations, demonstration and usage.

Communications absolutely still has a place in this new ecosystem, but it is less a 'have to have' and more a 'nice to have'. I contend that in a perfect world, paid media would be zero, because brands would have enough relationships, partnerships, customers, word-of-mouth, referrals and 'owned assets' to leverage. Your most credible spokespeople are your employees and your most influential salespeople are your customers. Under this umbrella, what we call 'non-media' or peer-to-peer (human-to-human) is both the lubricant and accelerant that greases the wheels and powers the new branding machine.

Traditional blunt branding relied on a misdirected mix of celebrity endorsement, borrowed interest, frequency and more frequency to force home a proof point. Now we have a much sharper weapon of choice: proof itself. Or the converse, which is the ability to expose untruths, disconnects, unsavory experiences or disappointment via a plethora of social channels.

Ultimately, we are judged not by what we say, but by what we do. This is true in life. And it is true now. More than ever. Business has finally caught up with humanity and hopefully based on its ability to adapt and evolve, it won't be caught out in the process.

Joseph Jaffe is author of *Death of the 30 Second TVC*. I've known Josef for around 10 years. We met at a conference together in Singapore and caught up with other speakers the night before the conference. We ended up getting incredibly drunk and playing a board game I invented (*The Analyst*) until the wee hours. The presentations the next day were a little average (apologies, conference organiser). Josef has been globally influential in championing alternative ways for brands to advertise beyond the 30-second TVC.

REFERENCES

Ariely, D. (2008). *Predictably Irrational: The Hidden Forces that Shape our Decisions.* New York: HarperCollins.

Barden, P. (2013). *Decoded: The Science behind What We Buy.* Chichester: John Wiley & Sons.

Brasel, S.A. & Gips, J. (2013). Tablets, touchscreens, and touchpads: How varying touch interfaces trigger psychological ownership and endowment. *Journal of Consumer Psychology.* In press.

Burns, W. (2012). When disgusting is good strategy. *Forbes,* 27 July. Accessed at www.forbes.com/sites/willburns/2012/07/27/when-disgusting-is-on-strategy.

Haefner, J.E., Deli-Gray, Z. & Rosenbloom, A. (2011). The importance of brand liking and brand trust in consumer decision making: Insights from Bulgarian and Hungarian consumers during the global economic crisis. *Managing Global Transitions,* 9(3), 249–73.

Kahneman, D. (2011). *Thinking, Fast and Slow.* New York: Macmillan.

MacLeod, C.M. (1991). Half a century of research on the Stroop effect: An integrative review. *Psychological Bulletin,* 109(2), 163–203.

Mossman, D. (1994). Assessing predictions of violence: Being accurate about accuracy. *Journal of Consulting and Clinical Psychology,* 62(4), 783–92.

Norman, D.A. (2004). *Emotional Design: Why We Love (or Hate) Everyday Things.* New York: Basic Books.

Pinaud, R., Tremere, L.A. & De Weerd, P. (eds) (2006). *Plasticity in the Visual System: From Genes to Circuits.* New York: Springer.

Poundstone, W. (2010). *Priceless: The Myth of Fair Value (and How to Take Advantage of It).* New York: Hill & Wang.

Schwartz, B. (2004). *The Paradox of Choice: Why More is Less.* New York: Ecco/HarperCollins.

Stroop, J.R. (1935). Studies of interference in serial verbal reactions. *Journal of Experimental Psychology,* 18(6), 643–62.

Thaler, R.H. & Benartzi, S. (2004). Save more tomorrow: Using behavioral economics to increase employee saving. *Journal of Political Economy,* 112(S1), S164–1.

Thaler, R.H. & Sunstein, C.R. (2008). *Nudge: Improving Decisions about Health, Wealth, and Happiness.* New Haven: Yale University Press.

The Simpsons (1992). The Otto Show, Season 3, Episode 22.

Venkataramanan, M. (2013). This is how current slot machines are cunningly designed to milk your wallet. *Wired,* 9 May. Accessed at http://www.wired.co.uk/magazine/archive/2013/06/start/you-have-been-played/viewgallery/304036.

COMMITMENT: HOW A SMALL REQUEST LEADS TO A BIGGER AGREEMENT

From little things big things grow.

    Paul Kelly, Australian singer and songwriter

Unless commitment is made, there are only promises and hopes; but no plans.

    Peter F Drucker, US management consultant

SPEED KILLS

At the beginning of the advertisement, you see several framed family photographs hanging on a lounge room wall. The song 'Pictures of You' plays. Seated on sofas holding photographs, a series of people wipe tears from their eyes. It becomes clear a loved one has died in a road accident. The ad demonstrates the devastating impact of road fatalities on the families left behind. In 2002, 397 people died on Victoria's roads (RACV 2012); by 2011, the number had dropped to 287 thanks, in part, to moving advertising campaigns such as 'Pictures of You', developed by Grey Advertising (see it on YouTube: www.youtube.com/watch?v=DOYEuEiNBKE&list=PL1F05D934105B4A26). But the story in rural Victoria was different, with fatalities on the rise. Could the next generation of country drivers be encouraged to take the pedal off the metal and drive safely?

Over nine years, John Thompson had the job of addressing road fatalities as Senior Manager of Road Safety and Marketing at the Victorian Transport Accident Commission (TAC). The TAC devised the successful 'Wipe Off 5' campaign featuring popular sports stars to encourage drivers to reduce their speed by just 5 km/h. The TAC also screened hard-hitting, emotional advertisements.

Driving along the Sunraysia Highway on his way to Mildura in 2010, Thompson's attention was captured by a sign that read, 'Welcome to Speed. Population: 45'. Surrounded by wheat and sheep farms, the town has just three stores: a fuel and machinery dealer, a general store and a post office. As John drove through Speed on that autumn day, he wondered: 'Could the town of Speed be used to highlight the dangers of speeding on rural roads?' I've known John for many years and when he came into Naked Communications in 2010, he was the type of client every advertising agency loves—one with the kernel of a good idea who is willing to do what it takes to turn it into a reality.

Driver behaviour is one of the most difficult behaviours to influence. Driving habits—good and bad—tend to become ingrained; and threats, such as large fines or losing your licence, need time to make an impact. Unlike drink driving, attitudes to speeding varies, with some viewing it as socially acceptable. Also, many people can, and do, get away with speeding.

A strategy to reduce speeding on rural roads could take years to make an impact and get results. As outlined in Chapter 3, there are three key components of behaviour change—thoughts, feelings and actions—with action the quickest way to get results. After much thought and discussion, John and I decided on a 'first step' strategy that wasn't about reducing the incidence of speeding per se, but about asking people to make an initial commitment to safer driving on rural roads. Over the next few weeks, the concept was mapped out on a flipchart until we developed this strategy: to rename the town of Speed to 'SpeedKills'. If 10,000 people clicked 'Like' on a customised Facebook page, the town would change its name, and the TAC would make a sizeable donation to the town's Lions Club. John loved the idea.

COMMITMENT TO CHANGE

When behaviour is either ingrained or not able to be changed in one step, securing a commitment to change is a small but positive first step. If you've ever attended a Tupperware party, you'll know what I mean. Your first purchase is often the first of many bigger purchases. If you've bought something from a door-to-door salesperson or 'Liked' a brand on Facebook, you may have experienced '**commitment**'.

To understand the power of commitment, let's go back almost 50 years to a study by Stanford University's Jonathan Freedman and Scott Fraser (1966). In the study, psychologists pretended to do market research on how homemakers use household cleaning products. In the middle of the day, they rang random households selected from the phonebook and explained they were researching cleaning products, asking the homemakers if they could spare five minutes to answer some questions. Most of them agreed and completed the survey. Three days later, they were telephoned again and asked if 'five or six men' could visit their house to do a thorough audit of their cleaning products. They were told it would take around two hours to complete. That's quite an imposition. A second group of homemakers was also asked if the group of men could visit to audit their cleaning products, but this group didn't have the initial five-minute phone call.

What do you think happened? It turns out the first group that received the initial five-minute phone call were more than twice as likely to agree to the request for the men to visit their house than the second group. This technique, known as the 'foot-in-the-door' technique holds that someone is more likely to agree to a request if they've already agreed to a smaller request.

This study has been repeated under various guises many times. Katie Baca-Motes et al. (2012) looked at whether hotel guests would 'commit' to eco-friendly behaviour during a hotel stay. The study lasted 31 days and involved 2416 participants. When people arrived at a hotel in California, they were asked to read a short statement about the hotel's commitment to eco-friendly behaviours. Some guests were asked if they would commit to being eco-friendly and reuse their towels. Others were asked if they would commit to being eco-friendly but also wear a pin to prove this 'commitment'. Guests that made a commitment to engage in eco-friendly behaviour during their stay were significantly more likely to do so. If the commitment was general (the first group), they were 25 per cent more likely to engage in eco-friendly behaviour. If the commitment was specific (the second group), they were 40 per cent more likely to be eco-friendly. Once people make a commitment, they are more likely to exhibit the behaviour.

This strategy has become a staple of influence theory. **People are more likely to complete larger tasks if you ask them to do a smaller task first**. And yes, the reason it's called the foot-in-the-door technique is because door-to-door salespeople are the experts at it. They will do whatever it takes to engage you in a conversation, as that's the best way to deliver their sales pitch. The longer you listen to the sales pitch, the more likely it is that you'll buy. The salesperson has a foot in the door (sometimes both literally and figuratively) and is closer to making a sale. It's a technique used by charities that collect donations in busy shopping centres. Their representative won't ask you for money straight up. They'll engage you first by asking 'How is your day going?' If you answer that question, you're more likely to open your wallet.

The psychological principle that underpins the commitment action spur is cognitive dissonance theory. As outlined in Chapter 3, when you take an action, you align your thoughts and feelings to match that action. When you take the action of committing to a particular behaviour, you set the stage for subsequent consistent behaviours (Cialdini 2007).

THE COMMITMENT TO RENAME SPEED

This principle informed our campaign to rename the town of Speed to 'SpeedKills'. The first step was a small but visible commitment to safer driving through the action of clicking 'Like' on Facebook. To encourage this, we filmed the town's 45 locals, who talked about the importance of slowing down when driving on rural roads. We gave them ownership of the campaign to increase compliance (rather than the TAC imposing it on them). They asked others to join the campaign to click 'Like' on Facebook to 'rename Speed'. Two of the town's older residents created an amusing video that explained how to 'Like' something on Facebook (you can see the video on YouTube: www.youtube.com/watch?v= qAZzWP3s5Jk&list=PL504DE3545B5707CD&index=5), while a younger resident, Gabby, wrote a song about slowing down on the roads. And instead of holding a car racing event, the town organised a slow car race, where the slowest car took first prize.

The campaign launched on 14 January 2011 and within 24 hours, 10,000 people visited the Facebook page and clicked 'Like'. We achieved the goal. But it didn't stop there. There was a call for town spokesman and sheep farmer, Phil Down, to change his name to Phil 'Slow' Down. He agreed to do so if the number of Facebook 'Likes' increased to 20,000. The target was achieved within a week. The campaign ran for six weeks and by its end, 35,500 had people clicked 'Like' on Facebook. In effect, 35,500 people publicly declared their support for reduced speeds on rural roads. This action was the first step—the commitment to safer, slower driving.

After analysing the Facebook data, we discovered that over a quarter of the 'Likes' were by young males, a group notoriously difficult to engage with on road safety messages. The campaign also received over 10 million impressions on Twitter. 'Rename Speed' was the seventh most liked non-profit cause on Facebook in Australia and New Zealand. The Facebook page received 15,000 comments and 1.3 million visitors and the video was viewed 83,000 times, with an average viewer ranking of 4.63 out of 5. As one Facebook contributor wrote, 'Congratulations to the small town of SpeedKills and thank you for making a difference to us all.'

The next month, on 18 February, the then CEO of the TAC and I went to Speedkills and gave the Lions Club a cheque for $10,000. This was also an opportunity for the TAC to receive positive media for being part of an innovative campaign. That day was also my birthday, so my wife came along and we ended up celebrating with Phil 'Slow' Down and his lovely family in Speed. You can see the story (of the campaign, not my birthday) in a three-minute case study on YouTube (www.youtube.com/watch?v=QPhiuu6RXbk).

DOES A FACEBOOK 'LIKE' INFLUENCE BEHAVIOUR?

Is there a connection between 'Liking' something on Facebook and behaviour change? In the 'Rename Speed' campaign, success was measured by community involvement. But the question of whether there's a link between a virtual commitment and subsequent behaviour is interesting, and one I decided to test. The findings were presented at the 2013 Society for Consumer Psychology Annual Conference held in San Diego.

In our study, 100 online participants were shown advertisements for a 'fake' new brand of chocolate bar called 'Chewychews', which was available in two flavours (see Figure 14.1).

Figure 14.1 Mock advertising for 'Chewychews'

After viewing the ads, a third of the participants were asked if they would purchase Chewychews. A second group was asked to 'Like' (or not) Chewychews on Facebook, before being asked if they would purchase them. The final group was asked for comments on how they felt about Chewychews (positive or negative), before being asked if they would purchase them.

The study revealed people who 'Liked' the brand on Facebook, or who wrote a comment, were more likely to purchase them, like them and recommend them to friends than those who only watched the ad (see Figure 14.2). So the smaller, and easier, commitment of liking the chocolate bar on Facebook influenced their purchasing decision. The action of clicking 'Like' on Facebook increased the likelihood of both purchase and recommendation.

Figure 14.2 The relation of exposure, liking and commenting to brand affinity and brand purchase

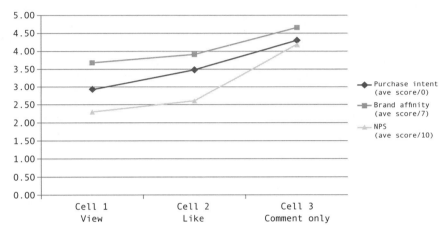

Facebook, Instagram and other social media platforms are becoming the marketer's tool of choice in securing a commitment towards their brand or cause. In online campaigns, when people click 'Like' they often receive a reward such as a free sample or discounted offer. As we've seen with Chewychews, a side effect is that this action makes you more likely to recommend and purchase the item. This is due to the commitment effect.

COMMITMENT TOWARDS A GOAL

Commitment has both push and pull factors. Asking people to make a small change in behaviour—one that encourages a larger change in the future—is an example of a push strategy. However, there's another way to use the commitment spur, and that's with a clearly articulated goal, which is a pull strategy.

Humans are goal-oriented, so if we set a goal, and start the journey, we'll generally strive to complete that goal. In a small but fascinating study in 1993, Ted Taylor and Steve Booth-Butterfield from West Virginia University tested whether the foot-in-the-door technique reduced the incidence of drink-driving. Over six weeks, they turned a local bar into a research laboratory. In the bar, two groups were randomly selected. Both groups were asked by the bartender to call a taxi if they drank more than the legal limit to drive: 'We want you to call a taxi if you've had too much to drink.' The first group was also asked by the bartender to sign a petition against drink-driving and were given a pamphlet about the dangers of drink-driving. Members of the second (control) group were not asked to sign the petition, nor were they given a pamphlet to read. What do you think happened? Those asked to sign the petition were far more likely to call a taxi than those in the control group. The small but public act of signing one's name on a petition against drink-driving influenced the ultimate behaviour to not drink and drive.

This goal-oriented behaviour can also be found in the consumer environment. Lee and Ariely (2006) conducted an interesting study at a convenience store. They analysed people's shopping behaviour and found the average basket contained around $4 worth of goods. Customers were then given discount vouchers. Half the customers received a voucher that said 'Spend $6 and receive $1 off'. The other half received a voucher that said 'Spend $2 and receive $1 off'.

The first group *increased* consumption from $4 to $6 to take advantage of the $1 off voucher. But customers that received the $1 off for a $2 purchase *reduced* their spending from the $4 average to around $2. Achieving the goal had become more important than the utility of the purchases.

Even if the original incentive or motivation is removed, once an agreement is made, people tend to honour it. Cialdini et al. (1978) noticed that car dealers often use this tactic. The car dealer will lure a buyer by offering a price that's lower than their competitors. But once the buyer agrees to the purchase, the dealer removes the price advantage by revealing the offer didn't include certain options that the buyer believed to be part of the deal. The actual price is much higher than the sticker price. Cialdini found that once the buyer had committed to the purchase, they stuck with it—even though they recognised both the reduced economic utility and the deception practised by the car dealer. **People feel a pressure to be consistent and act in accordance with their previous commitment or decision**. Cialdini et al. (1978) write, 'Once people said yes to something, they want to see that "yes" through.' The psychological underpinnings of commitment are strong in the world of technology and social media and we can now find even more ways to get people to make the first step towards whatever behaviour change we are trying to make.

SIMPLIFYING BEHAVIOUR CHANGE

According to CNN, BJ Fogg from Stanford University's Persuasive Technology Lab is one of the top 10 gurus you should know (Reingold & Tkaczyk 2008). He's a leader in the study of behaviour change and I've had the pleasure of meeting him several times. BJ has many beliefs about behaviour change and one of the strongest is that most people in the behaviour change business (advertisers included) spend way too much energy trying to increase people's motivation to change. Motivation often isn't the issue—it's the degree of difficulty to undertake the behaviour. His solution is to select simpler or easier behaviours. This is the thinking behind his 'Tiny Habits' program.

A tiny habit is something you:

- do at least *once a day*
- takes you *less than thirty seconds* to complete
- requires *little effort* (Fogg 2013).

In the introductory letter to his Tiny Habits course, BJ writes:

As you select Tiny Habits for this week, they must match the criteria above. (If you don't want to match the criteria, then please don't enrol with me. My method will frustrate you.) Simple is powerful. You'll see that this week. And you can expand the simple behavior in later weeks (for example, expand from flossing one tooth to all your teeth). But for this week, to benefit your own success and learning, please, please keep it simple.

Below are some examples of Tiny Habits. Note how they are written with an existing habit at the start ('After I…') combined with the new behavior you want.

'After I brush, I will floss one tooth.'
'After I pour my morning coffee, I will text my mom.'
'After I start the dishwasher, I will read one sentence from a book.'
'After I walk in my door from work, I will get out my work-out clothes.'
'After I sit down on the train, I will open my sketch notebook.'

This is the best example of commitment I've come across. The principle of larger change following a small change is well recognised, and vowing to keep the change specific, and anchored to something already occurring in your day, makes it even easier to carry out the behaviour change. So instead of pledging to lose weight next New Year's Eve, break it down and find three tiny habits to change instead. The Tiny Habits program works because people start off with small behaviour change and end up creating embedded habits. I wonder if the act of signing up to the Tiny Habits program also means people feel committed to BJ Fogg? He's one of the 10 modern gurus you should know, after all.[1]

COMMITMENT TO CHANGE THE WORLD (OR AT LEAST GET PEOPLE TO VOTE)

In 2010, the UK government set up a department called the Behavioural Insights Team, or Nudge Unit, named after Thaler and Sunstein's book *Nudge: Improving Decisions about Health, Wealth, and Happiness* (2008), discussed in Chapter 13. Its aim was to incorporate the latest understandings of human behaviour into public policy to provide more efficient services and save money for the government. Across the Atlantic, the US government, and President Barack Obama, noticed the positive influence of the Nudge team and decided to establish its own version, headed by Maya Shanker, a senior policy advisor in the Office of Science and Technology Policy at the White House. It's her job to create more accountable public policy. The recruitment campaign material claimed: 'A growing body of evidence suggests that insights from social and behavioural sciences can be used to help design public policies that work better, cost less, and help people to achieve their goals.' Governments around the world are embracing a new understanding of behaviour change to improve engagement.

---

1 I signed up to BJ's Tiny Habits program, but didn't end up doing any of the suggested activities. I had every intention of doing the program—but at the crucial time, and despite selecting an anchor, I didn't remember to do the tasks. Behaviour change is not simple! However, the course has had amazing reviews, and lots of positive endorsement (Chang 2013).

During Obama's 2012 re-election campaign, the Democrats gathered a 'dream team of behavioral scientists' (Carey 2012) to offer advice on getting people to vote—and, specifically, to vote for Obama. One technique when canvassing for votes door-to-door was to ask voters to sign an informal commitment to vote. The card included a picture of Obama in one corner. And that's it. It wasn't a pledge to vote Democrat. It was simply a 'pledge to vote' card that included an image of Barack Obama. According to the psychological principles of commitment, this small, voluntary action not only increased the likelihood the person would vote, but also that they would vote Democrat.

People like their actions to be consistent with behaviour they've already committed to. The take-home message is this: if seeking to influence someone else's behaviour, make a smaller request first.

WHEN COMMITMENT GETS WEIRD

Do you remember the now infamous KONY 2012 campaign? In case you missed it, or have forgotten about it already, KONY 2012 was the creation of US-based organisation Invisible Children, which produced a 30-minute video and campaign to highlight the plight of Ugandan children stolen from their families and enlisted as child soldiers. The man allegedly responsible for the kidnapping and abuse is Joseph Kony.

Invisible Children mapped out a campaign to galvanise and inspire people to sign a pledge and lobby cultural influencers (movie and music stars) and policy makers (political leaders and commentators) to use resources to find Kony and return the children to their families. The video is part documentary, part movie trailer and part music clip. You can see it on YouTube (www.youtube.com/watch?v=Y4MnpzG5Sqc). In it, Invisible Children founder Jason Russell tells the story of the stolen children through his young son, Gavin, and a Ugandan child soldier, Jacob. It's emotional and accessible. For $20, supporters received posters and armbands, with everyone to gather for an event called 'Cover the Night' in which cities across the globe would be covered in posters of Joseph Kony. Over 100 million people watched the video and thousands of people bought the kits, but when the night arrived, people did not turn up in anywhere near the numbers expected. So what happened?

Unfortunately for the cause, it all went a bit pear-shaped. The group's founder and front man, Jason Russell, had an apparent mental breakdown, the transparency of the organisation was questioned, and KONY 2012 was a fizzer. Despite significant attention through the evocative video, and despite asking viewers for a commitment, the campaign has not been considered a success (Carroll 2012). Here's my analysis of why.

1. *The organisation*—There were questions about the funding of Invisible Children, with grant money from religious donor groups such as the National Christian Foundation. The organisation was also criticised for spending large amounts of money creating videos.

2. *The message*—The content of the video was simplistic and, according to the Prime Minister of Uganda, Amama Mbabazi, inaccurate. In a nine-minute YouTube video retort, he said, 'The KONY 2012 campaign fails to make one crucial point clear. Joseph Kony is not in Uganda.' He added, 'Uganda is not in conflict. Uganda is a modern, developing country which enjoys peace, stability and security.'

3. *The action*—It was never clear how buying an action kit and showing your support during 'Cover the Night' could be directly related to capturing Joseph Kony. For a commitment to be successful, the initial action must be aligned with the desired behavioural change (for example, pledging to vote and then actually going on to vote).

4. *The leader*—To me, Invisible Children founder Jason Russell always seemed more of a cult leader than a saviour. He was more L Ron Hubbard than Mother Teresa. His bizarre behaviour during the campaign—including being filmed naked on a public street—further diminished his credibility.

Ultimately KONY 2012 failed because people no longer wanted to be associated with the organisation, not necessarily the cause itself. But the interesting thing for me wasn't that the movement bombed, but rather that very little has since been written about it. A few books have been published, but you would expect a campaign that attracted 100 million people and yet ended in massive failure to have been examined far more comprehensively. So, why wasn't it?

Let's first look at the grassroots supporters. Did you publicly declare support for Invisible Children and its cause to capture Joseph Kony? Did you take action and spread the message or buy an action kit? If so, did you subsequently hear about its failure to meet its target, and the controversy surrounding its leader? Did you then act to publicly renounce your affiliation with the cause? This situation is an ideal demonstration of the concept of cognitive dissonance (discussed in Chapter 3). When people act positively towards a goal, they align their thoughts and feelings to match that action. If they clicked 'Like' for KONY 2012, they publicly said, 'I support this cause' and consequently aligned their thoughts, feelings and actions to support Invisible Children and Jason Russell. But when negative information about the movement came to light, for most people it was very difficult to retract their 'Like'. When 'Cover the Night' came along, they didn't feel comfortable declaring that they were wrong or had been duped. They had already acted towards the cause, so to back out at the crucial moment would make them appear silly—both to themselves and to the people who had received their public declaration of support on social media. That's the power of action—and Jason Russell tapped into this. It's why there's been relative silence about the failure of the biggest social media experiments ever. The silence represents muted embarrassment from prior supporters and quiet smugness from detractors.

You can see a balanced postscript video on this case from Truth Loader on YouTube (www.youtube.com/watch?v=okmswBs4rdg). With 50,000 odd views, it's been seen a lot less than the 100 million or so that watched the original video.

KONY 2012 demonstrates the power of commitment. Even when a cause is proven to be less compelling, appealing or worthy of support than one might have originally thought, most people are very reluctant to drop their support, never mind publicly acknowledge their mistake. Transfer this commitment to a less controversial cause, or a legal sales transaction, and you can appreciate why advertisers are so keen to use it as a tool.

SUMMARY

Commitment is a powerful tool of influence and can be used for good or ill. It's an important first step to behaviour change. As seen in the foot-in-the-door experiments, asking someone to make a small commitment increases the likelihood of securing a greater one—you've already indicated your support for a cause or transaction and want to be consistent. If there's a positive commitment (or action) people are more likely to act in a manner consistent with that first action. Further, humans are goal-oriented. Sharing an overall goal, and getting people started on the path to that goal, is a great way to maximise their chance of being successful. When someone commits verbally or in writing to an idea or goal, they are more likely to honour that commitment. Similarly, the small action of 'Liking' a chocolate bar on Facebook or reducing speed on rural roads increases the likelihood of further, more significant action. Don't just ask people to do something. Talking at someone and then leaving with the task still to be done is, at best, missing a trick. Don't leave until you have a commitment from them that they will do whatever it is that needs to be done. A verbal commitment ('I'll do it') is better than nothing. A written commitment or 'pledge' is likely to work better than a verbal one. Getting people to start is even better than pledging, and so on. But as witnessed with KONY 2012, small commitments will be abandoned if the reality doesn't match the promise.

The Insider: Arjan Haring

I think we should first shift our attention to individuals. What behaviour change strategy should we apply given the individual we have in front of us? This is a break in focus with the current behavioural science. We have been busy with measuring group-level effects. But we already know that there is no one-size-fits-all approach. People react differently to different behaviour change methods. You need to learn from the interactions you have with someone what works best in their case. Technology will help us learn to change behaviour better, but technology first needs to learn more about how behaviour change experts (for example, car salesmen) interact with people.

Next to that I would say: don't ever give up. From my own experience with girls, things can look bleak, but you can always frame your way out of it. Back on the road to sunshine.

Arjan Haring is the founder of Science Rockstars. He and I are yet to meet, but we've bounced several ideas around online. Anyone who names his company Science Rockstars is an instant friend of mine!

REFERENCES

Baca-Motes, K., Brown, A., Gneezy, A., Keenan, E.A. & Nelson, L.D. (2012). Commitment and behavior change: Evidence from the field. *Journal of Consumer Research*, 39(5), 1070–84.

Carey, B. (2012). Academic 'dream team' helped Obama's effort. *New York Times*, 12 November. Accessed at www.nytimes.com/2012/11/13/health/dream-team-of-behavioral-scientists-advised-obama-campaign.html?_r=0.

Carroll, R. (2012). Kony 2012 Cover the Night fails to move from the internet to the streets. *The Guardian*, 22 April. Accessed at www.theguardian.com/world/2012/apr/21/kony-2012-campaign-uganda-warlord.

Chang, J. (2013). Tiny habits: Behavior scientist BJ Fogg explains a painless strategy to personal growth. *Success*. Accessed at www.success.com/article/tiny-habits.

Cialdini, R. (2007). *Influence: The Psychology of Persuasion*, New York: HarperCollins.

Cialdini, R., Cacioppo, J.T., Basset, R. & Miller, J.A. (1978). Low-ball procedure for producing compliance: Commitment then cost. *Journal of Personality and Social Psychology*, 36(5), 463–76.

Fogg, B.J. (2013). Join me. *Tiny Habits*. Accessed at http://tinyhabits.com/join.

Freedman, J.L. & Fraser, S.C. (1966). Compliance without pressure: The foot-in-the-door technique. *Journal of Personality and Social Psychology*, 4(2), 195–202.

Lee, L. & Ariely, D. (2006). Shopping goals, goal concreteness, and conditional promotions. *Journal of Consumer Research*, 33(1), 60–70.

RACV (2012). *Road Safety*. Accessed at www.racv.com.au/wps/wcm/connect/racv/Internet/Primary/road+safety/roads+_+traffic/safer+roads/How+many+people+are+killed+or+injured+on+our+roads.

Reingold, J. & Tkaczyk, C. (2008). 10 new gurus you should know. *CNNMoney*. Accessed at http://money.cnn.com/galleries/2008/fortune/0811/gallery.10_new_gurus.fortune.

Taylor, T. & Booth-Butterfield, S. (1993). Getting a foot in the door with drinking and driving: A field study of healthy influence. *Communication Research Reports*, 10(1), 95–101.

Thaler, R.H. & Sunstein, C.R. (2008). *Nudge: Improving Decisions about Health, Wealth, and Happiness*. New Haven: Yale University Press.

HOW TO BE GOOD

USING YOUR POWERS FOR GOOD

The thing I hate the most about advertising is that it attracts all the bright, creative and ambitious young people, leaving us mainly with the slow and self-obsessed to become our artists.

Banksy, British street artist

The trouble with the rat race is that even if you win, you're still a rat.

Lily Tomlin, US actress and writer

ALL I WANT IS A LITTLE RESPECT

The advertising profession doesn't enjoy the greatest reputation. In fact, of the 30 professions rated on their ethics and honesty by research powerhouse, Roy Morgan (2013), advertisers came 29th. Only nine per cent of respondents rated the ethics and honesty of advertisers as 'high' or 'very high'. This put us just above used car sellers (who've held the bottom spot for 30 years), and just below real estate agents and state politicians.

So that's the bad news. The good news is for the last three years the figure has improved. In 2011, only five per cent of respondents believed we performed our jobs with ethics and honesty. In 2012, it rose to eight per cent, and currently we are enjoying the heady heights of nearly one in 10 people claiming to respect advertisers. Now, despite the pretty low base, I believe the image of advertisers is improving. Over the last few years, we've seen globally successful TV shows about advertising such as *Mad Men* and *The Crazy Ones* (apparently inspired by Leo Burnett Chicago). In Australia, there's been the extremely successful *Gruen* series (*Transfer*, *Nation*, *Sweat* and *Planet*) that has turned several advertisers into household names. However, I don't think these shows are the reason advertising has become more respectable. I think it signifies that people are more interested in what advertisers have to say. And the single reason for this newfound respect is, I believe, that we are becoming more useful to the world.

We've just lived through the beautifully coined 'information age'. We have loads and loads of information, we are interconnected and sharing this wonderful information. Google and other companies have helped us 'organize all of the world's information' (Google's mission statement), and it's now at our fingertips. Yes, all of the world's information is available to everyone—including people much smarter than you and me. Yet even with these conditions, in which the smartest people have access to all of the world's information, we still struggle to make the world a better place. What significant problems have we solved through 'information'? Wars? They still happen. Crime? Getting worse. Poverty? Still happening and could be getting worse—hard to tell. Equality for humanity? Absolutely not. Global warming? Seems to be getting worse. Mental health? Seems to be getting worse. Did all this access to information help us predict the Global Financial Crisis? No. Does information encourage more people to ride a bike to work than drive a car? Can we convince a rich nation to give 10 per cent of its wealth to a poor nation? Can we stop men from sexually abusing women? No, no and no. Information, and its close cousin, rational debate, hasn't solved any of these issues. Without being a 'glass half empty' kind of guy, I wonder if information is useful in solving any of the world's big issues.

So where does one turn? One possibility is to an industry that knows how to influence and change behaviour. Why not turn to an industry that has convinced people to pay $10 for a beer, $1000 for a new barbecue and $100,000 for a new car? Why not seek insights from an industry that's made it normal to update your car every few years, your wardrobe every few months, and your toothbrush every few weeks?

Advertisers are the masters of manipulation and influence, and even though we may not understand fully how our craft works, we know it gets results. Other industries are curious and want advertisers to unbottle their tricks to help solve issues of significance. Do-gooders are getting into bed with the devil, potentially for the greater good. I've witnessed this first-hand. The techniques of advertising are being shared with the world—for good, not evil.

The aim of this book is to put advertising on the trajectory of helping rather than hindering. I've tried to distil what I've learned as a psychologist in advertising and trust you've found it useful. This final chapter adds some topspin to that information in the hope you'll use these behavioural change techniques for good.

THE DEBATE

Rory Sutherland is a charismatic and ebullient chap. He insists he's 'just an ad man', though he is head of the Institute of Practitioners in Advertisers (IPA), the UK's umbrella body for advertising. I caught up with Rory in early 2013 at a London pub, where we had a good chat about where advertising has been, where it's going, and how it will benefit by embracing an understanding of behavioural sciences.

Rory is a spokesperson for advertising and doesn't shy away from controversial topics. On the subject of advertising and ethics, Rory (Sutherland 2010, emphasis added) has said:

> The truth is that marketing raises enormous ethical questions every day—at least it does if you're doing it right. If this were not the case, the only possible explanations are either that you believe marketers are too ineffectual to make any difference, or you believe that marketing activities only affect people at the level of conscious argument. Neither of these possibilities appeals to me. I would rather be thought of as evil than useless.

There it is in plain black and white. Marketing is effective. It can, and does, make people do things. Advertisers can make people take up smoking. We can make them eat too much. We can make them laze around and not move. Marketing and advertising has the potential to do all of these things.

Interestingly, Rory could have been channelling Perry London (1964), who 50 years earlier said,

> 'We cannot, on the one hand, argue that our availability as professionals is worthwhile and justified, and on the other hand maintain that we are not in the business of changing people's behaviour.'

However, London wasn't talking about the advertising profession—he was talking about psychologists and clinical psychology.

Those practising the arts of influence or behaviour change need to decide if they want to do evil or do good. We need to be transparent about the power and influence that those in the behaviour change game can have over others. Further, we need to be honest about the fact that sometimes humans deceive themselves because of an inbuilt need to justify and make sense of our own behaviour. People can be very susceptible to behaviour change experts. I'm not sure what the answer is, but the quote, 'With great power comes great responsibility' (equally attributable to Voltaire and SpiderMan) comes to mind.

An encouraging sign that marketers and advertisers acknowledge that they're in the business of trying to change other people's behaviour—and therefore should be doing it ethically—is Unilever's 'Five Levers of Change' (Unilever 2011). Unilever is sharing the model in the hope that others will find it helpful and use it to inspire people to turn their concerns about sustainability into positive actions. The 'Five Levers for Change' are:

1. *Make it understood*—Sometimes people don't know about a behaviour and why they should do it. This lever raises awareness and encourages acceptance.

2. *Make it easy*—People are likely to take action if it's easy, but not if it requires extra effort. This lever establishes convenience and confidence.

3. *Make it desirable*—The new behaviour needs to fit with how people like to think of themselves, and how they like others to think of them. This lever is about self and society.

4. *Make it rewarding*—New behaviours need to articulate the tangible benefits that people care about. This lever demonstrates the proof and payoff.

5. *Make it a habit*—Once consumers have changed, it is important to create a strategy to help hold the behaviour in place over time. This lever is about reinforcing and reminding.

We now have a lot of information on how to change behaviour, and the Unilever principles are as useful a starting point for behaviour change as any I have seen. However, there's much more out there, and it's worth investigating which principles would best apply to your particular cause. For example, if you are a charity trying to raise money I suggest you read the excellent report by Sanders, Halpern and Service (2013), *Applying Behavioural Insights to Charitable Giving.*

If you don't get a chance to read this, then consider the following wonderful insight from psychologists De Bruyn and Prokopec (2013). If you are asking people to donate money to your cause, then do the following: have a row of options with donation amounts. Ensure the low option is on the left and the high option is on the right. To maximise the number of people donating and get the highest donations possible, do the following:

1. Ensure the left-hand option is as low as possible (say $1). The lower the amount that appears here, the more people you will get to donate.

2. Ensure the donation amounts escalate in size very quickly. The larger the increments are, the more money each person will donate.

So to maximise the amount of donations you receive, and to get the highest average donation possible, your options should look like those in Figure 15.1 (over the page).

Figure 15.1 Maximising donation levels

$1	$10	$100	$1000	$5000	$10,000

IS MARKETING ETHICAL?

Doug Gimesy is the founder and principal of consultancy The Framing Effect, which helps clients frame messages in the most persuasive manner. He also teaches marketing and business ethics at Monash University, Victoria. Doug is a passionate environmentalist, governor of the World Wildlife Fund (WWF) and a very good nature photographer. He takes the ethical side of persuasion very seriously. I was fortunate to attend one of his day-long seminars at Melbourne University, where he shared his theories on framing and the ways in which 'optimised' messaging gets people's attention.

Gimesy believes there are four levels of influence: coercion and manipulation, which are normally deemed unethical, and persuasion and education, which are deemed ethical (see Figure 15.2).

Figure 15.2 The unethical and ethical levels of influencing

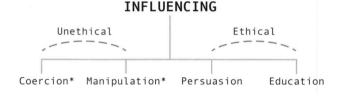

* Unless done purely as an act of paternalism

Source: Gimesy (2013).

Let's agree with Gimesy's contention that education is ethical and that advertising is not in the business of coercion. Therefore, the tension point is when persuasion becomes manipulation. The *Oxford Dictionary* (2013) defines 'persuade' and 'manipulate' as:

> *Persuade: To induce (someone) to do something through reasoning or argument:* it wasn't easy, but I persuaded him to do the right thing.

> *Manipulate: To control or influence (a person or situation) cleverly or unscrupulously:* the masses were deceived and manipulated by a tiny group.

Did you spot the dilemma? Persuasion is about convincing someone to take action based on 'reasoning or argument'. I don't think (nor do most others in advertising) that 'reasoning or argument' is an effective way to change behaviour. As discussed throughout this book (and highlighted by Sutherland above), most behaviour isn't processed rationally by the consumer. No matter whether an advertiser appeals to System 1 thinking or 'low-involvement processing', or asks people to play a game, these techniques don't ask a consumer to make a rational decision to purchase or not to purchase.

I have two things to say about this. First, to marketers and advertisers: **be careful when using your powers**. Remember that your ad is but one of thousands that are viewed by consumers. When you add all those views together, there's a cumulative pressure to consume. Be as positive as possible. However, as I write this I can't help thinking of the famous quote from the 'Socrates of San Francisco', Howard Gossage. Howard was an ad man in the *Mad Men* era and one of the first to talk openly about the morals and ethics of advertising. He said: 'To explain responsibility to advertising men is like trying to convince an eight-year-old that sexual intercourse is more fun than a chocolate ice cream cone' (O'Reilly & Tennant 2011).

If advertisers behave themselves, the next challenge is to the consumer. My advice is to **get educated**. There are very few voices to help the consumer understand the powers of marketing or explain how feeble-minded and vulnerable to persuasion we humans are. Most consumers still believe advertising doesn't work on them. It does—and you don't even need to be aware of the ads for them to have an effect! Hopefully this book is a useful part of that self-education process.

DON'T ADVERTISE THINGS THAT HARM

As an aside, I believe every brand or product has a right to market itself as long as it doesn't harm the self or others. The only legal product to fail this test is, in my opinion, cigarettes. Cigarettes, when used as the manufacturer intended, significantly harm you. Therefore, I don't think they should be marketed. My strong views against cigarettes could be based on personal experience; my father died at the age of 67 from cancer. He loved smoking so much he asked that his coffin be painted like a packet of Marlboro Red cigarettes (see Figure 15.3). He also asked me to deliver his eulogy: 'Adam, say whatever you like, but make sure they cremate me so I can light up one last time.' Yes, he had a good sense of humour.

My father's death was hardly the first that could be (at least partially) attributed to smoking, and it seems clear that ad agencies continued to accept accounts from the tobacco

Figure 15.3 My father's coffin

industry long after cigarettes were known to be lethal. As advertisers, we must be vigilant and strive to avoid such self-delusion in the name of making a buck. Are there brands or products available today that, if used exactly as the manufacturer intended, could cause harm? If so, we shouldn't advertise them.

There are two ways advertisers can use their powers for good—and by 'good' I mean in a manner that benefits and does not harm people. They are: a) using the powers of behaviour change to assist a good cause; and b) helping a not-so-good cause become better.

ASSISTING A GOOD CAUSE

This book outlines many good causes, such as Who Gives a Crap sustainable toilet paper, where 50 per cent of profits go to sanitation programs in the developing world. It also looks at ways to increase funding for community radio station, FBi, and how to maximise workplace safety for WorkSafe. Advertisers love doing work for causes with a positive impact both because these organisations are hungry for and open to creative ideas, and (somewhat more cynically) this kind of work is viewed favourably by awards bodies.

If you hope to influence behaviour for a good cause, use this book for inspiration and go forth and do good in the world. I've worked with several charities, including the Cancer Council NSW, Save the Children, the Australian Red Cross and Mind Shift—the National Self-Esteem Initiative, of which I'm patron. I'm often shocked at the amount of money wasted in the communications space through boring, ill-informed or poorly executed campaigns. This contributes to 'donor fatigue' in which people or nations lose interest in a particular cause (or causes) and stop donating. If a cause is for the greater good, you have a licence to grab people's attention by any means possible. Don't be afraid to be 'out there' or to create controversy.

When I worked for the Cancer Council NSW, the brief was to stop teenagers from thinking that tanning was cool. The organisation was enthusiastic about using youth media and messaging to appeal to teens and tweens (10–12-year-olds), as well as traditional media. They said we could be as attention-getting as we wanted to be. With this very clear brief, we decided to co-opt things that were cool to tweens and apply them to the action of resisting a tan. We enlisted the services of a very cool hip-hop artist called Lyrics Born and co-wrote a song, with a three-minute music video to go with it. Then we filled it with shocking content—sexy guys and girls, a hideously ugly animation of a singing melanoma, and a rapper called 'Al Bino' who rapped about how cool it is to stay white. We wrapped it up in a wonderfully dark title, 'It's a Beautiful Day for Cancer'. Although it is difficult to measure the campaign's success, I still enjoy the memory of being at a friend's party and seeing their child in a 'It's a Beautiful Day for Cancer' T-shirt singing the lyrics to himself. You can check out the song on YouTube (www.youtube.com/watch?v=rDE8HvGIt2U&oref=https%3A%2F%2Fwww.youtube.com%2Fwatch%3Fv%3DrDE8HvGIt2U&has_verified=1).

I really liked our earworm[1] campaign, but when I saw the campaign called 'Dumb Ways to Die' I instantly knew advertising agency McCann Melbourne had taken the idea to a

---

1 An earworm is an advertising expression for a song or jingle that has a tendency to play itself in your head over and over again.

whole new level. Metro Trains Melbourne wanted McCann to 'engage at-risk young people who were likely to become injured in or near a Metro train station'. It wanted young people to pay attention to, and talk about, a safety message. The campaign was developed after two key insights: deaths and accidents around trains are entirely preventable; and young people are digital natives and want to be part of the communications, not talked down to (Chan & Mills 2013). Using these insights, John Mescall, executive creative director at McCann Australia, developed the 'Dumb Ways to Die' concept—with a catchy song and accompanying digital strategy that became the most awarded piece of advertising work of all time. Some cynics claim this is because there are more award shows now, so it can't be considered the best work of all time. Regardless, it's up there with the best.

The campaign used four key principles:

1. Treat the campaign as entertainment not advertising.
2. Launch the song as you would any other song.
3. Amplify the campaign through social media and PR.
4. Ask people for a commitment.

The song and case study can be seen on YouTube (www.youtube.com/watch?v=IJNR2EpS0jw and www.youtube.com/watch?v=IxZ_ZznO2ek).

The song is the third most watched viral ad of all time, with more than 67 million views on YouTube. Data suggests train accidents decreased significantly in the year following the campaign, although a causal link between these two factors has yet to be made. Forty-four thousand people committed (via pledge) not to do dumb things around trains. Further, thousands more downloaded the song or played the Dumb Ways to Die game. However, given the amount of awareness it created, this level of interactivity appears small. I would have asked more of the listeners who engaged with this content. Regardless, I love this campaign. Did it change behaviour? Probably. However, human behaviour is complex and measuring behaviour change can be as difficult, or even more difficult, than creating it.

Even when a campaign is for a good cause, the principles don't really change.

1. Select the behaviour to change.
2. Assess it against motivation and ease.
3. Work out the right action spur to use.
4. Apply the spur with creative flair.

The campaign for 'A Beautiful Day for Cancer' had a very shocking video that made use of the evocation action spur. 'Dumb Ways to Die' was more complex and an excellent demonstration of reframing; that is, suggesting that being killed or injured at a train station because of risky behaviour is just plain dumb. No one wants to be thought of as dumb, especially young kids. It also used ownership (through content sharing) and commitment (through the pledge—which felt slightly peripheral to the campaign but was still there). To have 67 million YouTube views and almost 45,000 pledges is not a great rate of conversion.

It's easy to get it wrong when creating campaigns for good. An example of a campaign with good intentions was Red Cake Day, which asked people to bake red cupcakes to raise awareness of haemophilia. Like many great ideas in this space, the interactive ad communicated the actual cause, but it's unlikely it had much impact because:

1. Baking cupcakes is not a very visible or frequently occurring behaviour. People like to 'signal' to others when they are participating in a cause (by, for example, growing a moustache or wearing a red nose).

2. It asks too much of people. Baking cupcakes isn't easy. Further, some people don't bake at all.

3. It doesn't link very elegantly to the cause. What's baking got to do with haemophilia?

4. It feels a bit uncomfortable—linking blood with a red cake.

On the ease–motivation scale, the score is low. Contrast this with Movember, which asks men to grow a moustache during the month of November to raise money for prostate cancer research. It's a brilliant idea because it's easy for men to do (in most cases), highly visible, clearly communicates the cause and makes the cause feel cool or aspirational.

MAKING A NOT-SO-GOOD CAUSE BETTER

In 1997, I left a relationship with a girl called Rosie who was a quintessential intellectual, left-wing hippie type. She had a rather profound impact on my life and for a short time I wore a dress (why should men wear trousers and women wear dresses?) and didn't eat meat. There were other afflictions that went with this new-found liberation, including changing my name from Adam to Max (I've never actually changed it back, so according to the NSW Registry of Births Deaths and Marriages, it still is 'Max Adam Eric Ferrier').

At around this time, I heard a talk by founder of the Body Shop, the late Anita Roddick. She was an amazing speaker. I was moved by what she said and liked her advice for living an aware life of conscious consumption. At the end of her talk, she invited questions. I had a question about a new shoe Nike had just launched—its first 'green' shoe made from biodegradable materials. This was a time when Nike was synonymous with 'sweatshops'. I asked Anita if she thought Nike's hypocritical shoe should be supported by the general public. Should we buy this organic shoe from a company that uses child labour under horrific employment conditions? I was sure her answer would be, 'Of course not.' In fact, I think I asked the question in order to rant about how bad Nike was.

I was wrong.

Anita vehemently defended Nike and its organic shoe, and berated me for asking such a stupid question. She said of course we should support corporations when they do the right thing, not because they care or don't care. They are businesses that want to make money. They don't have feelings. When consumers support the 'good' shoe, the company will make more of them. When we ignore the bad shoe, it makes fewer of them. Anita spent some time answering my question as I stood at the microphone feeling smaller and smaller. However, her words had a significant impact that I still remember all these years later. When bad companies (and people) do good things, we should reward them. This will encourage more good behaviour.

We now live in a multimedia world where everyone has access to social media and the collective can find a platform. We have the power to influence the world and make corporations more accountable. Change.org is one of many websites that allow people to upload information about a cause and ask others to join it. And here's the thing: corporations are listening, and will continue to listen. As consumers become educated about the connection between their purchases and the impact of these, the more vocal they'll become in demanding that corporations source ethical products. A case in point is Nike, which has dropped subcontractors that use sweatshops.

Corporations derive value from making consumers genuinely happy as opposed to creating advertising that gives the perception of being a good corporate citizen. Some good examples include:

- Samsung Life Insurance's 'Bridge of Life' that uses lighting and messages of hope and compassion to dissuade people from using the bridge to commit suicide (see www.youtube.com/watch?v=LYMWPSKpRpE).

- Increased bone marrow donor registrations through pharmaceutical company Help Remedies and international bone marrow donor registry DKMS (www.youtube.com/watch?v=wwaGgXoHOFY)

- Paint company, Dulux, painting disenfranchised neighbourhoods around the world as part of the 'Let's Colour Project' (www.youtube.com/watch?v=rULv_FWsfCw).

Advertising dollars are funding these initiatives. Instead of traditional advertising, these corporations are using their advertising budget to do good works. It's easy to view these actions as a cynical grab for favourable corporate publicity—and a part of me does—but it's also easy to see these actions in a genuinely positive light. It should be encouraged.

Advertising is complicated and multifaceted. It no longer emanates from a TV or sits on outdoor ads passively transmitting its message. But it still concerns me that advertising has reached a supersaturated situation. Advertising's reach means it's an omnipresent force against the little ol' consumer. To all advertisers, I suggest you look at what you're giving the world versus what you are asking of it. If you pollute the world with ugly, gratuitously sexualised and sexist outdoor ads asking young men to buy your shoes, does it feel as though you're giving as much as you're taking? Or could those young men, who are potentially turned on by your crass advertising, be reached through less crass means? Are there more pro-social and positive ways to get their attention?

In my opinion, and it's only an opinion, one of the positive impacts of social media is that society's tolerance of unacceptable behaviour has diminished. As more people have a voice, and more people listen to that voice, small groups of people (described as 'clicktavists') can attract attention to particular issues. It's as if the sheer pervasiveness of advertising ends up annoying people to the point of action. As a consequence, São Paulo in Brazil and the American states of Hawaii, Alaska and Maine have placed a complete ban on outdoor advertising—with other metropolitan cities pushing for limits on their use.

CONCLUSION

Advertising is on a journey. It's moving from interruption and forced projection to promotion that relies on peer-to-peer recommendations—or that gives as much as it takes, such as creating apps or games. There's a saying that 'advertising is the tax you pay for an unremarkable product'. If you get the product right, the less you need to manipulate, persuade and coerce people to buy it.

So advertisers, use your powers of persuasion for good. And consumers, use your purchasing power to encourage the greater good.

The Insider: Alain de Botton

I think we need to make a distinction between influencing someone to do something good (make the world nicer, develop their talents, be kind) and influencing someone to do something bad (something slightly depressing, counterproductive or fruitless). Assuming the former is the goal, the key is to appeal to someone's 'better nature', which means not in any way making them feel guilty about their 'worse nature'. Give their less positive sides a chance to exit gratefully. Flattery is often seen in a bad light, but it is also a form of strategic exaggeration of the good—which helps to bring it more fully to life.

Alain de Botton is a writer, philosopher, TV presenter and entrepreneur. His books and TV programs discuss various contemporary subjects and themes, emphasising philosophy's relevance to everyday life. I've never met Alain, although we've exchanged emails over the years and follow each other on Twitter. He seems like a very nice man, and I was sincerely interested in his opinion to the Insider question.

The Insider: John Mescall

People derive enormous satisfaction from being a part of something bigger than themselves. It's the whole belongingness thing. So whenever you can, you should position the shift in behaviour you are attempting to elicit not so much as a plea for action, but as an invitation to join something brilliant.

As an individual, your actions can seem rather inconsequential: 'What does it really matter if I do the right thing or the wrong thing? I'm only one person.' But if you feel that you are part of a big idea or a movement ... your actions take on significance to yourself that far exceeds the relatively small thing you have done.

It's why Movember works so brilliantly well. It's why Kiva has to date managed to distribute nearly half a billion dollars in micro-loans. It's why the

Dumb Ways to Die campaign got millions of people to share a boring message about rail safety.

Create a sense of collectivism through an idea that's designed to attract people to it, and you will most likely succeed.

Cry poor, beg, plead or attempt to guilt or shock people into submission, and you will most likely fail.

John Mescall is executive creative director at McCann Erickson Australia. He's also creator of the world's most awarded advertising campaign (quite an achievement), 'Dumb Ways to Die', for Metro Trains. I've known John for many years. He has a reputation as one of the nicest (and funniest) guys in our industry. At the 2013 *Mumbrella* Awards, I was runner-up for 'Thinker of the Year'—John rightfully won.

REFERENCES

Chan, D. & Mills, A. (2013). *Dumb Ways to Die*. Accessed at http://effies.com.au/attachments/Bronze/Short%20term%20effects/Entry%2095%20DWTD%20O%20Short%20Term%20Effectiveness.pdf.

De Bruyn, A. & Prokopec, S. (2013). Opening a donor's wallet: The influence of appeal scales on likelihood and magnitude of donation. *Journal of Consumer Psychology*, 23(4), 496–502.

Gimesy, D. (2013). Gruen Planet chided over ad ethics. *B&T*, 16 September. Accessed at www.bandt.com.au/opinion/gruen-planet-chided-over-ad-ethics.

O'Reilly, T. & Tennant, M. (2011). *The Age of Persuasion: How Marketing Ate Our Culture*. Toronto: Knopf.

Oxford Dictionary (2013). Accessed at www.oxforddictionaries.com.

Roy Morgan (2013). *Roy Morgan Image of Professions Survey 2013*. Accessed at www.roymorgan.com/~/media/Files/Morgan%20Poll/2013/May/4888-ImageofProfessions2013April2013.pdf.

Sanders, M., Halpern, D. & Service, O. (2013). *Applying Behavioural Insights to Charitable Giving*. Cabinet Office Insights Team.

Sutherland, R. (2010). We can't run away from the ethical debates in marketing. *Market Leader*, Q1, 59.

Unilever (2011). *Inspiring Sustainable Living: Expert Insights into Consumer Behaviour and Unilever's 5 Levers of Change*. Accessed at www.unilever.com/images/slp_5-Levers-for-Change_tcm13-276807.pdf.

LIST OF VIDEOS

CHAPTER 1

- Theory for Volkswagen: http://www.youtube.com/watch?v=SByymar3bds

CHAPTER 3

- Albert Ellis and Gloria: www.youtube.com/watch?v=odnoF8V3g6g
- Festinger: https://www.youtube.com/watch?v=1kmVy1QPXn0
- Richard Wiseman: As if principle: https://www.youtube.com/watch?v=rBRUBrWR2ZE

CHAPTER 4

- Adam's Speech in Cannes: https://www.youtube.com/watch?v=RbJCR01WHhA

CHAPTER 5

- Daniel Kahneman: http://www.youtube.com/watch?v=KyM3d4gQGhM
- Ministry of Muffins TVC: http://www.youtube.com/watch?v=A7ryhvkREy4
- Reframing Carrots Case Study: http://www.youtube.com/watch?v=sDewR2jM138

CHAPTER 6

- Dark Side of Tanning: http://www.youtube.com/watch?v=6Giv9lopemY
- Sophie: http://www.youtube.com/watch?v=R4vkVHijdQk
- VW The Bark Side: http://www.youtube.com/watch?v=KqBfZ6vXPS8
- Rexona Rituals of Confidence: http://www.youtube.com/watch?v=QNlhkUZOnMM
- Drink Driving: www.youtube.com/watch?feature=player_embedded&v=YJDsH64sqNY
- Bupa: http://www.youtube.com/watch?v=Xn5J-2i2JmO

CHAPTER 7

- Milgram Experiment: https://www.youtube.com/watch?v=W147ybOdgpE
- Worksafe Video: https://www.youtube.com/watch?v=diRwtr-pq4U
- Asche Experiment: https://www.youtube.com/watch?v=qA-gbpt7Ts8
- Dove Campaign For Real Beauty Evolution Sketches: http://www.youtube.com/watch?v=XpaOjMXyJGk
- Best Job in the World Case Study: http://www.youtube.com/watch?v=74p9qSoKSzA
- Carrotmob Explainer Video: https://www.youtube.com/watch?v=AkGMVQl8_jI&feature=c4-overview-vl&list=PL70D8391CABB6A5BF
- Ask Richard Video: https://www.youtube.com/watch?v=jK8a7zu3E1w

CHAPTER 8

- McDonalds Name-it Burger: https://www.youtube.com/watch?v=yhu4kI6TZzg
- The Hawthorn Effect: https://www.youtube.com/watch?v=IxZoxN5IjFE
- Share a Coke: http://vimeo.com/46072805

CHAPTER 9

- Canal Water Case Study: http://www.youtube.com/watch?v=wvOh6fvIQPc
- Dr Stuart Brown at TED: http://www.ted.com/talks/stuart_brown_says_play_is_more_than_fun_it_s_vital.html
- Speed Camera Lottery: http://www.youtube.com/watch?v=iynzHWwJXaA
- Steal Banksy Art Series Hotels: http://www.youtube.com/watch?v=w08TVILY2LM

CHAPTER 10

- Wonder Bread I: http://www.youtube.com/watch?v=GEfWShkO4Ac
- Wonder Bread II: http://www.youtube.com/watch?v=vIxSSbjz1k8
- Wonder Bread III: http://www.youtube.com/watch?v=9TCuJ2hQcRo
- Art Series Hotel Overstay Checkout: http://www.youtube.com/watch?v=nkLY3GOU0tc
- IBM Smarter Cities: http://vimeo.com/69089787
- Tesco/Homeplus Case Study: http://www.youtube.com/watch?v=MGJifBHm8_s

CHAPTER 11

- The Bobo Doll Experiments: https://www.youtube.com/watch?v=hHHdovKHDNU
- Music Festival Dancing: http://www.youtbe.com/watch?v=GA8z7f7a2Pk
- Lynx Click: http://www.youtube.com/watch?v=b47J3kytnvg
- Dame Edna and Jarrah Coffee: https://www.youtube.com/watch?v=gEvE_FW2WKU

CHAPTER 12

- Who Gives a Crap Explainer video: http://www.youtube.com/watch? v=WdWZ8WVv6qk
- Who Gives a Crap Case Study: https://www.youtube.com/watch?v=rz1T-qXmx_I

CHAPTER 13

- Oxy: http://www.youtube.com/watch?v=l0cAaYW5Ri4

CHAPTER 14

- Pictures of You, TAC: http://www.youtube.com/watch?v=DOYEuEiNBKE&list=PL 1F05D934105B4A26
- Rename Speed Case TAC Study: https://www.youtube.com/watch?v=QPhiuu6RXbk
- How to Like a Brand on Facebook TAC: http://www.youtube.com/watch?v=qAZzW P3s5Jk&list=PL504DE3545B5707CD&index=5
- Kony2012: https://www.youtube.com/watch?v=Y4MnpzG5Sqc
- Kony2012: Postscript Video: https://www.youtube.com/watch?v=okmswBs4rdg

CHAPTER 15

- Beautiful Day For Cancer Song: https://www.youtube.com/watch?v=rDE8HvGIt2U &oref=https%3A%2F%2Fwww.youtube.com%2Fwatch%3Fv%3DrDE8HvGIt2U &has_verified=1
- Dumb Ways to Die Song: https://www.youtube.com/watch?v=IJNR2EpS0jw
- Dumb Ways to Die Case Study: http://effies.com.au/effies/attachments/9cd1869f-f2b4-49a0-bc3d-344b1653aa51.pdf
- Samsung Life Insurance Bridge of Life: http://www.youtube.com/watch?v=LYMWPSKpRpE
- Help and DKM with the Bone Marrow Donor Program: https://www.youtube.com/watch?v=wwaGgXoHOFY
- Dulux 'Let's Colour' Project — the making of video: http://www.youtube.com/watch?v=rULv_FWsfCw

Thanks for taking this action ☺ and doing this favour for me. As a consequence, you are a little bit more invested in me, and in this book. You've *acted* on my small request and will adjust your thoughts and feelings to align with that action. As you'll discover, action changes attitude faster than attitude changes action. When you ask someone to do you a small favour, they're more likely to view you positively because of that action. Now you can go back to page 29 and find out why this is the case.